The Nicene-Constantinopolitan Creed

πιστεύομεν εἰς ἕνα Θεὸν
πατέρα, παντοκράτορα,
ποιητὴν οὐρανοῦ καὶ γῆς,
ὁρατῶν τε πάντων καὶ ἀοράτων.

καὶ εἰς ἕνα κύριον Ἰησοῦν Χριστόν,
τὸν υἱὸν τοῦ Θεοῦ τὸν μονογενῆ,
τὸν ἐκ τοῦ πατρὸς γεννηθέντα
πρὸ πάντων τῶν αἰώνων,
φῶς ἐκ φωτός,
Θεὸν ἀληθινὸν ἐκ θεοῦ ἀληθινοῦ,
γεννηθέντα, οὐ ποιηθέντα,
ὁμοούσιον τῷ πατρὶ·
δι᾽ οὗ τὰ πάντα ἐγένετο·
τὸν δι᾽ ἡμᾶς τοὺς ἀνθρώπους
καὶ διὰ τὴν ἡμετέραν σωτηρίαν
κατελθόντα ἐκ τῶν οὐρανῶν
καὶ σαρκωθέντα ἐκ πνεύματος ἁγίου
καὶ Μαρίας τῆς παρθένου
καὶ ἐνανθρωπήσαντα,

σταυρωθέντα τε ὑπὲρ ἡμῶν
ἐπὶ Ποντίου Πιλάτου,
καὶ παθόντα καὶ ταφέντα,
καὶ ἀναστάντα τῇ τρίτῃ ἡμέρᾳ
κατὰ τὰς γραφάς,
καὶ ἀνελθόντα εἰς τοὺς οὐρανούς,
καὶ καθεζόμενον
ἐκ δεξιῶν τοῦ πατρός,
καὶ πάλιν ἐρχόμενον μετὰ δόξης
κρῖναι ζῶντας καὶ νεκρούς·
οὗ τῆς βασιλείας οὐκ ἔσται τέλος.

καὶ εἰς τὸ πνεῦμα τὸ ἅγιον,
τὸ κύριον, καὶ τὸ ζωοποιόν,
τὸ ἐκ τοῦ πατρὸς ἐκπορευόμενον,
τὸ σὺν πατρὶ καὶ υἱῷ
συμπροσκυνούμενον καὶ συνδοξαζόμενον,
τὸ λαλῆσαν διὰ τῶν προφητῶν·

εἰς μίαν, ἁγίαν, καθολικήν
καὶ ἀποστολικὴν ἐκκλησίαν·
ὁμολογοῦμεν ἓν βάπτισμα
εἰς ἄφεσιν ἁμαρτιῶν·
προσδοκῶμεν ἀνάστασιν νεκρῶν,
καὶ ζωὴν τοῦ μέλλοντος αἰῶνος. Ἀμήν.

Credo in unum Deum
Patrem omnipotentem;
factorem coeli et terrae,
visibilium omnium et invisibilium.

Et in unum Dominum Jesum Christum,
Filium Dei unigenitum,
et ex Patre natum
ante omnia saecula
Deum de Deo, Lumen de Lumine,
Deum verum de Deo vero,
genitum, non factum,
consubstantialem Patri;
per quem omnia facta sunt;
qui propter nos homines
et propter nostram salutem
descendit de coelis,
et incarnatus est de Spiritu Sancto
ex Maria virgine,
et homo factus est;

crucifixus etiam pro nobis
sub Pontio Pilato,
passus et sepultus est;
et resurrexit tertia die,
secundum Scripturas;
et ascendit in coelum,
sedet
ad dexteram Patris;
et iterum venturus est, cum gloria,
judicare vivos et mortuos;
cujus regni non erit finis.

Et in Spiritum Sanctum,
Dominum et vivificantem,
qui ex Patre Filioque procedit;
qui cum Patre et Filio
simul adoratur et conglorificatur;
qui locutus est per Prophetas.

Et unam, sanctam, catholicam
et apostolicam ecclesiam.
Confiteor unum baptisma
in remissionem peccatorum;
et expecto resurrectionem mortuorum,
et vitam venturi saeculi. Amen.

We believe in one God,
the Father, the Almighty,
maker of heaven and earth,
of all that is, seen and unseen.

We believe in one Lord, Jesus Christ,
the only Son of God,
eternally
begotten of the Father,
God from God, Light from Light,
true God from true God,
begotten, not made,
of one Being with the Father.
Through him all things were made.
For us
and for our salvation
he came down from heaven:
by the power of the Holy Spirit
he became incarnate from the Virgin Mary,
and was made man.

For our sake he was crucified
under Pontius Pilate;
he suffered death and was buried.
On the third day he rose again
in accordance with the Scriptures;
he ascended into heaven
and is seated
at the right hand of the Father.
He will come again in glory
to judge the living and the dead,
and his kingdom will have no end.

We believe in the Holy Spirit,
the Lord, the giver of life,
who proceeds from the Father and the Son.
With the Father and the Son
he is worshiped and glorified.
He has spoken through the Prophets.

We believe in one holy catholic
and apostolic Church.
We acknowledge one baptism
for the forgiveness of sins.
We look for the resurrection of the dead,
and the life of the world to come. Amen.

Billing Address:

Rick C Mastalka
2501 E WILLAMETTE LN
GREENWOOD VILLAGE, CO 80121-1634
USA

Shipping Address:

Rick C Mastalka
2501 E WILLAMETTE LN
GREENWOOD VILLAGE, CO 80121-1634
USA

Your order of March 14, 2010 (Order ID:104—5631394—7826623)

Qty	Item	Item Price	Total
	IN THIS SHIPMENT		
1	**We Believe in One God (Ancient Christian Doctrine)** (** P-4-N28E10 **) 0830825312 : 0830825312 0830825312 **Hardcover**	$31.50	$31.50

Subtotal		$31.50
Order Total		$31.50
Paid via Amex		$31.50
Balance Due		$0.00

This shipment completes your order.

Have feedback on how we packaged your order? Tell us at www.amazon.com/packaging.

(1 of 1)

SDwN3hWRxR

508/DwN3hWRxR/-1 of 1-/1P/second/6562736/0315-17:30/0315-01:31 V4

amazon.com
and you're done.

ANCIENT CHRISTIAN DOCTRINE

1

We Believe in One God

EDITED BY

GERALD L. BRAY

SERIES EDITOR

THOMAS C. ODEN

IVP Academic

An imprint of InterVarsity Press
Downers Grove, Illinois

InterVarsity Press
P.O. Box 1400, Downers Grove, IL 60515-1426
E-mail: email@ivpress.com

InterVarsity Press® is the book-publishing division of InterVarsity Christian Fellowship/USA®, a student movement active on campus at hundreds of universities, colleges and schools of nursing in the United States of America, and a member movement of the International Fellowship of Evangelical Students. For information about local and regional activities, write Public Relations Dept., InterVarsity Christian Fellowship/USA, 6400 Schroeder Rd., P.O. Box 7895, Madison, WI 53707-7895, or visit the IVCF website at <www.intervarsity.org>.

The Scripture quotations quoted herein are from the Revised Standard Version of the Bible, copyright 1946, 1952, 1971 by the Division of Christian Education of the National Council of the Churches of Christ in the U.S.A. Used by permission. All rights reserved.

Design: Cindy Kiple

Images: The Adoration of the Trinity, by Albrecht Dürer, at Kunsthistorisches Museum, Vienna, Austria. Erich Lessing/Art Resource, NY

ISBN 978-0-8308-2531-8

Printed in the United States of America ∞

Library of Congress Cataloging-in-Publication Data

We believe in one God/edited by Gerald L. Bray.
   p. cm.—(Ancient Christian doctrine; 1)
  Includes bibliographical references and indexes.
  ISBN 978-0-8308-2531-8 (cloth: alk. paper)
  1. God (Christianity)—History of doctrines—Early church, ca.
30-600. 2. Monotheism—History of doctrines. 3. Nicene Creed. I.
Bray, Gerald Lewis.
BT98.W4 2009
231'.1—dc22

2009000459

P	32	31	30	29	28	27	26	25	24	23	22	21	20	19	18	17	16	15	14	13	12	11	10	9	8	7	6	5	4	3	2	1
Y	37	36	35	34	33	32	31	30	29	28	27	26	25	24	23	22	21	20	19	18	17	16	15	14	13	12	11	10	09			

Contents

GENERAL INTRODUCTION

Ancient Christian Doctrine is a five-volume collection of doctrinal definitions organized around the key phrases of the Nicene-Constantinopolitan Creed (commonly called simply the Nicene Creed) as viewed by the foremost ancient Christian writers. The patristic period (c. A.D. 95-750) extends from Clement of Rome to John of Damascus. Geographically it stretches from Ethiopia to the Alps and from Spain to the Indus Valley. Classic Christian exegesis and doctrinal definition took decisive shape in this period. From the end of the New Testament to the Venerable Bede, biblical texts were intensely studied and their doctrine debated and defined.

In this series we are mining the prized ore of these early Christian intellectual labors. Here Christianity's rich doctrinal treasures are gathered, examined and organized as a commentary on the most respected doctrinal confession of the early church. The ancient Nicene text is the most convenient and reliable basis for holding together the whole fabric of early Christian teaching. Under each creedal phrase we present the most crucial doctrinal passages of key consensual interpreters of the early Christian centuries. A wide range of major issues of early Christian theology may be set forth as a phrase-by-phrase commentary on the Nicene Creed (The Creed of Nicaea, A.D. 325, The Constantinopolitan Creed of the 150 Fathers, 381).

The importance of the Creed and our purposes for the series can set forth under nine headings:

- explaining why early Christian teaching (*catechesis*) was so firmly linked with baptism

- recalling the terrible risks of saying "credo" under violent conditions of *persecution* during the perilous times when the creedal affirmations were being tested and refined

- showing why the Nicene Creed remains the most *authoritative* common confession of worldwide Christianity

- setting forth the *triune* order of all basic Christian teaching

- elucidating the basic *unity* of Christian teaching of one Lord, one faith, one baptism during this period of exponential growth

- showing how the *new* ecumenism is today being nourished and renewed by the *ancient* ecumenical consensus

- accounting for the widespread *readiness* of ordinary believers today to be reintroduced to basic Christian teaching

- clarifying the criteria for editorial *selection* and dynamic equivalency translation

- showing how nonprofessional readers might best *benefit* from this ancient wisdom

The Earliest Prebaptismal Teaching

The earliest summaries of Christian theology were lectures to prepare people for baptism. Our organization of key themes of Christian teaching will depend heavily on the thought sequence of those most influential early summaries by Cyril of Jerusalem (*Catechetical Lectures*), Gregory of Nyssa (*The Great Catechism*), John Chrysostom (*Baptismal Instructions*), Rufinus (*Commentary on the Apostles' Creed*) and Augustine (*Catechizing of the Uninstructed* and *On Faith and the Creed*).

This series brings together the earliest postbiblical, classic arguments about what each of these confessed points meant and how they are rightly grounded in sacred Scripture. It serves as a practical teaching guide to the earliest layers of classic Christian doctrine.

The roots of the Nicene Creed were scriptural summaries that were used in the earliest baptismal confessions. The Fathers of Nicaea and Constantinople said: This is what we have always believed! This is the baptism into which we were baptized.

The orderly teaching of early Christian doctrine arose out of a concrete and practical need: instructing those seeking Christian baptism in the basics of Christian doctrine. This teaching sought to express the commonly shared understanding of the unified meaning of the whole gist of Scripture. The purpose of the catechist was to draw the whole course of Christian teaching into a clear and simple statement. The early creeds offered a convenient way of putting together the entire narrative meaning of Old and New Testament Scripture into a simple, easily memorized affirmation of faith.

When Cyril of Jerusalem taught candidates the meaning of their baptism, he used the creed then commonly used in Jerusalem (A.D. 350) to organize and hold the lectures together. The teacher was expected to clarify and explain each phrase or article of the rule of faith and to defend it against false interpretations contrary to apostolic teaching.

This is why Christians all over the world still appeal to the early creeds, and especially to the most ecumenical of all ancient creeds, the Nicene Creed, as the most reliable confession of that one faith confessed throughout the world. Today we employ this same means to bring together the best thinking of early Christian teachers.

When Saying *Credo* Meant Life or Death

The Creed begins with a decisive Latin word: *credo*, "I believe" (or in the Greek, *pisteuomen*, "we believe"). Second and third century Christians who first said *credo* did not do so thoughtlessly. At times they uttered this word at the risk of their lives under threat of possible persecution, torture and death. Those prepared to suffer for and sacrifice their lives for their belief in God's good news are worthy of our careful attention.

To say *credo* in this way was to speak from the heart in direct defiance of the powers that be, precisely when those powers required direct denial of Christian faith. To say "I believe" is to reveal who one most deeply *is*, to confess one's essential belief, to state openly the truth that makes life worth living despite perilous consequences. One who says *credo* without willingness to suffer and, if necessary, die for the faith has not genuinely said *credo* in its deepest Christian sense as baptism: to die and rise again (Rom 6).

During times of persecution the baptismal confession typically was memorized, not only because it was unsafe to write it down, but also because written texts made other innocent people more susceptible to charges under civil authorities. More reliable was the quiet tradition faithfully passed on verbally through the *episkopoi* from the apostles. The bishops' primary task was to maintain accurate apostolic teaching without addition or subtraction. They, and the elders under their guidance, were charged with carefully guarding and defending the apostolic rule of faith for the eternal destiny and spiritual benefit of believers.

Christians have a right and a responsibility to know the meaning of their baptism. The purpose of this series is to clarify the ancient ecumenical faith into which Christians of all times and places are baptized. It is expected that all who are faithfully baptized will accurately understand what it means to believe in God the Father Almighty, in God the Son, and in God the Spirit.

Why Nicaea?

The Nicene Creed is the most authoritative common confession of worldwide Christianity. Hence this ancient confession serves as the most fitting framework for this whole series. It is commonly shared by very different cultures and languages: Christians of Coptic and Syriac and Armenian and Chinese and Roman and Greek language traditions, as well as modern languages. Like all ancient baptismal confessions, it is presented in three phases or articles corresponding with the three Persons of the one God attested in Scripture.

The first article confesses trust in "God, the Father, the Almighty, maker of heaven and earth, of all that is, seen and unseen." Explaining the scriptural grounding of this affirmation is the subject of this first volume of the series.

It is followed by confession of God the Son[2] and God the Holy Spirit,[3] in the overarching order in which God's self-disclosure unfolds in Scripture: *The Father sends the Son whose incarnate Word is made real in believers by the Spirit.* The whole revelation of God is summed up and brought into a unified biblical confession by this triune affirmation rightly understood. All other early ecumenical confessions, such as the Apostles' Creed and the Athanasian Creed (Quicunque vult) were organized in the same threefold way, to teach inquirers the significance of baptism in the name of God the Father, Son and Spirit.

There are two centuries of confessional prototypes before Nicaea. Their christological core is found in Philippians 2:6-11 which confesses one "who, though he was in the form of God, did not count equality with God a thing to be grasped, but emptied himself, taking the form of a servant, being born in the likeness of men. And being found in human form he humbled himself and became obedient unto death, even death on a cross. Therefore God has highly exalted him."

This same core confession appears repeatedly in the rule of faith we find in Ignatius (A.D. 107), the Epistula Apostolorum (c. 150), Justin Martyr (c. 165), the Presbyters of Smyrna (c. 180), Der Balyzeh Papyrus (c. 200), Tertullian (c. 200) and Hippolytus (c. 215), all in use and scrupulously committed to memory more than a century before Nicaea (325). All early creedal prototypes follow this same sequence of confession. Scripture itself provides the structural basis for the organization of baptismal teaching, and of this series.

As early as about 190, Irenaeus of Lyons summarized the faith of Christians in this memorable way, which anticipates the trajectory of this series: "The Church, though dispersed throughout the whole world, even to the ends of the earth, has received from the apostles, and their disciples, this faith: [She believes] in one God,

+ the Father Almighty, Maker of heaven, and earth, and the sea, and all things that are in them; and

+ in one Christ Jesus, the Son of God, who became incarnate for our salvation; and

+ in the Holy Spirit, who proclaimed through the prophets the dispensations of God."

This core outline of Christian teaching had already appeared prototypically in Matthew 28:19-20 in the formula for baptism, where the resurrected Lord concluded his earthly teaching with this summary charge to all subsequent believers: "Go therefore and *make disciples* of all nations, *baptizing* them in the name of the Father and of the Son and of the Holy Spirit, *teaching* them to observe all that I have commanded you; and lo, I am with you always, to the close of the age" (emphasis added). In this way, Jesus forever linked three crucial actions: baptizing and teaching and discipling. In all subsequent periods of Christian history these have remained intimately interwoven. Implicitly included in the command to baptize is the charge to teach its significance and to make disciples of all nations.

Today's Christian teaching still stems from early baptismal teaching. Christian theology came into being to explain Christian baptism. It was because the Creed first had a *baptismal* teaching function that it later came to have a *doctrinal* teaching function—for defense of the faith, for liturgical life, for scholastic and systematic theology, and for the training of persons charged with teaching the faith.

This series then is not a systematic theology by typical modern standards, but rather a compilation of authoritative patristic texts on the Nicene Creed. These texts form much of the doctrinal basis of virtually all subsequent systematic theology.

There remains a great deal of room for voluntary private opinion among believing Christians, provided those opinions are not blatantly opposed to the core confession of faith commonly held by all believers. Nothing is required of any believer other than that which is revealed by God through Scripture as necessary for salvation, as it has been affirmed generation after generation by common ecumenical consent. Since faith is voluntarily chosen, there can be no coercion in any genuine article of faith.

The Right Order of Classic Christian Teaching

Here is the short outline of the five volumes of Ancient Christian Doctrine:

Volume One: *We Believe in One God*—the knowledge of God the Father—the triune God revealed in creation, providence and human history (Gerald L. Bray, The Latimer Trust and Samford University).

Volume Two: *We Believe in One Lord Jesus Christ*—the coming of God the Son—the incarnate God, one person in two natures, truly God, truly human (John Anthony McGuckin, Union Theological Seminary and Columbia University).

Volume Three: *We Believe in the Crucified and Risen Lord*—the revelation of divine love—the reconciling work of Jesus Christ, his earthly ministry, death and resurrection (Mark J. Edwards, University of Oxford)

Volume Four: *We Believe in the Holy Spirit*—the ministry of God the Spirit—the person and work of the Holy Spirit in justification, salvation and the holy life (Joel C. Elowsky, Drew University)

Volume Five: *We Believe in One Holy Catholic and Apostolic Church*—the Triune God in the church and in history—the glory of God in the church and the fulfillment of history (Angelo Di Berardino, Augustinian Patristic Institute of Rome)

These topics of Christian teaching are not to be taken up in a haphazard, nonsequential way: "The teaching of all doctrine has a certain order, and there are some things which must be delivered first, others in the second place, and others in the third, and so all in their order; and if these things be delivered in their order, they become plain," for "he who enters rightly upon the road, will observe the second place in due order, and from the second will more easily find the third" (*Recognitions of Clement* 3.34). The best way to "enter the road" is by dealing first with the confession of "one God, the Father, the Almighty, maker of heaven and earth, of all that is, seen and unseen."

This series allows readers to crawl through the phrases of the Creed, as John McGuckin says, "in slow motion," to carefully show their biblical grounding, to challenge distortions of scriptural teaching, and to provide a plausible cohesion for the worshiping life of the baptized community. It offers readers direct access to the patristic teachers in their own straightforward language. It brings these great historic mentors into direct contact with the minds of believers today. Let all believers decide for themselves whether these mentors are telling the truth, but do not prevent them from speaking.

In these five volumes we are condensing their most durable thoughts and reasons on the core phrases of the ancient Creed. This is not just a casual exercise for theological voyeurs or for dilettantes. Rather it is a window into the earliest Christian reflection on the most decisive points of saving faith. The triune God, the saving work of Christ, and the power of the Holy Spirit in church and ministry are not optional but essential points of classic teaching commonly assumed among these living communities of Christian worship stretching out into vastly different cultures and centuries.

These arguments demand some intellectual sweat to grasp. They are worth the effort. What is worth doing is worth doing well, and what is consummately worth doing is worth doing incomparably well. So do not be afraid to think. With these mentors you are invited to think both on a cosmic scale and at the most personal and inward level.

How the Creed Teaches the Heart of Faith

The Creed offers the most reliable way to learn by heart the heart of faith. In teaching the cat-echetical creed used in Jerusalem in A.D. 350, Cyril of Jerusalem explained that believers are helped by the concise confession to keep closely to the center of faith as delivered by the apostles,

> which has been built up strongly out of all the Scriptures. For since all cannot read the Scriptures, some being hindered from the knowledge of them by lack of learning, and others because they lack leisure to study, in order that the soul should not be starved in ignorance, the church has condensed the whole teaching of the faith in a few lines. This summary I wish you both to commit to memory when I recite it, and to rehearse it with all diligence among yourselves, not writing it out on paper, but engraving it by the memory upon your heart, taking care while you rehearse it that no catechumen may happen to overhear the things which have been delivered to you. I wish you also to keep this as a provision through the whole course of your life, and beside this to receive no alternative teaching, even if we ourselves should change and contradict our present teaching. (*Catechetical Lectures* 5.12)

Memorize it for life. It is not too hard for anyone to grasp, if properly taught.

The Creed, says Rufinus, serves as a "short word" summarizing the whole of biblical faith, providing "standard teaching to converts," "a badge for distinguishing" those who preach Christ according to apostolic rule, constructed "out of living stones and pearls supplied by the Lord" (*Commentary on the Apostles' Creed*). Rufinus (345-410) was among the earliest of many classic commentators on the rule of faith. He shared the common assumption that the Holy Spirit had superintended its transmission in order that it "contain nothing ambiguous, obscure or incon-sistent." Poignantly, he explained, "The reason why the Creed is not written down on paper or parchment, but is retained in the believers' hearts, is to ensure that it has been learned from the tradition handed down from the Apostles, and not from written texts, which occasionally fall into the hands of unbelievers." Rufinus based his commentary on the personally remembered "text to which I pledged myself when I was baptized in the church of Aquileia."

In vastly different cultural settings around the world today, ordinary lay readers are asking how they might once again grasp the vital core of authentic baptismal teaching under the direct instruction of the greatest minds of the ancient church. This five-volume collection is a classic review of the most basic Christian arguments on those doctrines that have always been regarded as necessary for faithful baptism and discipleship.

Long before the early baptismal confessions became formal tests of faith, they were jubilant expressions of baptismal praise. They only became tests of faith as they became tested by false teaching or challenged by heresy. So first came doxology, the language of praise glorifying God, and only gradually in due time the *doxa* (praise) became *orthodoxa* (right praise, correct teach-ing). Later the *catechesis* (basic baptismal education) would be refined and extended into full scale theological reflection as an academic discipline.

This is why we now appeal to the Creed as the basis of our inquiry into the cohesion of early Christian teaching. It is a gathering up of the whole gist of scriptural teaching. The Creed is at heart a confession of the cumulative meaning of the prayers, liturgy and common acts of confession of the one, whole, united, embodied Christian community of all times and places. The Creed expresses the common sense of the faithful about what the scriptural revelation of God narrates and proclaims. It does so in a short form that seekers and youthful initiates may understand, and which all believers everywhere may confidently confirm as reliable biblical teaching.

As new ideas were tested, they were tested by this rule of baptismal faith. Arguments from Scripture were proposed both by heretics and orthodox and compared with the received consensus of the faithful. All voices appealed to canonical Scripture—some received consensually, others not. That is what the Nicene Creed symbolizes for the whole of ecumenical Christianity: It is the decisive *symbol* of faith in the classic sense that it *draws together (syn+ballō)* the essential elements of faith. This is why the study of classic Christian teaching was often called symbolics before it was called systematic theology.

Understandably, controversies arose over what should or should not be included in or implied from the rule of faith, the baptismal confession. Differences were reconciled by a collective attempt (through regional and general councils) to discern the common meaning of the whole of Scripture as viewed by the worldwide confessing community. These debates did not ask primarily about what the surrounding culture was likely to find congenial in Christian truth, but rather about how the Scriptures teach the revealed truth to all cultures in all languages and social contexts. Hence there is a catholic or universal claim embedded in each phrase of the Creed.

The consensus proved durable. It has survived for seventeen centuries through awesome challenges. The fact that we return to it as our centerpiece for these five volumes is proof that it has survived. It has made it easy to spot what is historically agreed as central for baptismal faith, as opposed to forms of speculation that by contrast are classified as "other than" (*haeresis*, heresy) the venerable multicultural consensus. The consensual orthodox faith definitions outlived the speculative attempts to "improve" upon them, such as those of Gnosticism and Arianism. The earliest documents of the New Testament (such as the Thessalonian and Corinthian letters) contain sharp distinctions between true and false belief and assume that true belief must be defended against false claims of disbelief.

This consensus set modest boundaries for the shared confession of the worldwide faithful. Many ideas were able to be freely examined within these boundaries. Many were permitted; some were considered out of bounds. When advocates of these nonconsensual views turned up purported texts by alleged apostles, they were judged and rejected in relation to the firm accord that had emerged confidently from the earliest communities of faith as expressed in their baptismal teaching. These became the rule of faith (*regula fidei*) for the worshiping community, the trustworthy rule by which the boundaries of scriptural teaching could be marked out.

The gradual clarification of the New Testament canon (list of books to be read in church) was needed as a defense against other floating documents that were contrary to the liturgy and hymns and catechetics stemming from the apostolic tradition. It closed the door against later documents falsely claiming apostolic authorship. It sharply marked those documents most widely acknowledged as fit always and everywhere for reading in Christian worship and fully trustable as doctrine. The four Gospels and the letters of Paul were from the outset widely agreed upon apostolic texts. All others were carefully examined as to apostolic claims. As this list of books became clearly defined, the basis became clearer upon which both consensual (orthodox) and nonconsensual (heretical) readings of the written Word could be assessed. Out of this canonical concord flowed continuing productions of liturgical expression, scriptural commentary, early theological treatises and moral discourse.

When each discrete Scripture text is clarified in relation to other texts, and all together by the whole flow and gist of the history of revelation, dogma becomes then historically and textually grounded. So we find in patristic comments on a given creedal phrase many other scriptural subtexts interwoven in order to illumine that text. These multiple references express the principle of thinking by analogy of faith—comparing text with text. The premise is that Scripture is explained by Scripture (*scripturam ex scriptura explicandam esse*).

Today we live amid a flurry of well-publicized efforts to revive ancient heresies. Some are desperate attempts to give even the weirdest ideas some faint aroma of legitimacy: DaVinci decoding, the grail as bloodline, the sexual relations of the Messiah, the insertion of ideological claims into Messianic interpretation, the new Gnostic elitism. Doting press attention has been given to these highly speculative forms of advocacy that promote long rejected documents and ideas. It has become a profitable media game to defend the poor heretics against the oppressive winners and elitists who wrote the rules of orthodoxy. The truth is the opposite: the most extreme elitism of all false claimants to Christian truth came from the Gnostics who were contemptuous of the naive consensus of uninformed believers, and who were never even interested in gaining the hearts of ordinary believers. Yet ordinary believers then and now could easily recognize that these later speculations did not match the authenticity, beauty and clarity of the original apostolic witnesses.

The New Ecumenism Nourished by the Old

To the extent that Christians today ignore the ancient rule of faith, they remain all the more vulnerable to these distortions. These ancient texts bring us back to the true meaning of ecumenism, following a century of often dubious modern ecumenical experimentation. They remind us of what believers universally believe and have believed from the beginning about the central affirmations of faith. This ancient faith is the rightful patrimony of all global Christians today, whether Protestant, Orthodox, Catholic or charismatic. Its wholeness rings true because it radiates the light of the Spirit and the warmth of divine grace.

The central task of the emerging new ecumenism is to listen clearly once again to the ancient consensus of apostolic faith throughout the world. What is being rediscovered is the time-tested faith of the one holy catholic apostolic community of worship in plain language without dying the death of a thousand qualifications.

There is a dawning awareness among Catholic, Protestant and Orthodox laity that vital ecumenical orthodox teaching stands in urgent need of deep grounding in its most consensual classic Christian sources. These ancient texts were written centuries before the plague of buzzwords that have so invaded the worshiping communities of our time. Today's communities of prayer, praise and service are steadily drawn toward these earliest Christian ecumenical sources for spiritual formation.

This collection itself reflects a lively ecumenical happening. Under this classic textual umbrella, it brings together Christians who have long distanced themselves from each other by competing historical memories. These texts welcome the gathering together of traditional Catholics with Protestant evangelicals and Eastern Orthodox with Pentecostals. How could it be so that such varied Christian traditions are able to find common inspiration in these classic sources? Why are these texts and studies so intrinsically ecumenical, so broadly *catholic* in their cultural range? Because all of these disparate modern communities have an equal right to appeal to the earliest apostolic traditions of teaching. All of these communions can, without a sacrifice of intellect, draw humbly together to listen to the same texts common to them all: Scripture and the earliest interpreters of Scripture. These classic texts have decisively shaped every contour of the subsequent history of doctrine in global Christianity.

Hence Protestants are recognizing the scriptural integrity of the pre-Lutheran fathers, while charismatics are being reawakened by the same Spirit who moved the ancient witnesses. Roman Catholics are once again beholding and owning their pre–Vatican II sources, while Orthodox are rejoicing in gracious awareness of all these unexpected recognitions. Cyril is not owned by Alexandria nor Leo by Rome. All believers have a right to the most faithful consensual teachers of God's revelation. These influential minds are the common possession of the whole church: African, Asian and European.

The international team of editors, translators and consultants for this series reflect the wide breadth of these ecumenical teaching traditions. They have searched insofar as possible for those texts that are most widely received generally by the whole church of all generations, East and West.

The future of dialogue between Protestants and Catholics and Orthodox on issues that have plagued them for centuries is now newly opened by the fathers on sticky questions such as justification, authority, Christology, holy living and the future of history. Evangelicals are finding in pre-Reformation believers a common faith to which Bible-believing Christians can appeal. Catholics and Orthodox are finding in the fathers a new birth of evangelization and mission.

Surprisingly, the most extensive new audience for patristic exegesis is found among the expanding worldwide audience of evangelical readers who are now mushrooming out of a history that has often been lacking in historical awareness. This is a tradition that has often been caricatured as literarily challenged and critically backward. We are now encountering well-educated Baptist and Pentecostal laity who are rediscovering that the Holy Spirit has a history. Both evangelicals and Catholics are recognizing their need for doctrinal resources that go far beyond those that have been made available to them either in their traditions of piety or scholarship.

As a theologian of a North American mainline denomination, this exercise has been for me like an ongoing seminar in learning to empathize simultaneously with the despair and hunger of both evangelical and catholic audiences. But why just now at this historical moment is this need for patristic wisdom felt particularly by both Catholic and evangelical communities? The evangelical tradition is far more famished for these sources, having been longer denied vital sustenance from them. While the Catholic tradition has been attending actively to its recent modern magisterial tradition, it has until recently lost sight of much of the ancient magisterial (patristic) tradition. So the doctrinal definitions here presented are equally pertinent to the needs of both Catholics and Protestants.

The new ecumenism is now being powerfully nurtured by the oldest ecumenical wisdom because the modern ecumenical experiments have left behind them a smoldering path of moral devastation, because time-tested wisdom is still true and ripe for rediscovery, and because God the Spirit has promised not to allow the faithful to forget altogether the core of scriptural truth.

Why This Rediscovery Is Occurring Today

It has been a long time since any deliberate attempt has been made to produce this sort of standard doctrinal benchmark. Our editors are aware of their responsibility in undertaking the first ecumenical endeavor in recent literature to present the teachings of the church fathers as a phrase-by-phrase commentary on the Creed.

Three forces are at work to draw our global lay Christian readers once again toward careful reexamination of these arguments and texts:

* a growing recognition of the social relevance of classic Christian teaching and the hazards of ignoring it

* deepening demoralization about the practical moral outcomes of supposedly scientific biblical criticism

* a dawning recognition that the ancient doctrinal consensus is already shared inwardly and actively by Christians of all continents and of vastly different times and places

These converging recognitions are found among the growing worldwide lay and clerical readers of Roman, Eastern, Protestant and charismatic traditions.

The predecessor of this collection, the Ancient Christian Commentary on Scripture (ACCS), has spawned numerous other projects. That twenty-nine volume commentary has elicited many requests that it be followed by a doctrinal series organized around key points of classic Christian teaching. The ACCS has provided much of the method and inspiration for attempting this demanding series on Ancient Christian Doctrine (ACD). Our editors have benefited greatly from the huge searchable digital data base created by the ACCS research team. These two projects are quite different but entirely complementary and resonant—the one focusing on patristic exegesis and the other on patristic doctrinal reflection.

An extensive project such as this requires a well-focused objective that has served constantly as its organizing principle. Its center informs each step along the way, to wisely manage the tensions inherent in its complexity.

The varied audiences of this collection (lay, clergy and academic) are a much broader vineyard than the highly technical and specialized scholarly field of patristic studies as conceived in the academy. They are not limited to the Western university scholars concentrating on the study of the history of the transmission of the text or to those with highly focused interests in textual stemma or historical critical issues or comparative cultural studies. Though these remain crucial concerns for specialists, they are not the burning interest of Ancient Christian Doctrine. The editors welcome all who want to think with the early church about the plain sense, theological wisdom, and moral and spiritual meaning of the central Christian doctrines based on those texts most widely honored as authoritative by believers of all times, cultures and places. These texts have fed the fertile imagination of the global faithful for most of two millennia.

Only in an ancillary way do we have in mind as our particular audience the esteemed guild of Western patristic academics, who we expect carefully to assess our translations and methods utilizing rigorous standards, which we welcome. If these brilliant texts are rendered clearly enough to find their way to the useful hearing of ordinary lay readers to serve them practically, we expect they also will be found useful by academics and courses in Scripture studies, church history, historical theology and Christian education. This exercise does not pit theology against critical theory or history against faith. Instead, it employs critical methods and brings them into the service of clear classic statements of faith.

The editors have chosen and ordered these selections primarily for a combined pastoral and general lay reading audience that is seeking plainly to rediscover the vital truth and meaning contained in the texts of classic Christianity. Most lay readers are students of Scripture far more than of technical theology or history as such. The faithful regularly ponder the written Word seeking to make cohesive sense out of the whole testimony of the prophets and apostles. Our editors' text selections intend to serve this audience of lay students of Scripture in addition to working pastors who seek to instruct and look after the spiritual lives of their parishioners. We are at the same time determined to work according to rigorous requirements of academic readers who will find uses of these volumes in curricula in theology and history. These students and teachers have to date had access to many of these texts only in dated or inadequate translations.

The texts of Scripture and tradition resist capture by modern ideological interests. A series dedicated to allowing ancient Christian teachers to speak for themselves in their own idioms will resist becoming fixated on the narrower world of contemporary criticism, however well intentioned. We are determined to make available to our present-day pastoral and lay audience the multicultural, transgenerational, multilingual resources of the ancient ecumenical Christian tradition.

This is not to imply that all patristic writers agree in detail on all points. Even casual readers will immediately see that within the wide and ranging boundaries of common orthodoxy, excluding outright denials of ecumenical teaching, there are many legitimate ways of expressing the truth of Christianity. These are often strongly affected by wide varieties of social environments and contexts.

Selection and Translation Criteria

It is fitting here to add some notes on editorial selection and translation philosophy. Our volume editors have sought to understand the historical, social, economic and political contexts of the selections excerpted from these ancient texts and, where necessary, to comment on them. Our mission, however, is not primarily to discuss these contexts extensively or to display them in the references. Nor are we primarily interested in the social location of the text or the philological history of particular words or on their potential political implications, however interesting or evocative these may be. Those texts that stand on their own easily and brilliantly without the need of extensive contextualization are the texts we have most preferred in this study.

Whenever possible we have opted for metaphors and terms that are normally used by unpretentious communicators today. Linguistic experts are free to disagree with our translations, but it should be remembered that the purpose of this collection is to allow the ancient Christian writers to speak for themselves to ordinary readers in the present generation. It is not necessary to have a classical Greek or Latin education in order to grasp their intent or experience their benefit. We have sought out editors who are sympathetic to the needs of lay persons, and who are deeply familiar with the patristic literature in its full range, and who intuitively understand the dilemma of communicating the gospel today in cross-cultural settings.

In keeping with these translation principles, we have chosen to use ICET version for the English rendering of the Creed. ICET was the International Consultation on English Texts, convened in 1969 by the International Commission on English in the Liturgy and whose task was completed in 1975 with the publication of *Prayers We Have in Common*. It has since been superseded by the English Language Liturgical Consultation (ELLC) convened in 1985. Though the ELLC and other groups have produced other English versions of the Nicene Creed, we have chosen to use the ICET version in this series since it is not only contemporary but also in wide use through its adoption in the Episcopal Book of Common Prayer and the Lutheran Book of Worship in current use.

In the commentary, we have tended to edit out those passages that do not have enduring relevance, penetrating significance, cross-cultural applicability and practical relevance. We hope they will also have rhetorical strength and self-evident persuasive power, so as not to require extensive explanation. In addition to seeking substantive intellectual argument, we have sought out selections that are pungent, memorable, brief and quotable, rather than extensive technical analyses or detailed editorial opinions.

We seek the most representative comments that best reflect the mind of the believing church of all times and cultures. We are less interested in odd tributaries or fantastic interpretations of a given idea than in those texts that fairly represent the central flow of the great ecumenical doctrinal stream. The focus here is on the unembellished texts of the ancient Christian writers themselves, not mediated by modern commentators' views or opinions. Those who insist on limiting the definition of theology to what recent theologians have opined are hardly intending to become key players in the textual definitions of classic ecumenical teaching. Our purpose is not to engage in critical speculations on textual variants or cultural contexts, however useful those exercises may be, but to present the most discerning comments of the ancient Christian writers with a minimum of distraction from modern commentators.

The editors of this collection have been meticulous about commissioning translators and consultants who have a record of honoring this consensual tradition. They have sought out worldclass scholars who are preeminent in international theological and patristic scholarship, and at the same time wise to the heart of the classic teaching consensus. The editing of this series has been viewed not only as an academic exercise with legitimate peer review in the academic community, but also as a solemn vocation, a task primarily undertaken before God and not only before human critics.

Some skeptical critics imagine they have a right to exercise a kind of curial censorship over ancient texts based on entirely speculative critical premises. They imagine they have the right to stamp their personal imprimatur on any sacred text as if it were their own property. This reminds the faithful of the third century African maxim to not follow the *traditors* in turning over Scripture to its secular and persecuting critics. Open season is over for frivolous revisionary redefinitions of classic dogma. The killing fields are being reclaimed and the graves marked.

The era of nineteenth- and twentieth-century systematic theology has been skewed by an increasing philosophical bias toward moral relativism. Historical knowledge is sometimes presumed to be limited to reductionist premises and pseudo-scientific methods. The editors of this series have lived through dozens of cycles of literary and historical criticism that view the ancient texts out of ever-narrowing secularist premises. Trendy preachers have desperately sought to advance these approaches, yet often found the hearers' hearts unmoved. There is often left only a residue of dismal awareness of the speculative excesses and spiritual limitations and hubris of much recent academic theology.

The clearest evidence of the prevailing modern neglect of classic ecumenical teaching is that so many of the fathers' most authoritative sources have remained untranslated into modern languages at a time when heretical sources are more widely available than ever and actively promoted. Even in supposedly religionless China such deep neglect has not befallen the classic Buddhist, Taoist and Confucian textual sources.

How to Benefit from These Texts

Please remember the self-imposed limitations of these volumes: (1) the focus is on primary sources, not secondary historical or literary comments; (2) the audience includes lay readers and not professionals alone; and (3) the purpose is core doctrinal instruction based on patristic consensus.

These extracts were either translated by the volume editor or quoted or adapted from various published sources. In each case we have tended to prefer a translation that presents the text in plain English, using a dynamic equivalency method that translates phrase-by-phrase and meaning by meaning rather than word by word. If a single asterisk (*) accompanies a reference, that means that a previous translation has been slightly amended by the editor, while a double asterisk (**) indicates that a translation has been substantially amended.

Each set of excerpts is preceded by two overviews. First is a section designed to put the excerpts within their *historical context*. Where wording of the Creed reflects the culmination of discussions of highly controverted issues, readers are offered a brief summary of the controversy and the issues at stake in order that they can make more sense of the selections set forth. Where doctrine developed harmoniously without much controversy, that fact is noted and a brief description of the development of the doctrine is supplied. Following the historical context is an overview of the excerpts, designed to provide a brief précis of the ensuing section's arguments. Readers are given a concise glimpse into the cumulative argument of the patristic comment on a particular phrase of the Nicene text. The overview attempts to state the gist of patristic reasoning on a cluster of related questions, looking for a natural way of unifying the flow of the overall argument.

Readers may wish to pursue biographical background as needed from other sources such as the definitive *Encyclopedia of the Early Church* (originally published by Oxford University Press and now available from James Clarke, Ltd.). A significantly expanded Italian version, *Nuovo dizionario patristico e di antichità cristiane*, is now available and will be issued in English as the *Encyclopedia of Ancient Christianity* in 2012. These wonderful volumes have been edited by one of our distinguished volume editors, Angelo Di Berardino. Since biographical information on each ancient Christian writer is in abundant supply in many general reference works, patrologies, dictionaries and encyclopedias, there is no reason for the Ancient Christian Doctrine series to duplicate these efforts. Nevertheless, readers will find in the last volume a timeline of all the writers or anonymous texts quoted in the series, with brief identification of time, place and office.

At times the notes will point to problems in the transmission of the text or anomalies or conflicts among the source texts. No literature is ever transmitted over centuries by handwritten manuscripts without the risk of some text variations intruding. Because we are working with very ancient texts, we employ those methods of inquiry appropriate to the study of such texts. The work of textual critics in these fields has been invaluable in providing us with the most authoritative and reliable versions of ancient texts currently available. In the annotations the editors have identified many of the Scripture allusions and historical references embedded within the texts.

Some may wonder if or when this collection will be available in digital form. We hope these five volumes will follow the twenty-nine volumes of the Ancient Christian Commentary on Scripture into a digital CD-ROM or similar format and become available in searchable form.

Keep in mind that much that the fathers say runs counter to our familiar modern assumptions about physics, cosmology, psychology and social process. Modernity is fiercely antitraditional. So if modern readers are to benefit from historic wisdom, they must find in their hearts some capacity for compassionate imagination to reach back into the thought and language worlds of the early Christian writers. A little tolerance for premodern concepts is required for them to have a chance to be heard and perhaps to correct some of the absurdities and exaggerations of modern consciousness.

Thus we commend to readers this patristic commentary on an ecumenical understanding of the Nicene Creed. Our editors have provided a model for the study of the history of doctrine as creedal commentary. We are grateful to our experienced volume editors who come from widely different Christian traditions of interpretation: Catholic, Orthodox, Anglican and Protestant. Our board of reference includes leading scholars from major teaching traditions: Metropolitan Kallistos Ware (Orthodox), Fr. Augustine di Noia of the Congregation of the Doctrine of the Faith (Catholic), Principal Stephen Sykes of Durham (former Anglican bishop of Ely), and Dr. James I. Packer of Vancouver (Anglican evangelical). We are indebted to the Ecumenical Patriarch of Constantinople Bartholomew and Avery Cardinal Dulles of New York for their wise counsel on the needs and requirements of the Ancient Christian Doctrine series.

The reason the consensual interpreters of canonical Scripture were called fathers is that they were widely regarded by believers as trustworthy protectors and engenderers of apostolic faith. They did not promote their own private inventive speculations but the truth of the apostolic testimony as consensually received. By the seventh century their views were being taught from Britain to Persia and from the equatorial headwaters of the Nile to the Rhine Valley. In its journey through history, Christianity has honored those consensual ecumenical teachers who by common consent were reliable transmitters of apostolic teaching.

Thomas C. Oden
General Editor

A Guide to Using The Commentaries in the Ancient Christian Doctrine Series

Several features have been incorporated into the design of this commentary series. The following comments are intended to assist readers in making full use of each of the volumes.

Sections of the Creed

The five commentaries are first and foremost a phrase-by-phrase commentary on the Nicene-Constantinopolitan Creed. The portion of the Creed for each individual volume has been set in three languages—Greek, Latin and English—with the appropriate phrase under consideration highlighted in bold font in each language. Numerous English translations have been developed in recent years; we have used the ICET version of 1975 because of its current wide use.

Historical Contexts and Overviews

Following each section of the Creed is a short section labeled HISTORICAL CONTEXT. Where wording of the Creed reflects the culmination of discussions of highly controverted issues, readers are offered a brief summary of the controversy and the issues at stake in order for them to make more sense of the selections set forth. Where doctrine developed harmoniously without much controversy, that fact is noted and a brief description of the development of the doctrine is supplied. Following the historical context is a section labeled OVERVIEW, designed to provide a brief précis of the ensuing section's excerpts. It tracks a reasonably cohesive thread of argument among patristic comments, even though they are derived from diverse sources and generations.

Topical Headings

An abundance of varied patristic comment is available for each phrase of the Creed. At the same time the Creed itself forms a skeleton for supporting the larger doctrinal convictions of the church. Thus the commentary on the Creed can show the full range of the church's systematic theological concerns. For this reason we have broken the sections of the Creed into two levels. First are subsections that group common themes within the patristic comments. Then each individual patristic comment is tagged by a key phrase, metaphor or idea that suggests the essence of the excerpt.

Identifying the Patristic Texts

Following the topical heading of each excerpt, the name of the patristic commentator is given. An English translation of the patristic comment is then provided. This is immediately followed by the title of the patristic work in English and the appropriate textual reference—usually book, section and subsection. If the notation differs significantly between the English-language source footnoted and other sources, alternate references appear in the notes.

The Footnotes

Readers who wish to pursue a deeper investigation of the patristic works cited in this commentary will find the footnotes especially valuable. A footnote number directs the reader to the notes at the bottom of the right-hand column, where in addition to other notations (clarifications or biblical cross references) is found information on English translations (where available) or standard original language editions of the work cited. An abbreviated citation (normally citing the book, volume and page number) of the work is provided. A key to the abbreviations is provided in the front matter. Where there is any serious ambiguity or textual problem in the selection, we have tried to reflect the best available textual tradition. Where original language texts have remained untranslated into English, we provide new translations. Wherever current English translations are already well rendered, they are utilized, but where necessary they are stylistically updated. A single asterisk (*) indicates that a previous English translation has been updated to modern English or amended for easier reading. A double asterisk (**) indicates either that a new translation has been provided or that some extant translation has been significantly amended.

Outline of Contents, List of Ancient Authors and Texts Cited, and Index

In lieu of a subject index, a full outline of the sections and subsections has been included in the back matter of each volume. This should aid readers in finding specific theological content and make the volumes all the more useful for the study of historical and systematic theology. Each volume contains a list of ancient authors and texts cited, as well as a full Scripture index.

Biographical Sketches and Timeline

Many readers will find helpful brief biographical sketches of the patristic writers as well as a timeline placing them within the proper century and geographical location. Rather than repeating the sketches and timeline in each volume, we have decided to gather them at the conclusion of volume five. Similarly, we have supplied the general introduction to the series only in volume one. For any readers who have not purchased the whole set, the general introduction, sketches and timeline may be found online at www.ivpress.com by searching for the series information and following the appropriate links.

Abbreviations

AF	J. B. Lightfoot and J. R. Harmer, trans. *The Apostolic Fathers.* Edited by Michael W. Holmes. Grand Rapids, Mich.: Baker, 1992.
AHSIS	*The Ascetical Homilies of St. Isaac the Syrian.* Boston: The Holy Transfiguration Monastery, 1984.
ANF	A. Roberts and J. Donaldson, eds. Ante-Nicene Fathers. 10 vols. Buffalo, N.Y.: Christian Literature, 1885-1896. Reprint, Grand Rapids, Mich.: Eerdmans, 1951-1956; Reprint, Peabody, Mass.: Hendrickson, 1994.
AnMar	Anecdota Maredsolana. 4 vols. Maredsoli, 1893-1903.
BLC	*The Book of the Laws of Countries: Dialogue on Fate of Bardaisan of Edessa.* Translated by H. J. W. Drijvers. Assen, 1965.
CApol	I. C. T. Otto, ed. Corpus apologetarum Christianorum saeculi secundi. 9 vols. Jena, 1851-1881.
CConf	Augustine. *Confessions.* Translated by Henry Chadwick. Oxford: Oxford University Press, 1991.
DCA	Franz Xavier von Funk, ed. *Didascalia et Constitutiones Apostolorum.* Paderborn: Ferdinandi Schoeningh, 1905.
ESCN	Gustav Bickell, ed. *Ephraemi Syri carmina Nisibena.* Leipzig, 1866.
ESHS	Theodore Joseph Lamy, ed. *Sancti Ephraem Syri hymni et sermones.* 4 vols., Mechelen, Belgium, 1882-1902.
ESOO	J. S. Assemani, ed. *Sancti Patris nostri Ephraem Syri Opera omnia.* 6 vols. Rome, 1732-1746.
FC	Fathers of the Church: A New Translation. Washington, D.C.: Catholic University of America Press, 1947-.
ICET	International Consultation on English Texts.
lxx	Septuagint
NPNF	P. Schaff et al., eds. A Select Library of the Nicene and Post-Nicene Fathers of the Christian Church, 2 series (14 vols. each). Buffalo, N.Y.: Christian Literature, 1887-1894. Reprint, Grand Rapids, Mich.: Eerdmans, 1952-1956; Reprint, Peabody, Mass.: Hendrickson, 1994.
PG	J.-P. Migne, ed. Patrologiae cursus completus. Series Graeca. 166 volumes. Paris: Migne, 1857-1886.
PL	J.-P. Migne, ed. Patrologiae cursus completus. Series Latina. 221 volumes. Paris: Migne, 1844-1864.

PS   Ignacio Ortiz de Urbina, ed. *Patrologia Syriaca*. Rome: Pont. Institutum Orientalium Studiorum, 1965.

TOSS   Petrus Battifol, ed. *Tractatus Origenis de libris Sanctarum Scripturarum*. Paris, 1900.

INTRODUCTION

The First Article of the Creed

The first article of the Nicene-Constantinopolitan Creed, popularly known as the Nicene Creed, is both the shortest and probably also the oldest, because it can be found (with only minor variations) as far back as the first baptismal confessions of the earliest Christians. In the historical development of the creeds, brevity and antiquity usually go together, and it is remarkable that this article survived the theological upheavals of the fourth century virtually unaltered.

The Form of the Article

It is not difficult to demonstrate that the doctrine that it contains was taught in the church from the very beginning, and with the significant exception of the word *Father*, it can even be traced back to the opening pages of the Old Testament. It is the only article of the creed to which a practicing Jew can assent without serious difficulty, though he or she might find the combination of the words *Father* and *Almighty* somewhat unusual. In a real sense, therefore, the first article of the creed is a confession common to both biblical Testaments, and its all-embracing nature may be one reason why it survived the ups and downs of early church doctrinal controversy substantially unchanged.

In its present form, the words of the article are those that were recited at the second session of the council of Chalcedon (October 25, 451), though virtually identical texts can be found in the Eastern churches[1] in the fourth century and recognizably similar forms appear a hundred years before that. It is true that the Western (Latin-speaking) church had a different tradition, which is now enshrined in the so-called Apostles' Creed, but although it appears to have developed independently, it cannot be said to depart from the Eastern versions in any matter of substance. On the contrary, the available evidence suggests that the Western form was supplemented from the East sometime after the late fourth century, as the Nicene Creed became better known and more widely used in the Latin world, and so the two great branches of the early church joined hands to confess the faith that they had always held in common.

The variations that occur in different forms of the article can be listed as follows:

1. *We believe/I believe.* The form of the creed officially proclaimed in 451 used the plural because it was the common confession of the entire synod. This reflected a practice that went

---

[1]The word *Eastern* is used here to refer to those churches whose classical liturgies and literatures were composed in Greek, Coptic, Syriac or Armenian.

back to the first council of Nicaea in 325 and even earlier, and it carries with it a certain sense of authority. However, the singular form is considerably more ancient, and it probably goes back to early baptismal confessions. There is no theological difference between the two forms, each of which can be found in regular use today.

2. *In one God/in God.* The inclusion of the word *one* is generally believed to be an Eastern phenomenon, though some scholars have claimed that there are a few early Western creeds that have it too. It makes no theological difference, though the inclusion of "one" can be said to reinforce biblical monotheism.

3. *The Father Almighty/the Father, the Almighty.* Many modern forms of the creed (although not the ICET version used in this series) print the words *Father Almighty* as if they belonged together, though there is considerable evidence to support the view that they were originally separate terms. The two words are never found together in the Bible, and before the end of the second century, it was not common to link them in this way. Historically, and to some extent theologically, it is therefore better to treat the two words as distinct from each other.

4. *Maker of heaven and earth, of all that is, seen and unseen.* Creedal formulations prior to the Nicene-Constantinopolitan tended to stress one side of this expression or the other. In general terms, it seems that the form "maker of heaven and earth" is more Western and the form "maker of all that is, seen and unseen" is more Eastern, though there is no evidence to suggest that the varieties were ever intended to convey a different meaning. The present form of the creed combines both. In all cases, the belief confessed is that God has made everything that exists out of nothing. The words "heaven and earth" are found in Genesis 1:1 and may therefore be said to be more obviously biblical, but the idea that the visible world was created out of nothing occurs in Hebrews 11:2. This is not quite the same thing as saying that God created both the visible and the invisible worlds, but the inference is easily drawn, and the Nicene Creed combines both traditions. The only possible difference between the two phrases is that the former concentrates on the lower creation and says nothing about angelic beings, who played a prominent part in the theology of the early church, whereas the latter would appear to include them. But if the addition of the second phrase was designed to provide a reference to the spiritual creatures, this would have been intended as a clarification of the former statement, not as a difference from, or as an addition to, its basic theology.

The Greek version says *Maker*, which the Latin sometimes translates as "Creator" and sometimes as "Maker." English versions until recently preferred "Maker," but some recent ones have substituted "Creator," perhaps in order to emphasize that the creation was made out of nothing and not out of some preexisting matter. If so, that distinction was not intended in the original texts, all of which assumed that creation came into being ex nihilo.

The Sources of Christian Belief

The first article of the Nicene Creed presupposes that there is an objective body of teaching that Christians are expected to confess as their faith. This idea seems normal and natural to us, but it was a novelty in the ancient world. Neither Judaism nor any pagan religion or philosophy could claim to have a closely defined set of beliefs that everyone adhering to it was expected to profess publicly and defend against all comers. Jews were generally born into their faith, and the relatively few converts were obliged to submit not to a body of doctrine as such but to the prescriptions of the law. These could be very demanding, particularly when grown men were expected to undergo circumcision, and the requirement seems to have been quite a deterrent in many cases. Certainly there was a substantial number of Gentiles, known in the New Testament as "God-fearers," who adhered to Jewish synagogues but did not become full members of the community, presumably because the barriers were set too high for them. Paganism, by contrast, was notoriously receptive to almost any kind of belief, and one of the biggest problems pagans faced, even within the recognized philosophical schools, was to establish some sort of coherence in their world view. Eclecticism and syncretism were common among them, and the available evidence strongly suggests that this tendency was growing in the first Christian centuries as new syntheses of Greek and Eastern (Syrian, Egyptian and Persian) ideas continued to emerge in the late Roman world.

In sharp contrast to this, Christians had a clearly defined and coherent set of beliefs, which were contained in their Scriptures. These consisted of the Old Testament, inherited intact from Judaism, and the writings of the apostles and their immediate followers, which were gradually collected together and recognized as a New Testament. Together, they formed a canon, or rule of faith, and Christians believed that everything essential to their confession was contained in them. The precise boundaries of the canon were not established until the fourth century, but it is clear from the evidence that most of the books that are now in the Bible were accepted as authoritative long before that. As far as the Old Testament is concerned, it was the Hebrew canon that was universally recognized, although most people read it in a Greek translation, particularly in the famous version composed sometime after 250 b.c. and attributed to seventy scholars of Alexandria.[2] That translation included a number of additional books that were not recognized by Palestinian Jews as canonical, and although the early Christians sometimes referred to them, they did not normally place them on the same level of authority as the other Old Testament Scriptures.[3] It was not until the time of Augustine (354-430) that any prominent Christian writer defended the authority of these additional books, but even after that they were seldom commented on or used to any significant extent to establish points of doctrine.

As far as the New Testament is concerned, the early church accepted the writings that were used in its preaching and teaching ministry, which were generally regarded as coming from the apostles or their immediate circle and carried their authority. There was never any doubt about the four Gospels, the Acts of the Apostles or the thirteen letters of Paul. Questions arose only in connection with some of the books that are now placed at the end of our Bibles, and the doubts

---

[2]This is why we know it as the Septuagint (lxx), from the Latin word for seventy.
[3]Today they are known as the Apocrypha, or deuterocanonical books, and are sometimes printed between the Old and New Testaments in our Bibles.

mainly concerned the problem of authorship. Hebrews was eventually accepted because it clearly came from the Pauline circle, even though nobody could quite decide who wrote it. First Peter and 1 John were generally agreed to have come from those apostles, and so they were accepted as canonical, but 2 Peter, 2 and 3 John and the book of Revelation were questioned because it was not certain who their authors were. James was widely accepted as the work of the brother of Jesus, but Jude was doubted by some, because nobody knew for sure who he was. In the end, these books were received into the canon because they had proved their worth in the church's ministry, and rightly or wrongly, they were attributed to the apostles whose names they bore.

The Scriptures were universally believed to have been given by God, who used prophets and apostles as his instruments for conveying his Word to the church. Their divine origin and content gave them a status that was unrivaled by any other authority, and it is safe to say that there was no doctrine taught in the early Christian communities that did not stem in some way from them. It is true that some of the church fathers drew extravagant conclusions from certain verses of Scripture, which we would not accept today, but that does not invalidate the principle that all doctrine taught publicly in the church had to have a scriptural foundation. A good example of how this worked can be found in the interpretation frequently given to Genesis 6:1, to the effect that when the angels ("sons of God") fell to earth, they married human women and so produced the race of demons that plagues the created order to this day. No modern scholar would accept this interpretation of that text, but even in ancient times, John Chrysostom rejected it on the ground that angelic beings do not have physical bodies like ours, and so they are unable to engage in sexual intercourse with humans. As a result of this more sophisticated approach, the earlier interpretation faded out and is seldom found after the end of the fourth century. Yet however dubious the original ancient interpretation is, it must be said that the Fathers would not have taught such a doctrine concerning the origin of demons if they had not felt able to find it somewhere in the Bible. They went wrong not because they introduced alien ideas into Christian theology but because they lacked the historical and cultural knowledge that would have enabled them to interpret the text with historical precision. Even today, when such knowledge is more widely available, scholars do not agree about the true meaning of this verse, so we are hardly in a position to criticize the ancient fathers of the church on this score!

It is also important to note that when there were doubts about the canonicity of a particular book, the Fathers were careful not to base their doctrine exclusively on it. They did not hesitate to warn Christians against drawing conclusions from what was doubtful but urged them to accept only what was known to be authentic. In the end, the doubts regarding some of the disputed books were resolved because it was possible to show that they taught the same doctrine as the books that were universally recognized, after which they were accepted as authoritative. Here it is important to note the procedure that the early church followed, as much as the conclusions to which it came. The Fathers went from the certain to the doubtful and tested the latter by their conformity with the former—a pragmatic approach that reflects the great authority that the universally recognized books had in the canon.

The apostolic provenance of the New Testament books was guaranteed by the fact that they were recognized by the churches that had been founded by the apostles themselves. The Fathers' argument was that the churches mentioned in the New Testament as apostolic foundations had preserved the apostles' teaching intact, and they pointed to the remarkable agreement that existed among those churches with respect to the texts of the apostolic writings. They were well aware that there were a large number of pseudo-apostolic books in circulation, but since they were not accepted by the apostolically founded churches, they were excluded from the canon. It is important to emphasize that the Fathers understood these apostolic churches to be guardians of the apostles' legacy and not as authorities who were empowered to determine what that legacy was. There was never any suggestion that the leaders of those churches should pronounce on the canonicity of the books in their possession, nor was a council ever held to determine the status of the disputed books. The latter eventually became normative by constant use, not by any official decree. In the end the consensus of the church was unanimous. By the middle of the fourth century, the present canon was fully established, and after that, it was hardly ever questioned by anyone. The previously disputed books were mostly accepted and the clearly pseudepigraphical ones were universally rejected—all without any official pronouncement on the subject.

The Fathers believed that what we now call the infallibility and inerrancy of the biblical texts were a logical consequence of their divine origin, but they had a more relaxed understanding of these terms than would normally be the case today. This was not because they had any difficulty with the principle of infallibility or inerrancy but because they understood the practical problems that dogged the accurate transmission of texts in the ancient world. The copying of manuscripts was always a risky business, and there were few, if any, available that were totally free from scribal corruptions of one kind or another. Ancient readers were accustomed to dealing with this, and they saw no problem about making what they believed were obvious and necessary corrections to faulty texts. Modern textual study has shown that what seemed obvious to them was not always correct, and scholars have sometimes been able to reconstitute more primitive readings that differ from the versions found in the Fathers. The variations are seldom very serious from a theological point of view, but they exist, with the result that it is not always possible to follow patristic arguments based on textual exegesis by using a modern translation.[4]

Another feature of patristic interpretation is that a number of the Fathers believed that God had deliberately placed obscurities in the Bible in order to attract our attention and make us inquire more deeply into the real meaning of the text. According to them, this was often to be found not in the literal meaning of the words, which might not make sense in some cases, but in some hidden, spiritual interpretation, which the awkwardness of the literal reading was meant to point toward. The Fathers therefore believed that the infallibility of the Bible, which in principle they accepted, in practice demanded an allegorical interpretation of certain parts of it, a conclu-

---

[4]As a general rule, it is often the case that the patristic readings are closer to the Authorized (King James) Version of the English Bible than to most modern translations.

sion that is foreign to most modern defenders of infallibility and inerrancy.

It should also be said that the Fathers recognized that there were some apostolic traditions that had been handed down in the churches but had not found their way into the written texts from which they drew their doctrinal authority. These traditions were almost all connected with worship or with ritual observances of various kinds (like the signing with the cross at baptism) that the Fathers regarded as lawful because of their apostolic provenance but that they did not teach as infallible truth or impose on everyone as essential. Their main concern was to authenticate existing practices that were useful but had no written authority to back them up, not to add to the deposit of revealed truth that they had received in the Scriptures.

The Emergence of a Creedal Pattern

Although the supreme authority of the Bible was never questioned in the early church, from a very early time its teaching was summarized in short statements of belief that individual Christians were meant to learn and recite on appropriate occasions. There were a large number of these statements in circulation across the Christian world, and many examples of them have come down to us from the second century and later.

Common to them all is a trinitarian pattern, which remained fundamental even in the fourth century, when church leaders began to compose creeds for particular confessional purposes. Also very common, though perhaps not universal, was some connection with baptism, which had to be administered in the triune name to be valid.[5] Most scholars now agree that candidates for baptism were asked a number of questions about their faith, to which they were expected to give precise responses that reflected the essentials of Christian doctrine. These questions seem to have been framed along the lines of *Do you believe in God the Father? Do you believe in God the Son? Do you believe in God the Holy Spirit?* which is supposed to account for the three-article pattern of the responses preserved in the form of proto-creeds—one for each person of the Trinity.

For a long time, the most important thing about these formulas was their general pattern and content, not their precise wording. For example, we possess three different versions of what looks very much like an early form of the Apostles' Creed in the writings of Tertullian (fl. c. 186-212), all of which are immediately recognizable as such but none of which is identical in wording or detailed content. If one person could reproduce what he called "the rule of faith" in three different ways, it shows that there was no fixed formula even in a single church, so that trying to trace genealogies of creeds in this early period is doomed to frustration. It is possible to say that some phrases like "God the Father Almighty" became fairly stereotyped early on, since they can be found in almost every proto-creed known to us from about A.D. 200 onwards, but how can we account for the fact that Western (Latin) creedal formulas had no clause corresponding to "creator of heaven and earth," which seems to have been introduced there only after the spread of the Nicene Creed in the fifth century? Though this is puzzling, it can easily be shown that the

---

[5]See Mt 28:19.

Western churches taught the doctrine that this phrase contains; its absence from the formulas cannot be regarded as a denial or even as an underemphasis of its teaching. As far as the first article of the creed is concerned, there is nothing to prove that the doctrine it proclaims was ever unknown in the church and everything to suggest that it was taught in substantially its present form from the beginning, whether it was officially confessed in this way or not.

It is true that when creeds began to be composed deliberately, as expressions of the church's faith in the face of heresy, there was no difficulty in adopting the longer form of the first article, which has survived virtually unchanged to the present time. The developments that occurred elsewhere in the creed under the pressures of fourth-century theological controversies had no impact on the first article, even when a case could be made for expanding it to deal with some of the issues raised at that time. From a modern perspective, it is striking to note that the word *Almighty*, applied to the Father, was never extended to cover the other persons of the Trinity, even though the applicability of this term to the Son was one of the issues at the heart of the Arian controversy. Evidently, the phrase "Father Almighty" was by this time sacrosanct and no longer susceptible to further expansion, with the result that the first article of the Nicene Creed now has a curiously archaic flavor. Yet whatever else may be said about it, there can be no doubt that the first article represents a doctrinal position that had been proclaimed by the church from the earliest days of its existence and continued to set the tone of theological confession throughout the controversies that gave rise to the later, standardized version of the creed as we know it.

The Doctrine of the First Article

This doctrine can be summed up in a single word—monotheism. Scholars debate whether the early Israelites were monotheists in the strict sense, since there is at least a possibility that they worshiped Yahweh, the God of Israel, as one deity among many.[6] But whatever truth there may be in that idea, it is clear that by the time of Jesus, Jews were monotheistic in the modern sense of the term. The only argument was whether pagan gods were demons or illusions—that is, did they exist in some form, or were they nonexistent? For most Jews this must have been an academic question, of little practical significance for their lives, which were lived in separation from the non-Jewish (Gentile) world around them. Christians found it more difficult to ignore the issue, because they were engaged in active evangelism among pagans and therefore had to deal with the claims made for their gods. It is probably fair to say that the more intellectual the Christian, the more he would be inclined to argue that pagan gods were nonexistent. But the reality of the early church was that many believers came from the lower classes of society, where belief in demon possession was extremely prevalent. Christians in that milieu could not afford to be too intellectual in their approach, and what we find is an insistence that pagan temples were the haunts of demonic forces, against which Christians were protected by their faith in God and by the intervention of guardian angels, who watched over them on a daily and individual basis.

---

[6]This is known technically as henotheism, rather than as monotheism, which implies that only one God actually exists.

But even on this interpretation, it is obvious that no Christian ever imagined that the pagan gods were real in the sense that the claims made for them were true. There was only one God, and he was the God of the Bible, the God of Abraham, Isaac and Jacob (Israel), who had now revealed himself in the world as the Lord Jesus Christ.

This core belief set Christians apart from the pagan world, but it also cut them off from their Jewish roots. Jews did not believe that God had become a man and did not accept that the messianic promises of the Old Testament had been fulfilled in the way that Christians claimed. Explaining how God could appear on earth and yet remain in heaven was not easy, and it forced the early Christians to develop what we now know as trinitarian doctrine. The first element in this was to confess God as Father. This was the teaching of Jesus, and it is clear from the Gospels that it was meant to be understood in the context of his self-understanding as the Son. The early Christians knew this and did not hesitate to argue for a Father-Son relationship in the Godhead,[7] but they also knew that the word *Father* was ambiguous. It could be used to mean no more than that God was the Creator of the universe—its "father" in the sense of being its source or originator. That idea was present in Judaism and was almost a commonplace in the Hellenistic world, which included the Jews of the diaspora. For that reason, it can frequently be found in the writings of the second-century apologists, whose first concern was to make Christianity comprehensible and acceptable to intellectuals living in that environment.

Nevertheless, it would be wrong to suggest that they promoted a universalistic understanding of the term *Father* at the expense of the more restricted New Testament usage, since both can be found in their works and there is no apparent tension between them. On the contrary, it is clear that the more general understanding of the word was gradually deemphasized, so that by the fourth century it had apparently become undesirable to speak in such terms and the word *Father* was thenceforth largely restricted to its trinitarian context.

That God was almighty went without saying to anyone who accepted the divine inspiration of the Old Testament, but it is remarkable that this title for Yahweh was scarcely used by the apostles. Outside the book of Revelation, which is a special case, it occurs only once in the New Testament, in 2 Corinthians 6:18, which is a quotation of 2 Samuel 7:8. It can hardly be said that the apostles did not believe that God was almighty, since they clearly accepted the Old Testament teaching on the subject, but it was not thought necessary to put special emphasis on this, presumably because it was too obvious to need defending. However, it is important to bear in mind that the words underlying the translation "Almighty" are nouns in Hebrew and Greek, not adjectives. God is named El-Shaddai (Hebrew) and Pantocrator (Greek)—the one who rules over everything.

The force of this teaching was not lost on the early Christians, for whom it was a way of affirming that there could be no god or principle in the universe opposed to the power of the

---

[7]The Holy Spirit was not excluded from this, but he was not related to the Father in the same way as the Son clearly was, and less consideration was given to him before the fourth century.

Almighty. In particular, this meant that Satan and his angels could not hold any effective power over Christians, even if they were allowed to operate relatively freely on earth. Nor was it possible for Christians to hold to the kind of dualism that divided the world into spirit (essentially good) and matter (essentially evil). The existence of one almighty God precluded such an understanding of reality, since matter too must have been created by him and come under his jurisdiction, making it essentially just as good as spirit.

This was one of the most basic Christian doctrines, which characterized its mission in the Greco-Roman world more clearly than perhaps anything else. The unity of spirit and matter under the aegis of a good, almighty God was the essential precondition for two other doctrines that stand out as specifically Christian: the incarnation of the Son and the resurrection of the flesh. Neither of these would have been possible without the prior assertion of the goodness of the material world and the controlling power of God over it, which the term *Almighty* serves to emphasize.

From the mid-second century onwards it became customary to connect the terms *Father* and *Almighty*, so much so that it is now difficult to imagine that they had separate origins. Later on, the term *Almighty* underwent another, more subtle development, apparently thanks to the fact that Latin had no exact equivalent for the Greek *Pantocrator* but had to use the adjective *omnipotens* instead. Reflection on the word *Almighty* as an adjective describing the divine being, rather than as a noun indicating a divine title, led Christians to affirm that God is capable of doing anything he chooses to do. There is no sign that this had ever been denied, but stating it as boldly as that led to certain difficulties. For instance, can God do things that go against his nature? Today it might be argued that if God were to do something we call bad, it would be good for him, since he is good in himself, and his decision to do whatever it was would be determined by that fact. God would not choose to do something bad, because his will is perfectly good, and such a choice would therefore be excluded. The Fathers argued that the divine omnipotence could not fall into a logical contradiction, because in their eyes that would compromise the supreme goodness and greatness of God.

Here it seems that we are dealing with an accidental, but nevertheless important, development of Christian theology that is not openly stated in the Bible but is nevertheless implied by its teaching. Even if the development owes something to an inadequate Latin translation of the Greek word *Pantocrator*, it is still true that God has to be omnipotent in order to be himself and that he could not function as Pantocrator if this were not so. The theological reflection of the Fathers may have gone beyond the strict letter of the biblical text (without their realizing it, in this instance), but their conclusions are still valid, both because they are implied in what is stated and because what is stated cannot be properly understood otherwise. In the doctrine of divine omnipotence, we have an excellent example of how the church fathers remained within the mindset of the Bible, even as they were led to develop its teaching further in an effort to bring out its underlying meaning.

That God should be acknowledged as the creator of heaven and earth merely repeats the assertions of Genesis 1, and it seems that for many early Christians, particularly in the Western (Latin) church, that was already implied by the term *Almighty*. It was in the East that this phrase was first included in the creedal formulas, either by saying that God was the "maker of heaven and earth" or more commonly that he was the "maker of all things, seen and unseen." The first of these formulations is more obviously biblical and the second more philosophical, but the Greek-speaking churches may have been inclined to prefer the latter, since to them it would have been clearer in meaning. Later the two phrases were combined, and both entered the Nicene Creed as we now have it.

The Patristic Sources

The early development of the first article, and its relatively uncontroversial passage through the theological storms of later times, means that much of the material most relevant to its interpretation can be found in the writings of the Fathers who lived before the legalization of Christianity in A.D. 313. The fundamental character of Christian monotheism means that it could hardly have been otherwise, and as we have already suggested, it is almost impossible to imagine how the christological controversies of the fourth and fifth centuries could have taken place without a prior development of the doctrine of the good Creator God. This means that the writings of the first few centuries are particularly rich in references to the issues under consideration in this volume, and in most cases later commentators did little more than expand and develop what they had to say. The works of Justin Martyr, Irenaeus, Tertullian and Origen are for the most part readily available in English translation, though the last of these is less well served than the others. Much the same can be said for writers like Clement of Alexandria, Cyprian, Novatian and Lactantius, who are other major sources for these doctrines and for this period. The witness of later centuries, though less original, is also of interest, partly because it is often more detailed and explores aspects of the issues that had not previously received much treatment, but mainly because it confirms the continuity of Christian teaching from the earliest times in spite of the many changes that the church underwent in the fourth and fifth centuries. The bedrock of the church's beliefs remained unaltered, and in the first article of the creed we can be confident that we are being transported back to the earliest days of the apostolic preaching.

Today the main issue of controversy is not whether the first article of the creed faithfully reflects the teachings of the New Testament and the earliest fathers of the church but whether those writings are truly representative of the Christian community (or communities) as it then existed. Anyone who reads Irenaeus or Tertullian will soon become aware of the conflicts that were raging in the church around A.D. 200, concerning the teachings of people whom we nowadays tend to group together as Gnostics. Both Irenaeus and Tertullian spent a great deal of time refuting Gnostic beliefs, and in the process both writers offer us a number of quotations that are suitable illustrations for the doctrines taught in the first article of the creed. But who or what did Irenaeus and Tertullian represent? How normative were (or are) the arguments that they put forward for the church in general?

For many centuries it was assumed without question that men like them were the defenders of the orthodox view of the church, which was the teaching of the vast majority of Christians and the official doctrine of the leading apostolic churches. Virtually nothing was known about the heretics whom they combated, other than what enemies like Irenaeus and Tertullian said about them, and this naturally contributed to the feeling that Valentinus and Marcion had never played a significant part in the life of the church. Their teachings appeared to be so bizarre and inconsistent that it was hard to imagine that they had ever had any followers to speak of, and it was generally assumed that once they were gone, their breakaway movements vanished without trace.

This traditional view began to be challenged in the early nineteenth century, when a new way of looking at church history was developed at Tübingen (and later elsewhere) in Germany. Scholars like August Neander classified heretics of the second century as Gnostics. They did not coin this word, which has an ancient pedigree, but they invested it with a new and more technical meaning than it had previously had. There had been a small group of heretics in ancient times who went by the name *Gnostici*, but who they were or what they believed is unknown, and they must have been fairly insignificant. By contrast, Clement of Alexandria (d. c. 215) used the word *gnostic* in a positive sense, to refer to someone whom we would probably now call spiritual.[8] Neander, however, used the word to refer to people who tried to create a synthesis of pagan and Christian beliefs. Given that there was an almost infinite variety of pagan ideas to choose from, it is hardly surprising to discover that Gnostics came in many different shapes and sizes. They did not form a single group and are best described as representatives of a syncretism that is not uncommon when different religious and philosophical traditions come into contact with each other. Later on, it would be argued by Walter Bauer[9] and others that the Gnostic phenomenon was not an aberration but formed part of the mainstream church in the earliest period and that so-called Gnostics may have been the majority in many if not in most of the churches for more than a hundred years.

Readers of the relevant patristic texts will not get the impression that the ancient church was full of Gnostics in the sense intended by the Tübingen school, but there is no doubt that people with syncretistic doctrines were around and that the Fathers felt obliged to combat their teachings at some length. Marcion, who rejected the Old Testament and relegated the Jewish God to a secondary status, was not typically Gnostic and is usually treated separately nowadays, but the others held to a certain pattern of beliefs that is immediately recognizable. It was an agglomeration of ideas that can be explained most easily as an attempt to graft the spirit-matter duality of ancient paganism onto a biblical and usually specifically Christian framework. Jesus was portrayed as a miracle worker from childhood, whose chief aim was to exalt the spirit over matter and deliver his followers from the latter's clutches. This could be done by spiritual experiences

---

[8]This must be borne in mind because the translator of Clement's works in the ANF series (ANF 2:163-604) does not hesitate to use the word *Gnostic* in this way, which is confusing to modern readers who are used to understanding it differently.

[9]Walter Bauer, *Rechtgläubigkeit und Ketzerei im ältesten Christentum* (Tübingen: Mohr, 1934).

that would purify the soul by distancing it as much as possible from the taints of this world, and in particular from the lusts of the flesh. To this end, some Christians developed a complicated mythology in which Adam, Eve and the serpent were given symbolic meanings and a celestial hierarchy, consisting of abstract eons and the so-called pleroma ("fullness"), was devised to aid the soul in its ascent into the divine mystery. There were many different versions of this, but the general outline is clear enough.

Bauer's classic work on the subject appeared in 1934. He argued that the early church was a mixed company of people holding a wide variety of beliefs and that sometime in the late second century there was a takeover by what later became the orthodox party. These people, of whom Irenaeus would be a prime example, narrowed the range of doctrinal options acceptable in the church, and dissidents were pushed to the sidelines. Fortunately (from Bauer's point of view) traces of them and their beliefs survived on the edges of the Christian world, and from them we can reconstruct what the earlier situation must have been like. Bauer's views were refuted in some detail by H. E. W. Turner, in a series of Bampton Lectures that he gave in 1954 and published in the same year.[10] That should have been the end of the story, but Bauer's work was translated into English in 1972[11] and has since enjoyed a wide popularity in parts of the English-speaking world, where Turner's refutation seems to have been forgotten.

Because of this, it is now necessary to defend the classical fathers of the early church against the charge that they were a small and unrepresentative minority who happened to take control of the church at a key moment in its development and who were thus able to obscure the historical truth in their own interests. Fortunately, the best refutation of such ideas is the reading of the Fathers themselves. Everyone agrees that the different Gnostics had convoluted and obscure systems of thought, which would have been clear only to those who were specially initiated into the cult—which is what Gnostics supposedly were. If the Fathers had been like them, they would simply have produced another obscure theological system, which would have been equally opaque to outsiders. But they did not do this. Instead, they appealed to the clarity, the openness and the recognized antiquity of the Scriptures as the best proof that what the so-called Gnostics were teaching was not only wrong; it was historically impossible.

Far from spurring the orthodox to construct a competing theological system, the Gnostics appear to have retarded the development of systematic theology by forcing the church fathers to restrict their defense to an appeal to the precise wording of the biblical texts alone.[12] Any attempt to move beyond the apostolic writings was resisted as an illegitimate departure from the deposit of divine revelation, and even in the fourth century, when it was increasingly necessary

---

[10]H. E. W. Turner, *The Pattern of Christian Truth: A Study in the Relations Between Orthodoxy and Heresy in the Early Church* (London: Mowbray, 1954).

[11]Walter Bauer, *Orthodoxy and Heresy in Earliest Christianity* (London: SCM, 1972).

[12]"Scripture alone" in this sense does not mean exactly the same thing as the Protestant principle of *sola Scriptura*. Protestants do not normally object to systematic theology; they merely expect it to be grounded in scriptural evidence and principles.

to devise theological terminology capable of defeating Arius and his followers, resistance to this was still very strong, for the same reason. It ought to be equally obvious (though apparently it is not) that the church before the time of Constantine had no means of relegating its dissidents to a marginal role. Had they been as numerous as Bauer claimed, they could not have been dislodged from the cities in which they were preaching, and even if they could have been excluded from the church, there would have been no way of preventing them from starting their own worshiping communities, which is what most of them did, or any way of hindering the growth of these breakaway movements.

Had the Gnostics been really influential, it is hard to see why the Roman authorities, who were trying to persecute and extirpate the church, did not take advantage of the situation by trying to play one group off against the other. They could presumably have split the church into a hundred warring parties if they had wanted to, but nothing like that ever happened. Instead, by the time the Arian controversy began in 318, Basil, Valentinus, Hermogenes and Marcion were to all intents and purposes forgotten. The survival of their ideas in the sands of Upper Egypt can be explained by a number of other factors, remoteness being one of them.[13] Modern discoveries have given us a more objective picture of what these groups were like, but they have not overturned the traditional picture of an essentially orthodox church that was called to combat new and alien heresies in its midst. We can therefore state with complete confidence that the writings of the classical church fathers remain primary witnesses for what the early church believed and taught and that the underpinning they provide for the first article of the Nicene Creed represents the authentic tradition of Christian teaching, not a late and somewhat totalitarian deviation from it. Bauer's thesis and its variants will doubtless continue to circulate, but students of early Christian doctrine do not have to worry that the magisterial church fathers are unrepresentative of the beliefs of the mainstream Christian communities in ancient times.

The Selections in This Volume

The patristic texts chosen for inclusion in the present volume have been selected primarily because of the light that they shed on the first article of the creed and the doctrines that it contains. It will be obvious that before the fourth century, none of the writers concerned was commenting on the creed as such, though the doctrine of the first article is sufficiently fundamental and universal that it is not difficult to find expositions of its themes that are as valuable as if they were commentaries on the actual text. It is also true that the Fathers often alluded to these doctrines in passing, when their main concern was to discuss something else, and in these cases it has been necessary to edit out the extraneous material, unless it sheds some particular light on the concerns of the first article.

This problem is particularly delicate when it comes to trinitarian texts, many of which are pri-

---

[13]It is just as likely that the Nag Hammadi community represented a group that had gone off to the country to seek obscurity as that it was a lingering survival of what had previously been a majority view in the Egyptian church. We simply do not know.

marily concerned to prove the divinity of the Son or the Holy Spirit or both. In cases where the role of the Father is highlighted in some particular way that deserves to be recorded, the text has been included here, but readers will have to supplement such examples with material in the other volumes in this series if they wish to have a complete picture of the patristic doctrine of the Trinity. Likewise, it would have been very easy to include long portions of patristic writings about creation, which some of the Fathers examined in great detail, but here too a line had to be drawn, and it is the scope of the first article of the creed that has determined the parameters of what would be included. The article is concerned primarily with the identity of the Creator, not with the mechanics of the creation, with the result that in this volume only those texts that emphasize or explain the work of God have been consistently selected, although there is also a sampling of the other kind of texts, particularly when they illuminate some aspect of the divine plan.

Care has also been taken to achieve a balance in the use of the available source material. Often the Fathers copied one another or repeated themselves in much the same terms, and unless a particular passage adds its own special twist to the doctrine, there seemed to be little justification for including multiple quotations that are effectively the same. In such cases, the more ancient sources have generally been preferred, and it has been assumed that later writers merely followed the tradition. However, when it can be shown that a later author contested or altered earlier opinions, care has been taken to include this as well. It is therefore possible to follow the course of theological development over time without having to produce a comprehensive collection of every relevant text.

Quotations have been arranged in broadly chronological order within given thematic categories. This means that every quotation within each category needs to be looked at in order to get a complete picture and that similar topics within a particular theme are not grouped together if they are attested, as most of them are, in different centuries. The indexes should be of help here and ought to be consulted by anyone trying to do a systematic search for a particular topic, whether it is a designated theme or not. It must also be remembered that in the ancient world, contemporaries or near contemporaries seldom knew of each other's work and were therefore not dependent on one another. This is less true of the fourth and fifth centuries, when Christianity was a public religion and men like the Cappadocian fathers (Basil the Great, Gregory of Nazianzus and Gregory of Nyssa) clearly did work together. Somewhat later, even strangers like Augustine and Jerome corresponded with each other and followed what they were doing. But this situation can only rarely be projected back into the time of persecution, so that even prominent writers, like Tertullian and Origen, lived and worked in complete ignorance of each other. It is therefore all the more remarkable to observe the extent to which they agree with one another and demonstrate that the communion of saints was an intellectual as well as a physical and a spiritual reality.

Most of the material dating from the age of persecution is now available in English translation, and in some cases there are multiple versions to choose from. In this volume, the texts have been freshly translated from the original languages, but with some attention being paid to the vocabulary and style of the more important existing translations, particularly where technical theological terminology is concerned. The fact that the series known as the Ante-Nicene Fathers (ANF) is still the most commonly used one has been acknowledged in the footnotes, but that series has been used in the translations themselves only to the extent that it has stood the test of scholarship and time. Otherwise it has been altered or replaced by more satisfactory modern renderings.

The post-Nicene sources are both more extensive than the earlier ones and less fully translated into English. To some extent the two series known as the Nicene and Post-Nicene Fathers (NPNF) still provide a classic starting point for most students, and when a text has been translated in that series, reference to it has been given here, whether it has been used in preparing this edition or not. Other existing translations have also been consulted, but in every case the translation used here has come first and foremost from the original or, where the original is missing, the extant Latin text. These can mostly be found in J.-P. Migne's classic Patrologia Graeca and Patrologia Latina, which remains the standard source for the Fathers as a whole and to which reference is invariably given, for much the same reason as applies to the ANF and the NPNF. Where there are more reliable, critical editions these have been used instead, and the translations have been modified accordingly. Among modern English translations, the Fathers of the Church series (Catholic University of America Press), Ancient Christian Writers (Paulist), Cistercian Studies Series (Cistercian), Message of the Fathers of the Church (Michael Glazier, Liturgical Press), and Texts and Studies (Cambridge) may be singled out for special mention. As for modern critical editions of patristic texts, the series Sources Chrétiennes, Corpus Christianorum, Corpus Scriptorum Christianorum Orientalium, Corpus Scriptorum Ecclesiasticorum Latinorum, Texte und Untersuchungen zur Geschichte der altchristlichen Literatur, Die Griechischen Christlichen Schriftsteller, Patrologia Orientalis, Patrologia Syriaca, Biblioteca Patristica, Les Pères dans la foi, Collana de Testi Patristici, Letture Cristiane Delle Origini, Letture Cristiane del Primo Millennio, Cultura Christiana Antica, Bibliotheca de Patristica, Thesarus Linguae Latinae, Thesaurus Linguae Graecae and the Cetedoc series, which offers in digital form the volumes of Corpus Christianorum, are all significant. The last of these has been particularly important in establishing the text of many of the selections translated here.

In conclusion, it ought to be said that the choice of selections for this volume has been guided throughout by the desire to find texts that will not only convey the authentic flavor of the early church's beliefs but also provide usable material for the spiritual growth of modern readers. This volume is one of a series that is primarily intended to foster the edification of Christian believers, even as it may also provide valuable assistance to scholars and others who are less concerned with that aspect. In saying this, we are merely following the Fathers, whose only concern in writing was to glorify God and make known his salvation in Jesus Christ. If this book contributes to that aim, it will have served its purpose well and brought honor to those whose memory and teaching it seeks to preserve and communicate afresh to a new generation.

WE BELIEVE IN ONE GOD

WE BELIEVE

πιστεύομεν εἰς ἕνα Θεὸν	**Credo** *in unum Deum*	*We believe* in one God,
πατέρα, παντοκράτορα,	*Patrem omnipotentem;*	the Father, the Almighty,
ποιητὴν οὐρανοῦ καὶ γῆς,	*factorem coeli et terrae,*	maker of heaven and earth,
ὁρατῶν τε πάντων καὶ ἀοράτων.	*visibilium omnium et invisibilium.*	of all that is, seen and unseen.

HISTORICAL CONTEXT: It was the general belief of the church fathers, which they articulated with great force from the second century onwards, that the apostles of Jesus had left their teaching in the form of letters and memoirs. They had either sent these to, or deposited them with, the churches that they themselves founded. Those churches were therefore recognized by all as the guardians of that apostolic faith, which quickly came to be summarized in the shape of a rule. This rule did not have a fixed form at first, but it was structured according to a trinitarian pattern, and all members of the church were expected to subscribe to it. The evidence suggests that this was done publicly at baptism, but it may have been repeated periodically at other times.

The church differed from other religious and philosophical groups in that it had a precise form of teaching, which was enshrined in holy Scripture, particularly in the canonical books of the New Testament. This clarity and precision was trumpeted as a great blessing to church members, not least because possession of the written gospel made it possible for them to distinguish true from false doctrine. In a world where Christian teachings were unfamiliar and often went against commonly

received ideas, errors and corruptions were probably inevitable, and the leaders of the church were constantly trying to protect its members from distortions.

The early Christians accepted that God spoke to people through the natural order, but they did not rate this very highly because it had failed to convert pagans to the truth. Only the Scriptures were capable of doing this. The Jews of the Old Testament who had believed the teaching of Scripture were saved in Christ, even though they had no direct knowledge of him. Since the coming of Jesus, however, conscious belief in him was essential for salvation, and this was the unanimous teaching of the New Testament. By the middle of the second century, it was generally accepted that there were four authentic Gospels, which lost none of their divine authority for being slightly different from one another in form and content. The Pauline corpus was also accepted as canonical, along with the epistle to the Hebrews, although there were some who questioned this last book because it did not appear to come from the apostle Paul.

The early Christians were uncertain whether to ascribe 2 and 3 John to the author of the Gospel that bears his name (as well as of 1

John), and there were also doubts expressed about the Johannine authorship of the book of Revelation. The Petrine corpus was regarded as being especially complex, because there was so much that circulated under the name of Peter but was clearly inauthentic. Only his first epistle was universally recognized as genuine, though the second one was gradually admitted to the canon as time went on. Some also questioned Jude, though it was eventually included in the canon as well. The reason for these doubts was that the apostolic origins of these books were uncertain, and it was universally agreed that only apostolic writings could form part of the New Testament. This meant that no new books could be written once the apostles had died, and after about 200 it was generally accepted that there were no books of genuinely apostolic origin that were still waiting to be discovered. Even before that time, Irenaeus and others had insisted that the church already possessed the fullness of the apostles' teaching, so that there was no secret doctrine of theirs that was still waiting to be revealed.

The ancient church never admitted any doctrinal authority other than that of holy Scripture. The role of the bishops and clergy was to protect and expound the sacred texts correctly, and the great councils of the church were called to pronounce on what the authentic biblical message was whenever controversies about it arose. There was no sign that any individual bishop or small group of bishops had the authority to make definitive pronouncements on matters of doctrine, something that could be done only by a council of all the bishops. Even after that, their statements were submitted to the judgment of the church as a whole, and only those that were found to be in agreement with the teaching of Scripture were retained as authoritative.

The Fathers were reluctant to grant authority to any nonbiblical traditions, though they recognized that there were certain rituals and liturgical practices that had probably come down to them from the apostles and could therefore claim a legitimate place in worship. However, it must be stressed that this did not affect matters of doctrine, which could be decided only on the basis of the biblical text. This was generally recognized to be the Hebrew Old Testament and the indisputably genuine books of the New Testament, which by the fourth century had been fixed at the present twenty-seven in number. The Greek Septuagint was widely used and preferred by some, notably by Augustine, but the weight of scholarly authority was against it. It is particularly interesting to note that Jerome, the great translator of the Bible into Latin, insisted that the Hebrew text was the only authentic one, and he used it as the basis of his own version, which formed most of the standard Latin Vulgate in the Middle Ages.

OVERVIEW: Our faith is grounded in the teachings of the Lord (IGNATIUS). A common apostolic faith is found in all the churches where the apostles preached, and it is summarized in the rule of faith. It is the duty of church leaders to maintain the purity of that faith by rejecting new and unbiblical doctrines (IRENAEUS, TERTULLIAN).

The distinctive heart of Christianity is its faith in the Trinity (ATHANASIUS), which is itself the ultimate rule of faith (PHOEBADIUS) on which the creed is based (EPIPHANIUS). Faith is the necessary prelude to understanding (BASIL, RUFINUS) and the witness of the church to this faith is crucial to our acceptance of it (AUGUSTINE). At stake is the question of truth, which only the church and the gospel proclaim (FULGENTIUS).

It is possible to know that there is a God by contemplating nature, because he created it (ORIGEN, EUSEBIUS, AMBROSE, JEROME, AUGUSTINE, JOHN OF DAMASCUS). The order of the universe points to a rational being as its creator (ORIGEN, EPHREM, BASIL), and only a fool would deny this (HILARY). Yet what we see in nature is only a shadow of the divine reality (Gregory of Nazianzus). God dwells beyond the limits of mere nature, which we must transcend if we are ever to know God (Arnobius, Lactantius, Didymus, Augustine). Human beings possess a soul that knows God by its nature (Tertullian), and they also have a conscience, which is an important means of knowing God (Chrysostom).

True and complete revelation is found only in the Word of God, incarnate in Jesus Christ and written down for us in holy Scripture. The Bible is the ultimate proof of the truth of our faith (Clement of Alexandria, Origen). Christ is both the author of Scripture and its subject (Augustine). It contains the teachings of Christ, faithfully transmitted by his disciples (Cyprian). Holy Scripture is inspired by God the Holy Spirit (Clement of Rome, Athenagoras). This inspiration took many forms, but all of them are equally valid (Epiphanius).

The apostles communicated everything they knew about God to their disciples, so there is no hidden or secret message still waiting to be revealed (Irenaeus, Tertullian). Holy Scripture is rational and consistent (Methodius), and minor discrepancies do not detract from this (Tertullian), though faulty manuscripts must be corrected (Jerome, Augustine). Scripture has a spiritual purpose, which is the edification of believers in their faith (Justin Martyr, Clement of Alexandria, Tertullian). It is more ancient than any pagan philosophy or Christian heresy, and therefore more authoritative (Theophilus, Tertullian). The Bible is uniquely authoritative and sufficient in all matters of faith and doctrine (Tertullian, Augustine). Its truth is vindicated by the power of God at work in the church (Origen). Scripture may sometimes report things that are false, but only in the context of a wider message that is infallibly true (Augustine). We need to hear and obey this message because we are inherently sinful and liable to go astray if we do not (Chrysostom).

The canon of Scripture contains the Hebrew Old Testament, which is to be preferred to the Greek Septuagint translation (Melito, Athanasius, Cyril of Jerusalem, Jerome), though the latter was also composed under divine guidance (Clement of Alexandria), and most people find it easier to consult than the Hebrew original (Augustine). The Old Testament has been fulfilled in Christ (Augustine), but those who followed its teaching before he came into the world were saved by it (Chrysostom). The New Testament includes all authentic apostolic teaching and nothing else (Eusebius, Athanasius). Some books, especially 2 Peter, are of doubtfully apostolic origin and should be used with caution (Origen, Augustine). But even if some of the human authors of the Scriptures are unknown to us, this does not matter, because their true author is God (Theodoret, Gregory the Great). All authentic apostolic tradition can be found in Scripture, but there are some ritual and liturgical customs that have been handed down from the apostles and may be used in the church, even though they have no explicit written authority behind them (Irenaeus, Tertullian, Basil, Chrysostom). We must respect tradition in interpreting the Scriptures (Epiphanius) and universal custom has the force of divine law (Jerome, Augustine). We can have confidence in them because of the unbroken succession of apostolic teaching and authority in the church (Theodoret) and because they are universally accepted and observed (Vincent).

Understanding the true meaning of the Scriptures is difficult (Augustine), even though the text has been adapted to suit the understanding of our limited human minds (Epiphanius). The literal sense is not always clear, and the text has to be searched carefully in order for its true spiritual meaning to be discerned (Gregory of Nyssa, Augustine).

Every part of Scripture has been inspired for a particular purpose (JOHN OF DAMASCUS). The Bible gives us eternal life (JUSTIN MARTYR), tells us what will happen in the future (THEOPHILUS) and reveals the secrets of true wisdom (CLEMENT OF ALEXANDRIA). Most importantly, it teaches us the way of salvation (CLEMENT OF ALEXANDRIA) and helps us grow in the knowledge of God (TERTULLIAN). Quotations from the Old Testament in the New are not always exact (JEROME), and often more than one interpretation of a text is possible (AUGUSTINE). Even the prophets and apostles grew in wisdom and understanding during the course of their careers (GREGORY THE GREAT).

The Form and Content of Our Faith

BELIEVING CHRIST'S TEACHINGS IN THE CHURCH. IGNATIUS OF ANTIOCH: Try hard to be well-grounded in the teachings of the Lord and the apostles, so that whatever you do may turn out well, both in body and spirit, in faith and love, in the Son, the Father and the Holy Spirit, in the beginning and at the end, along with your distinguished bishop, the beautifully woven spiritual crown of your eldership and the deacons who do God's will. Be subject both to the bishop and to one another, as Christ was to the Father, and as the apostles were to Christ and to the Father, so that your unity may be both physical and spiritual. To THE MAGNESIANS 13.[1]

THE WORLDWIDE CHURCH HOLDS ONE AND THE SAME FAITH. IRENAEUS: Although the church is dispersed throughout the world, even to the ends of the earth, it has received this common faith from the apostles and their disciples:

> [We believe] in one God, the Father Almighty, Maker of heaven and earth and the sea, and everything that is in them
>
> And in one Christ Jesus, the Son of God,

who became incarnate for our salvation

> And in the Holy Spirit, who proclaimed the [divine] dispensations through the prophets, including the advents, the birth from a virgin, the passion, the resurrection from the dead and the bodily ascension into heaven of the beloved Christ Jesus our Lord, as well as his [future] coming from heaven in the glory of the Father, when he will "gather all things in one."[2]
>
> And to raise up again all flesh of the whole human race, in order that "every knee should bow and every tongue confess"[3] to Christ Jesus, our Lord and God, our Savior and king, according to the will of the invisible Father, and that he should execute righteous judgment toward all.
>
> That he may send "the spirits of wickedness"[4] and the angels who transgressed and became apostates, together with the ungodly and unrighteous, wicked and profane among human beings, into everlasting fire, but in the exercise of his grace may grant immortality to the righteous and holy, and to those who have kept his commandments and persevered in his love and may clothe them with everlasting glory.

As I have already observed, the church has received this preaching and this faith, even though it is scattered throughout the world, and carefully preserves it intact, as if it were living in a single house. The church believes these doctrines as if it had only one soul and one heart, and it proclaims them and hands them on in perfect harmony, as if it spoke with only one voice. The languages of the world may be dissimilar, but the message of the tradition is one and the same. . . . Just as the sun is the same wherever it shines, so is the preaching of

---

[1]PG 3:672-73; cf. ANF 1:64. [2]Eph 1:10. [3]Phil 2:10-11. [4]Eph 6:12.

the truth the same everywhere in the world, enlightening everyone who wants to come to a knowledge of the truth. No church leader, however gifted he may be, will teach anything different from this, because no one is greater than the Master. Nor will anyone of inferior eloquence do harm to our tradition, because our faith is always one and the same. For this reason, the gifted teacher can add nothing to it, nor can the less gifted take anything away from it. Just because some people have more or less intelligence than others, it does not follow that they should add or subtract doctrines accordingly. AGAINST HERESIES 1.10.1-3.[5]

FIND THE TRUTH AND BELIEVE IT. TERTULLIAN: There is a particular and definite truth taught by Christ, which the Gentiles ought to believe. This is what they are called to seek so that once they have found it, they can believe it. You cannot go on forever looking for something that has already been taught as the one definite truth. You must seek until you have found it, and when you have found it, then you ought to believe it. After that, you have nothing else to worry about, because there is no further truth to be believed and nothing more to go looking for. If you have any doubts about this, we can prove our point because we have Christ's teaching in our possession. PRESCRIPTIONS AGAINST HERETICS 9.[6]

THERE IS ONLY ONE RULE OF FAITH. TERTULLIAN: The rule of faith is altogether one, alone immutable and irreformable. It is the rule of believing in only one Almighty God, the Creator of the universe, and in his Son Jesus Christ, born of the Virgin Mary, crucified under Pontius Pilate, raised again the third day from the dead, received into the heavens, sitting now at the right hand of the Father, destined to come to judge the living and the dead through the resurrection of the flesh as well [as of the soul]. This law of faith is constant, but other points of discipline and

behavior are open to correction as the grace of God operates and progresses to the [perfect] end. ON THE VEILING OF VIRGINS 1.[7]

THE RULE OF FAITH AND HUMAN HISTORY. TERTULLIAN: The rule of faith prescribes the belief that there is only one God and that he is none other than the Creator of the world, who produced all things out of nothing by his Word, which he sent forth. This Word is called his Son, and under the name of God he was seen in different ways by the patriarchs, heard at all times in the prophets, and was at last brought down by the Spirit and power of the Father into the Virgin Mary, was made flesh in her womb, and being born of her, came out as Jesus Christ. He preaches this new law and the new promise of the kingdom of heaven. He worked miracles. Having been crucified, he rose again on the third day, and having ascended into heaven, he sat at the right hand of the Father. From there he sent the power of the Holy Spirit to guide those who believe. He will come again with glory to take the saints into the enjoyment of everlasting life and of the heavenly promises. He will condemn the wicked to everlasting fire after both these types of people (i.e., the good and the evil) have been resurrected and given back their flesh. We shall prove that Christ taught this rule, and the only questions it raises among us are those that are provoked by heretics. PRESCRIPTIONS AGAINST HERETICS 13-14.[8]

WE MUST BELIEVE SOME THINGS AND REJECT OTHERS. APHRAHAT: This is faith, when a person believes in God the Lord of all, who made the heavens and the earth, the seas and all that is in them, and he made Adam in his image. He gave the law to Moses, he sent of his Spirit upon the prophets, he sent moreover his Christ into the world. Furthermore, a per-

---

[5]PG 7:549-53; cf. ANF 1:330-31. [6]PL 2:23; cf. ANF 3:248. [7]PL 2:889; cf. ANF 4:27. [8]PL 2:26-27; cf. ANF 3:249.

son should believe in the resurrection from the dead and should also believe in the sacrament of baptism. This is the faith of the church of God.

A person ought to separate himself from the observance of hours and sabbaths and moons and seasons, and divinations and sorceries and astrology and magic, from fornication and from festive music, from vain doctrines that are the instruments of the evil one, from the blandishment of honeyed words, from blasphemy and from adultery. A person should not bear false witness or speak with a double tongue. These are the works of the faith that is based on the true Rock, which is Christ, on whom the whole building has been erected. DEMONSTRATIONS 1.19.[9]

THE COMMON FAITH OF THE CHURCH.
ATHANASIUS: When the fathers of the council of Nicaea wrote about the date of Easter, they prefaced their remarks with the words "It seemed good to us," but when they wrote about the faith, they put "Thus believes the Catholic church" in order to show that their opinions were not something new but derived from the apostles. ON SYNODS 1.5.[10]

THE TRINITY IS THE HEART OF OUR FAITH. ATHANASIUS: Let us see what the tradition, doctrine and faith of the universal church was from the very beginning, what the Lord handed on, what the apostles preached and what the Fathers have preserved. The church is founded on this faith, and if anyone goes beyond its bounds, he no longer has the right to call himself a Christian. Therefore the Trinity of Father, Son and Holy Spirit is both holy and perfect and contains nothing alien or additional to the faith. It is not a mixture of the Creator and his creatures but is in its entirety possessed of the power to create and bring into being.[11] Each member of the Trinity is like the others and shares the same divine nature, just as each one participates in

the single action and activity of God. For the Father makes everything by his Word in the Holy Spirit, thereby preserving the unity of the Trinity. . . . Moreover, the Trinity is not a trinity in name only, but genuinely exists as a single entity. For just as the Father truly exists, so also his Word truly exists, who is also and above all God himself. Nor is it the case that the Holy Spirit does not exist, for he too is really there [in God]. . . . In order that believers should understand that this is the faith of the church, . . . the Lord sent his apostles, teaching them to lay this foundation for the church. As he said: . . . "Baptize them in the name of the Father, and of the Son, and of the Holy Spirit."[12] FOUR LETTERS TO SERAPION 1.28.[13]

THE RULE OF FAITH IS THE TRINITY. PHOEBADIUS OF AGEN: We must hold to the rule that says that the Father is in the Son and the Son in the Father, which preserves one substance in the two persons and recognizes this dispensation of the divine nature. Therefore the Father is God and the Son is God, because the Son is God in God the Father. If this causes someone to stumble, let him hear from us that the Spirit is from God. The Son is the second person in him, and the Holy Spirit is the third. As the Lord said, "I shall ask my Father, and he will give you another comforter."[14] For this reason, the Spirit is distinct from the Son, just as the Son is distinct from the Father. The third person is the Spirit, just as the second person is the Son, but all three are one God—the three are one. This we believe, this we hold, because it is this that we have received from the prophets, this that the Gospels have said to us, this that the apostles have passed on, this to which the martyrs witnessed by their deaths. By this we cling in

[9]PS 1:44-45; cf. NPNF 2 13:352. [10]PG 26:688; cf. NPNF 2 4:453. [11]This statement is intended to counteract the Arians, who claimed that the Father was the Creator and that the Son and Holy Spirit were both creatures. [12]Mt 28:19. [13]PG 26:593-96. [14]Jn 14:16.

our minds to the faith against which "even if an angel from heaven should declare anything, let him be anathema."[15] BOOK AGAINST THE ARIANS 22.[16]

THE CREED IS BASED ON THE TRINITY.
EPIPHANIUS OF SALAMIS: The Antiochenes confess that Father, Son and Holy Spirit are consubstantial, three hypostases, one essence, one divinity. They say that this is the true faith, which has been handed down from our ancestors, that it is the faith of the prophets, the Evangelists and the apostles, which our own fathers and bishops confessed when they assembled at the council of Nicaea, which was held in the reign of the great and most blessed Emperor Constantine. PANARION 73.34.[17]

THE PRIMACY OF FAITH. BASIL THE GREAT: Let faith in the teachings about God prevail—faith and not proof. This is the faith that leads the mind toward assent more than rational arguments do, the faith that is born not of mathematical necessities but from the inner workings of the Holy Spirit. HOMILIES ON THE PSALMS 115.1.[18]

BELIEF IS THE FOUNDATION OF LIFE.
RUFINUS OF AQUILEIA: "I believe" is placed first in the creed[19] because the apostle Paul, writing to the Hebrews, says, "Whoever comes to God must first of all believe that he is, and that he is the rewarder of those who believe in him."[20] The prophet also says, "Unless you believe, you will not understand."[21] Therefore, in order for the way of understanding to be open to you, you must confess your belief, for nobody embarks on the sea or trusts himself to it unless he first believes that he will have a safe journey. Neither does the farmer commit his seed to the furrows or scatter his grain over the earth unless he believes that the showers will come, along with the warmth of the sun, by which the earth will produce and multiply their fruits. In short, nothing in life can be

done unless there is first of all a willingness to believe. It is hardly a matter of wonder, then, if in coming to God, we first of all profess that we believe, since without belief, even ordinary life is impossible. COMMENTARY ON THE APOSTLES' CREED 3.[22]

THE CHURCH IS THE BASIS OF OUR FAITH.
AUGUSTINE: If you come across somebody who does not yet believe the gospel, what would you say if he says to you, "I do not believe"? I myself would not believe the gospel if the authority of the universal church had not persuaded me to. AGAINST THE LETTER OF A MANICHAEAN 5.6.[23]

TRUTH IS ONE. FULGENTIUS OF RUSPE: True religion consists of the worship of the one true God. . . . For truth itself is the one God. Just as there is no truth other than the one truth, so there is no true God other than the one true God. It is not possible to say that there are two true gods, because by its nature, truth is one and cannot be divided. LETTER 8.4.10.[24]

Knowledge of God in Nature

THE HUMAN SOUL KNOWS GOD BY ITS NATURE. TERTULLIAN: The object of our worship is the one God, who by his commanding Word, his arranging wisdom and his mighty power brought forth out of nothing the entire mass of our world, with all its array of elements, bodies and spirits for the glory of his majesty. The Greeks recognize this and for that reason have called it the cosmos. The eye cannot see God, although he is spiritually visible. He is incomprehensible, though he is manifested by grace. He is beyond our utmost thought, though our human faculties conceive of him. He is therefore real and great in equal

---

[15]Gal 1:8. [16]PL 20:30. [17]PG 42:468. [18]PG 30:104. [19]Rufinus was referring to the Apostles' Creed, but the principle is the same for the Nicene Creed. [20]Heb 11:6. [21]Is 7:9; see also Dan 12:10. [22]PL 21:339-40; cf. NPNF 2 3:543. [23]PL 42:176. [24]PL 65:365.

measure. Things that can be seen, handled and conceived are by nature inferior to the eyes that see them, the hands that touch them and the minds that discover them, but the infinite is known only to itself. Paradoxically, it is this that gives us some idea of who God really is. He is beyond our conception, but the very fact that we cannot grasp him gives us some idea of what he really is. He is presented to our minds in his transcendent greatness, at once both known and unknown. The crowning guilt of humankind is found right here, in that they will not acknowledge the One of whom they cannot possibly be ignorant. Do you prefer the works of his hands, so numerous and so great, that both contain you and sustain you, that both minister to your enjoyment and strike you with awe, or would you rather have it from the witness of the soul itself? Though it is under the oppressive bondage of the body, led astray by depraving customs, enervated by lusts and passions, in slavery to false gods, whenever it comes to itself, as if out of a sleep or sickness, it speaks of God. Phrases like "God is great and good," "May God grant it" are on every lip. It bears witness to the fact that God is judge, exclaiming, "God sees," and "I commend myself to God," and "God will repay me." O noble testimony of the soul, which is Christian by nature! By using expressions such as these, the soul looks not to the seat of earthly government but to the heavens. It knows that it is there that the throne of the living God is found, because it came down from there itself. Apology 17.[25]

Natural Knowledge of God Is Possible.

ORIGEN: Although nobody can speak with certainty about God the Father, it is nevertheless possible for some knowledge of him to be gained through the visible creation and the natural feelings of the human mind. Moreover, it is possible for such knowledge to be confirmed by holy Scripture. On First Principles 1.3.1.[26]

God Wants Us to Know Him.

ORIGEN: Since God is not known by wicked people, he wants to make himself known. This is not because he thinks that he does not receive the proper degree of reverence but because knowing him will free people from their unhappiness. Against Celsus 4.6.[27]

Serious-minded and Upright People Believe in the One God.

ORIGEN: The truth revealed by Jesus is fully investigated by everyone who wishes to obtain a perfect knowledge of Christianity and who knows that "the mouth of the righteous speaks wisdom, and his tongue talks of judgment; the law of God is in his heart."[28] Even those who have not gone into these matters in detail, either because they have no knowledge or inclination to do so or because they do not have Jesus to lead them into a rational view of religion, still believe in the most high God and in his only-begotten Son, the Word who is also God. Furthermore, they often exhibit in their character a high degree of seriousness, purity and integrity, while those who call themselves wise have despised these virtues and have wallowed in the filth of homosexuality, in lawless lust, "men doing unseemly things with other men."[29] Against Celsus 7.49.[30]

The Limits of Human Knowledge.

ARNOBIUS OF SICCA: Christ says that it is none of our business to inquire into such things as the origin of souls, the causes of the existence of evil, whether the sun is bigger than the earth or whether the moon shines with its own light or one borrowed from elsewhere. What benefit is there in knowing such things? Leave them to God. What matters to you is the salvation of your own soul, which is in danger. Unless you dedicate yourselves to the knowl-

---

[25]PL 1:431-33; cf. ANF 3:31-32. [26]PG 11:147; cf. ANF 4:252.
[27]PG 11:1036; cf. ANF 4:499. [28]Ps 37:30-31 (36:30-31 LXX).
[29]Rom 1:27. [30]PG 11:1492; cf. ANF 4:631.

edge of the supreme God, a cruel death awaits you when you are finally set free from the body. You will not be suddenly annihilated but destroyed by the bitterness of a grievous and long-protracted punishment. AGAINST THE NATIONS 2.61.[31]

GOD'S TRUTH CANNOT BE UNDERSTOOD BY UNAIDED HUMAN EFFORTS.

LACTANTIUS: The truth, which is the secret of the most high God, who created all things, cannot be understood by our own ability and perception. If human thought could reach the counsels and dispositions of that eternal majesty, there would be no difference between God and humankind. Because it was impossible for God's ways to be known by our own efforts, God did not permit us to wander in search of the light of wisdom without any tangible result but opened his eyes and made the investigation of truth his own gift. His purpose was to show the nothingness of human wisdom and to point out to erring human beings how they could find immortality. DIVINE INSTITUTES PREFACE.[32]

NATURE LEADS TO BELIEF IN GOD.

EUSEBIUS OF CAESAREA: Nature and the human mind discover for themselves, or rather they are taught by God, that beautiful and useful things exist that point to the name and substance of God. For what everyone assumes by natural reason has been instilled in every rational and intelligent creature by the Creator of all things, using our natural thought processes as the medium for this. Nobody has deduced this sort of thing by some natural logical process. PREPARATION FOR THE GOSPEL 2.6.[33]

ORDER POINTS TO SOMEONE WHO MAINTAINS IT.

EPHREM THE SYRIAN: I saw houses and knew that the householders were in residence. I saw the world, and I understood providence. I saw a ship sink without anyone to steer it, and I noticed the pointless behavior of human beings who were not steered by God.

I saw different cities and states well organized and understood that everything holds together by the ordering of God. The flock depends on the shepherd, and everything that exists on earth grows by [the power of] God. SELF-EXAMINATION.[34]

NATURAL KNOWLEDGE LEADS TO FAITH AND WORSHIP.

BASIL THE GREAT: The knowledge that God exists comes before faith in him, as we can see by looking at creation. For we recognize wisdom, power and goodness and "understand all his invisible things from the creation of the world,"[35] and in this way we accept the ruler of these things as our own Lord. Since God is the creator of the entire world and we are a part of that world, God is our creator also. Faith follows on our recognition of this, and worship follows faith. LETTERS 235.1.[36]

A SHADOW OF THE DIVINE REALITY.

GREGORY OF NAZIANZUS: It is not only the peace of God that passes all understanding and knowledge[37] or only the things that God has stored up as promises for the righteous, that "eye has not seen, nor ear heard, nor mind conceived"[38] except in a very small degree, or the accurate knowledge of the creation. For even of this, I would have you know that you have only a shadow when you hear the words "I will consider the heavens, the work of your fingers, the moon and the stars"[39] and the settled order therein, not as if he were considering them now but as destined to do so hereafter. But far more important than they are is that nature that is above them, out of which they spring—the incomprehensible and illimitable—not, I mean, as to the fact of his being but as to its nature. For our preaching is not empty or our faith vain,[40] nor is this the doctrine

---

[31]PL 5:907-8; cf. ANF 6:457. [32]PL 6:113; cf. ANF 7:9. [33]PG 21:140. [34]ESOO 1:123. [35]Rom 1:20. [36]PG 32:872. [37]Phil 4:7. [38]Is 64:4; 1 Cor 2:9. [39]Ps 8:3 (8:4 LXX). [40]1 Cor 15:14.

we proclaim, for we would not have you take our candid statement as a starting point for a quibbling denial of God or of arrogance on account of our confession of ignorance. For it is one thing to be persuaded of the existence of a thing and quite another to know what it is. On Theology, Theological Orations 2(28).5.[41]

Only Fools Deny the Existence of God. Hilary of Poitiers: The fool has said in his heart, "There is no God."[42] For if he tried to say it out loud, it would be shown by the judgment of public opinion that he indeed is a fool. For who can look at the world and not sense that there is a God? But it often happens that while necessity forces us to confess the existence of the true God, the experience of reverses persuades us that he does not exist, and what we believe against our faith we express with the thoughts of an unbelieving heart. Homilies on the Psalms 52.2.[43]

The Limits to the Natural Knowledge of God. Didymus the Blind: Because God exists beyond the invisible, beyond what is most secretly hidden and beyond what any mind can fathom, not only can he not come within the range of our vision or feeling, but neither can he be studied by the mind of the angels, because he is incomprehensible and inaccessible. That God exists is known to everyone, but to understand what he is or how he exists . . . is the most difficult thing that there is in the natural world. On the Trinity 3.16.[44]

Faith and Reason. Ambrose: It is good for faith to come before reason, lest we should appear to be demanding rational proofs from other people as well as from the Lord our God. How wrong it would be if we were to believe people's testimonies on the basis of what others say about them, yet not believe God's Word when he talks about himself. On Abraham 1.3.21.[45]

The Heavens Declare the Glory of God. Ambrose: Heaven and earth are the sum of all visible things, which point not only to the order of this world but also to invisible things of whose existence they constitute one of the arguments, as the prophetic word states: "The heavens declare the glory of God, and the firmament shows his handiwork."[46] The apostle Paul says essentially the same thing when he writes, "The invisible things are understood by means of the visible."[47] We easily understand him to be the maker of angels, dominions and powers, who in a moment of his dominion brought the great beauty of the world into being out of nothing and granted substance to things and causes that did not exist. Six Days of Creation 1.4.16.[48]

Our Conscience Reveals the Existence of God. Chrysostom: One way of knowing God is through the universal nature of things, but there is another way that is no less important—the way that is provided by conscience. . . . The understanding of good and evil is rooted in us, and our inner conscience makes it all clear to us. Thus there are two teachers who have been given to us from the beginning, creation and conscience, which have taught the human race without ever uttering a word. Sermons on Hannah 1.3.[49]

We All Know God by Nature. Jerome: We—and all the human race—know God by nature. There are no nations anywhere who do not naturally understand their Creator. Even if they worship stones and wood, they nevertheless understand that there is something bigger than themselves and mistakenly assume that they have wisdom, which is simply that there is no nation that does not know God by nature. Homilies on the Psalms 95(96).[50]

---

[41]PG 36:32; cf. NPNF 2 7:290. [42]Ps 14:1 (13:1 lxx). [43]PL 9:325-26. [44]PG 39:873. [45]PL 14:428. [46]Ps 19:1 (18:1 lxx). [47]Rom 1:20. [48]PL 14:130. [49]PG 54:636. [50]AnMar 3.2.137.

MIRACLES OF NATURE POINT US TO WHAT LIES BEHIND THEM. AUGUSTINE: The miracles performed by our Lord Jesus Christ are divine works that incite the human mind to rise to the knowledge of God on the basis of what has been seen. It is because God is not a substance that can be seen with the eyes, and because the daily miracles that he performs in governing the world and administering the entire universe are taken for granted, he has reserved certain works that go beyond the ordinary course of nature, which he performs from time to time in order that those who pay little heed to his everyday works may be astonished by them. . . . Obviously, the government of the whole world is a greater thing than merely filling five thousand people with five loaves of bread, but nobody marvels at the former, and the latter astonishes everyone—not because it is greater but because it is rare. In the miracle of the loaves and the fishes the senses are exposed to something that ought to claim the attention of the mind, and the eyes see something that ought to engage our understanding, so that we might admire the invisible God through his visible works, and being raised to faith and cleansed by it, we might desire to see him even invisibly. TRACTATES ON THE GOSPEL OF JOHN 24.1.[51]

GOD IS KNOWN TO ALL RATIONAL CREATURES. AUGUSTINE: The name of God must have been known in some way to the whole of creation, and thus to people of every nation, before they believed in Christ. For the energy of the Godhead is such that it cannot be completely hidden from any rational creature who makes use of his reason. With the exception of a few whose nature has become outrageously depraved, the entire human race acknowledges God as the maker of this world. In this respect, God was known to all nations before they received the teaching of Christ. TRACTATES ON THE GOSPEL OF JOHN 106.4.[52]

EVEN THE UNGODLY KNOW GOD. AUGUSTINE: How do the ungodly obtain the truth? Has God ever spoken to them? Have they ever accepted the law, the way the people of Israel did through Moses? How have they managed to discover the truth while still in their iniquity? Listen to the following, which explains this: "What may be known about God is plain to them, because God has made it plain to them."[53] Has he made it plain to people to whom he did not give the law? Listen to how he did this. "God's invisible qualities have been clearly seen through the things that he has made."[54] Search the world, the hosts of heaven, the splendor and arrangement of the stars. . . . Search everything, and see whether anything gives you the impression that God did not make it. Even the noble philosophers sought these things, and from art they recognized the artificer. SERMONS 141.2.2.[55]

GOD HAS REVEALED HIMSELF IN NATURE. JOHN OF DAMASCUS: God is ineffable and incomprehensible . . . but he has not left us in absolute ignorance. He has implanted the knowledge of his existence in everyone by nature. The creation, its preservation and its government all proclaim the majesty of the divine nature. ORTHODOX FAITH 1.1.[56]

The Word of God Revealed in Christ, Proclaimed and Written in Scripture

THE BIBLE IS THE BASIS OF OUR KNOWLEDGE. CLEMENT OF ALEXANDRIA: The Lord is the source of our teaching—we have him by the prophets, the Gospel and the blessed apostles, speaking "in different ways and at many times,"[57] leading from the beginning of knowledge to the end. If anyone thinks that another origin was necessary, it would be impossible

[51]PL 35:1592-93; cf. NPNF 1 7:158. [52]PL 35:1910; cf. NPNF 1 7:400. [53]Rom 1:19. [54]Rom 1:20. [55]PL 38:776. [56]PG 94:789; cf. NPNF 2 9.2:1. [57]Heb. 1:1.

to find one. Whoever believes the Scriptures and the voice of the Lord is being faithful. The Bible is the criterion of our knowledge. What is subjected to scrutiny is not believed until it is subjected to this test, so that whatever needs to be examined in this way cannot be regarded as our first principle. Therefore, as is only reasonable, we grasp the undemonstrable first principle by faith, and then we receive abundant proof of the truth of the first principle from the first principle itself. In this way we are trained up by the voice of the Lord to a knowledge of the truth. STROMATEIS 7.16.[58]

THE BIBLE ALONE PROVES THAT GOD HAS A SON. ORIGEN: Everyone who perceives that there is a Providence agrees that God, who created and ordered all things, is himself unbegotten and recognizes that he is the parent of the universe. To say that he has a Son is a statement that is not made by us alone. It may seem to be an incredible assertion to some of those who enjoy a reputation as philosophers among the Greeks and barbarians, although there are some even among them who have entertained a notion of his existence, because they acknowledge that everything was created by the Word or reason (Logos) of God. We, however, in conformity with our belief in that doctrine, which we certainly hold to have been divinely inspired, believe that there is no other way to explain and bring within the reach of human understanding the higher and diviner Logos as the Son of God than by means of those Scriptures that alone were inspired by the Holy Spirit—the Gospels and Epistles, the Law and the Prophets, as Christ himself declared. ON FIRST PRINCIPLES 1.3.1.[59]

CHRIST'S TEACHING IS VALID FOR ALL TIME. CYPRIAN: If the Lord has commanded something and the command is backed up by the apostle Paul, to the effect that as often as we eat the bread and drink the cup, we do it in remembrance of the Lord, we must do as he

did if we are going to claim that we are observing the commandment. We must not depart from the gospel precepts. Disciples should observe and do exactly what the Master taught and did. The blessed apostle teaches: "I am amazed that you have so soon departed from him who called you into grace and gone after another gospel, which is no gospel at all. There are some who would trouble you and pervert the gospel of Christ. If an apostle or an angel from heaven preaches or teaches anything other than what Christ has taught once for all and his disciples have preached, let him be anathema."[60] LETTERS 63.10.[61]

THE BIBLE PROCLAIMS THE ONLY TRUE GOD. TREATISE ON REBAPTISM: Whoever believes in another God or receives a Christ other than the one declared in the Old and New Testaments is a heretic, because the Bible clearly declares the Father Almighty, creator of all things, and his Son. TREATISE ON REBAPTISM 13.[62]

THE OLD TESTAMENT SAINTS WERE SAVED WITHOUT CONFESSING CHRIST. CHRYSOSTOM: "What then?"one may say. "Were they wronged, who lived before his coming?" By no means, for people might then be saved even though they had not confessed Christ. For this was not required of them, but only not to worship idols and to know the true God. "For the Lord your God," it is said, "is one Lord."[63] Therefore the Maccabees were admired, because for the observance of the Law they suffered what they did suffer,[64] and the three children[65] and many others too among the Jews, having shown forth a very virtuous life and having maintained the standard of this their knowledge, had nothing more required of them. For then it was sufficient for salva-

---

[58]PG 9:532; cf. ANF 2:551. [59]PG 11:145-46; cf. ANF 4:251-52. [60]Gal 1:6-9. [61]PL 4:381-82; cf. ANF 5:361. [62]PL 3:1247; cf. ANF 5:674-75. [63]Deut 6:4. [64]2 Macc 7:1-41. [65]Dan 3:1-30.

tion, as I have said already, to know God only, but now it is so no more. There is need also of the knowledge of Christ. Homilies on the Gospel of Matthew 36.[66]

Christ Is the Author of the Scriptures. Augustine: Christ our mediator, having spoken what he thought was sufficient first by the prophets and then by his own lips and afterwards by the apostles, has also produced the Scripture that is called canonical. This has paramount authority, and we assent to it in all matters of which we ought not to be ignorant yet cannot know by ourselves. We can obtain knowledge of visible objects by the testimony of our own senses, . . . but when it comes to things that are not accessible to our senses, we need the witness of others, since we cannot know them by ourselves, and we trust the people who have seen and borne witness to what they describe. City of God 11.3.[67]

To Stimulate Faith. Augustine: The miracles of Christ were published in order to produce faith, and the faith that they produced gave them even greater prominence. They are read in congregations so that they may be believed, but they would not be read unless they were believed. Even now miracles are wrought in the name of Christ, . . . but they are not so brilliant and obvious as to cause them to be published with the glory that accompanied the earlier miracles. City of God 22.8.1.[68]

Old Testament Typologies Fulfilled. Augustine: The things in the Law and the Prophets that Christians do not observe are only the types of what they do observe. These types were figures of things to come and are necessarily taken away when the things themselves are fully revealed in Christ, so that by this very removal the Law and the Prophets may be fulfilled. Against Faustus, a Manichaean 18.4.[69]

The Inspiration of Scripture

The Holy Spirit Inspired the Scriptures. Clement of Rome: You love to argue, brothers, and are experts in things that have nothing to do with salvation. Look carefully into the Scriptures, which are the true utterances of the Holy Spirit. Observe that there is nothing unjust or counterfeit in them. You will not find in them any suggestion that the righteous were cast off by people who were themselves holy. 1 Clement 1.45.[70]

The Scriptures Are Divine Prophecies. Clement of Rome: Beloved, you understand the holy Scriptures very well. You have looked deeply into the prophecies of God. 1 Clement 1.53.[71]

The Prophets Were Musical Instruments. Athenagoras: We have the prophets as witnesses of the things we understand and believe. Men like Moses, Isaiah, Jeremiah and the other prophets declared things about God and the things of God. It would be irrational of us to disbelieve God's Spirit and accept mere human opinions instead, for God moved the mouths of the prophets as if they were musical instruments. A Plea Regarding Christians 9.[72]

The Apostles Told Us Everything They Knew. Irenaeus: If the apostles had possessed hidden knowledge that they were in the habit of sharing privately with those who were "perfect," then surely they would have committed this knowledge to those whom they were putting in charge of the churches. After all, the apostles wanted their successors to be

---

[66]PG 57:417; cf. NPNF 1 10:241. [67]PL 41:318; cf. NPNF 1 2:206. [68]PL 41:760; cf. NPNF 1 2:484-85. [69]PL 42:345; cf. NPNF 1 4:237. [70]PG 1:300-301; cf. ANF 1:17. [71]PG 1:316; cf. ANF 1:19. [72]PG 6:905-8; cf. ANF 2:133.

perfect and blameless in all things. AGAINST HERESIES 3.3.1.[73]

TRUTH DEPOSITED WITH THE CHURCH.
IRENAEUS: There is no need to go looking for the truth, because it can easily be obtained from the church. The apostles deposited everything they knew with the church, just as a rich person might leave everything he has in a bank, so that anyone who wants to draw out the water of life can do so freely from the church. AGAINST HERESIES 3.4.1.[74]

THE SCRIPTURES ARE ALWAYS TRUE.
TERTULLIAN: The statements of holy Scripture never disagree with the truth. A corrupt tree will never yield good fruit unless a better nature is grafted into it, nor will a good tree produce bad fruit, except by the same process. Stones will become children of Abraham if they are educated in Abraham's faith, and a generation of vipers will bring forth the fruits of repentance if they reject the poison of their malignant nature. ON THE SOUL 21.[75]

ALL SCRIPTURE IS EQUALLY INSPIRED BY GOD. TERTULLIAN: The apostle Paul was guided by the same Spirit as the author of Genesis was, and the same is true of all the Scriptures. ON PRAYER 22.[76]

THE WHOLE TRUTH AND NOTHING BUT THE TRUTH. TERTULLIAN: The apostles would have found it impossible to convert either Jews or Gentiles unless they had "set forth in order"[77] the things that they wanted them to believe. Once the churches were well-grounded in their faith, the apostles would not have withheld anything from them in order to grant it to a few select individuals. Even supposing that they held intimate discussions among a few friends, it is incredible that these could have been of such a kind as to introduce another rule of faith, different from and contrary to the one that they

were proclaiming throughout the churches. How could they have spoken of one God in the church and another at home? PRESCRIPTIONS AGAINST HERETICS 26.[78]

THE TRUTH OF SCRIPTURE IS VINDICATED BY THE POWER OF GOD. ORIGEN: Just as the doctrine of providence is not weakened (in the eyes of those who have assented to it) merely by the fact that some events cannot be explained, so the divinity of Scripture, which extends to all of it, is not diminished because of our inability to discover in every verse the hidden splendor of the doctrines that are concealed in common and unattractive phraseology. . . . For we have this treasure in earthen vessels, so that the excellence of the power of God may shine forth, and no one will think that it comes from mere human beings like us. For if the common methods of proving things had been able to produce conviction regarding the truth of the Bible, then our faith would have been regarded as resting on the wisdom of people rather than on the power of God. But now it is clear to everyone who cares to look that the word and preaching have not prevailed among the people "by persuasive words of wisdom but by demonstration of the Spirit and of power."[79] ON FIRST PRINCIPLES 4.1.7.[80]

THE INSPIRATION OF THE ONE HOLY SPIRIT. MURATORIAN FRAGMENT: Although different things are taught in the different Gospels, there is no difference with respect to the faith of believers, because all of them were inspired by the same controlling Spirit. . . . We should not be surprised to find that John mentions the same things in his first epistle, . . . claiming to have been both the eyewitness and hearer of the matters he describes, as also the

---

[73]PG 7:848; cf. ANF 1:415. [74]PG 7:855; cf. ANF 1:416-17. [75]PG 2:685; cf. ANF 3:202. [76]PL 1:1185; cf. ANF 3:687. [77]Lk 1:1. [78]PL 2:38-39; cf. ANF 3:255. [79]1 Cor 2:4. [80]PG 11:356; cf. ANF 4:355.

historian of all the wonderful deeds of our Lord, in the order in which they occurred. MURATORIAN FRAGMENT 1.[81]

SCRIPTURE IS A RATIONAL AND CONSISTENT WHOLE. METHODIUS: Why does the Lord say that "heaven and earth shall pass away"[82] or the prophet Isaiah declare that "the heaven shall perish as smoke, and the earth shall grow old like a garment"[83] when it is clear that the universe will not be destroyed? The answer is that Scripture usually calls the change from this world to a better and more glorious one "destruction," because the earlier form is lost in the transformation of all things into a state of greater splendor. There is no contradiction or absurdity in holy Scripture. It is not the world but the "fashion of the world"[84] that passes away. . . . The creation will perish in order that it may be renewed, not destroyed forever, so that we who are spiritually renewed may dwell in a new world, where there will be no sorrow. ON THE RESURRECTION 1.9.[85]

THE MANY FORMS OF DIVINE INSPIRATION. EPIPHANIUS OF SALAMIS: Moses did not write anything contrary to the will of God but rather legislated at the direction of the Holy Spirit, which makes it clear that his legislation is the law of God. Everywhere God gives laws, some of which relate to particular circumstances, some of which are foreshadowings of what is to come and some of which are a revelation of those future blessings with which our Lord Jesus Christ filled us when he came. PANARION 33.9.[86]

SCRIPTURE IS ADAPTED TO OUR UNDERSTANDING. EPIPHANIUS OF SALAMIS: Human nature cannot see God because the visible cannot see the invisible. But the invisible God, in his mercy and power to give strength to the weak, made it possible for us to perceive the invisible. We do not see what is invisible and

infinite to its full extent but only in so far as our limited human nature can understand it. Strengthened by his power and might, our weak nature can rise to the contemplation of the Almighty. Furthermore, there are no contradictions in holy Scripture, nor will you find in them any statement that is opposed to any other. PANARION 70.7.[87]

THE AMAZING DEPTH OF THE SCRIPTURES. AUGUSTINE: What wonderful profundity there is in your sayings! The surface meaning lies open before us and attracts beginners. Yet the depth is amazing, my God, the depth is amazing! To meditate on it is to experience awe— the awe of adoration before its transcendence and the trembling of love. I hate the enemies of Scripture.[88] I wish that you would kill them with a two-edged sword.[89] Then they would no longer be its enemies. The sense in which I wish them dead is this—I love them, and so want them to die to themselves that they might live in you.[90] CONFESSIONS 12.14.17.[91]

THE DIFFERENCE BETWEEN THE TWO TESTAMENTS. AUGUSTINE: Put very briefly, the difference between the two Testaments can best be expressed in two words—fear and love. Fear is for the old person and love for the new, yet each has come from and is connected with the most merciful dispensation of the one God. AGAINST ADIMANTUS 17.2.[92]

SCRIPTURE CONTAINS THINGS THAT ARE FALSE IN THEMSELVES. AUGUSTINE: Although the Gospels are completely true in everything they say, not everything that is contained in them can be regarded as true, since the truthful Scripture of the Gospel records that the Jews said many false and ungodly

---

[81]PL 3:185-87; cf. ANF 5:603. [82]Mt 24:35. [83]Is 51:6. [84]1 Cor 7:31. [85]PG 18:276; cf. ANF 6:366. [86]PG 41:572-73. [87]PG 42:349-52. [88]Ps 139:21 (138:21 LXX). [89]Ps 149:6. [90]Rom 14:7-8; 2 Cor 5:14-15. [91]PL 32:832; cf. NPNF 1 1:180. [92]PL 42:159.

things. Similarly in Job, where many people are presented as having spoken, you have to consider not just what is said but who is saying it. When we look into this and test ourselves by the witness of the holy writings, we realize that it is nowhere said that we must believe something, even if it is written in the Gospel, if the Evangelist mentions that he has recorded something that in itself is not to be believed. To Orosius 9.12.[93]

Every Part of Scripture Is Inspired for a Purpose. John of Damascus: All Scripture is given by inspiration of God and is therefore certainly profitable.[94] This is why it is most proper and useful for every soul to search the Scriptures. Just as the tree planted by the waterside gives its fruit in the right season,[95] so also the soul watered by the divine Scriptures will do the same. In the Bible we are encouraged to practice every virtue and dissuaded from every vice. . . . If we do not understand what we read, let us not give up but rather persevere, discuss and inquire as to the meaning. Orthodox Faith 4.17.[96]

The Spiritual Purpose of the Scriptures

The Scriptures Give Us Eternal Life. Justin Martyr: Moses and the prophets were far more ancient than any of your Greek philosophers. Therefore, abandon their delusions and read the divine histories of the prophets, so that you may discover the true religion from them. They do not present you with artful discourses, nor do they speak speciously and plausibly—for this is what people who want to rob you of the truth are wont to do—but they use the words and expressions that come to mind with great simplicity and declare to you whatever the Holy Spirit, who descended on them, chose to teach through them. Renounce the errors of your ancestors and read the prophecies of the sacred writings. Learn from them what will give you eternal life. Horta-tory Address to the Greeks 35.[97]

The Scriptures Are Our Guide to the Future. Theophilus of Antioch: Do not be skeptical, but believe. I myself used to be an unbeliever, but now I have taken these things into consideration and have changed my mind. I met with the sacred Scriptures of the holy prophets, who by the Spirit of God foretold things that have already happened, and in the same order. They have also foretold things that are happening right now, again in the right order, and they have foretold things that are still to come, once more in the order of their future occurrence. Having considered the fulfillment of prophecies already accomplished, I became a believer, and I urge you to do the same, lest the eternal punishments foretold for unbelievers should torment you in your unbelief. . . . Pay reverent attention to the holy Scriptures, and they will make your way plainer for escaping from eternal punishment and obtaining God's eternal prize. The God who formed the mouth for speech, the ear for hearing and the eye for seeing will examine all things and pass righteous judgment, giving each person the reward he deserves. . . . You asked me to show you my God, and here he is. To Autolycus 1.14.[98]

The Secret of True Wisdom. Clement of Alexandria: The wise person who has been persuaded to obey the commandments will become wiser by his knowledge, and the intelligent person will acquire power. He will understand parables and obscure sayings, the oracles and enigmas of the wise.[99] Those inspired by God and those who have been converted through them do not produce spurious words, nor do they trick people with

---

[93]PL 42:676. [94]2 Tim 3:16. [95]Ps 1:3. [96]PG 94:1176-77; cf. NPNF 2 9.2:89. [97]PG 6:304; cf. ANF 1:287-88. [98]PG 6:1044-45; cf. ANF 2:93. [99]See Prov 1:2-6.

their clever words, as the Sophists do. On the contrary, those who possess the Holy Spirit "search the deep things of God"[100] and thus grasp the secrets that are in the prophecies. It is forbidden to impart holy things to dogs, as long as they remain beasts. Those who are jealous and disturbed, and whose behavior is still pagan, should never be allowed to dip into the divine and clear stream of the living water. . . . But the person who believes the Scriptures correctly hears in them the voice of God, who gave them to us. STROMATEIS 2.2.[101]

THE SCRIPTURES TEACH US THE WAY OF SALVATION. CLEMENT OF ALEXANDRIA: I could produce ten thousand texts of Scripture of which "not one jot or title shall pass away"[102] but will be fulfilled. For the mouth of the Lord the Holy Spirit has spoken these things. "My son, do not despise the chastening of the Lord or be discouraged when he rebukes you."[103] What great love for us! The Lord does not speak to us as a teacher to his pupils, as a master to his servants or as God to his people, but as a father to his children. The spirit of godliness tells us that only God can make us be like him. It is this teaching that the apostle Paul calls truly divine. "From childhood, Timothy, you have known the holy Scriptures, which are able to make you wise unto salvation, through faith in Christ Jesus."[104] Those writings that sanctify and deify are truly holy in themselves. For that reason, the apostle Paul calls the Scriptures "inspired of God and profitable for doctrine, reproof, correction."[105] No one will be as impressed by the sayings of the saints as he will be by the words of the Lord himself, the one who loves us. EXHORTATION TO THE GREEKS 9.[106]

THE SCRIPTURES TEACH US HOW TO GROW IN FAITH AND KNOWLEDGE OF GOD. TERTULLIAN: In order that we might acquire a fuller and more authoritative knowledge both

of himself and of his counsels and will, God has added a written revelation for the benefit of everyone whose heart is set on seeking him, so that by seeking he may find, and by finding believe, and by believing obey. From the first, he sent messengers into the world—those whose stainless righteousness made them worthy to know the Most High. He revealed to them, people abundantly endowed with the Holy Spirit, that they might proclaim that there is only one God, who made all things, who formed humankind from the dust of the ground—for he is the true Prometheus who put order into the world by arranging the seasons and their course. These have further set before us the proofs he has given of his majesty in his judgments by floods and fires, the rules appointed by him for securing his favor, as well as the retribution in store. . . . We, too, used to laugh at these things. We are of your stock and nature, for people are made, not born, Christians. The preachers of whom we have spoken are called prophets, from the office that belongs to them of predicting the future. Their words, along with the miracles that they performed in order for people to have faith in their divine authority, are recorded in the literary treasures that they have left us and that are open to all. . . .

The Jews too read them publicly and are in the habit of going to hear them every sabbath. Whoever pays attention to them will find God in them; whoever takes the trouble to understand will be compelled to believe. Their great antiquity, first of all, claims authority for these writings. You too make it almost a religious requirement that things should be very old. Well, I tell you that all your sacred books and objects put together are not as ancient as even one of our prophets. If you have heard of Moses, . . . let me tell you that he is five hundred years older than Homer. The other prophets

---

[100]1 Cor 2:10. [101]PG 8:937-41; cf. ANF 2:348-49. [102]Mt 5:18. [103]Prov 3:11. [104]2 Tim 3:15. [105]2 Tim 3:16. [106]ANF 2:195-96.

came later, but every one of them is older than the first of your philosophers, legislators and historians.[107]. . .

There is another thing of even greater importance—the majesty of our Scriptures. If you doubt that they are as old as we say, we offer proof of their divine character. You can persuade yourselves of this right here, without bothering to do any research into the matter. Your instructors—the world, the times we live in and the events described—are all before you. Everything now taking place around you was announced beforehand—the swallowing up of cities by the earth, the theft of islands by the sea, wars that cause both internal and external convulsions, the collision of kingdom with kingdom, famines, pestilence, local massacres and widespread genocides, the exaltation of the lowly and the humbling of the proud, the decline of righteousness, the growth of sin, the fall-off of interest in all good things, the disorder of the seasons, the appearance of monsters—all this was foreseen and predicted before it happened. When we suffer calamities, we read of them in the Scriptures. As we examine them, they are proved to be right. The truth of a prophecy, in my opinion, is the evidence that it has come from above. We have an assured faith with regard to future events because they have already been prophesied to us. They have been uttered by the same voices and are written in the same books—all inspired by one and the same Spirit. APOLOGY 18-20.[108]

THE LETTER KILLS, BUT THE SPIRIT GIVES LIFE. GREGORY OF NYSSA: "Every Scripture is given by inspiration of God and is profitable for doctrine, for reproof, for correction, for instruction in righteousness."[109] Such a gift as this is not within anyone's reach, for the divine intention lies hidden under the body of Scripture, as if under a veil—some legislative enactment or some historical narrative being cast over the truths that are contemplated by the mind. This is why the apostle Paul tells us

that those who look at the body of Scripture "have a veil over their heart"[110] and are unable to look at the glory of the spiritual law because of the veil that has been cast over the face of the lawgiver. This is why Paul says, "The letter kills, but the spirit gives life,"[111] showing that very often the obvious interpretation, if it is not the one that fits with the overall sense, has an effect contrary to the life that is indicated by the spirit, seeing that this lays down for everyone the perfection of virtue in freedom from passion, while the history contained in the writings sometimes includes such incongruous facts as to make the obvious sense of the passage a message of death rather than one of life. Thus it is that those who handle the text in too literal a manner have a veil cast over their eyes, whereas those who turn to contemplate the God of whom the Scriptures speak receive the revelation of divine glory that lies behind the letter of the text. AGAINST EUNOMIUS 7.1.[112]

GOD WANTS US TO BE CHRISTIANS, NOT SCIENTISTS. AUGUSTINE: You have said that Mani has taught you the beginning, the middle and the end of the world, as well as how and why it was made. But with respect to the course of the sun and moon and the other things that you have mentioned, you will not read in the Scriptures that the Lord said, "I am sending you a Comforter who will teach you about the course of the sun and moon." He wanted to make us Christians, not scientists! AGAINST FELIX THE MANICHAEAN 1.10.[113]

ALL STORIES HAVE A SPIRITUAL PURPOSE. CYRIL OF ALEXANDRIA: Those who reject a story recounted in holy Scripture because of

---

[107] This is not strictly accurate, but the general point—that the Hebrew Scriptures are mostly older than the writings of the main Greek and Roman philosophers—is true. [108] PL 1:377-91; cf. ANF 3:32-33. [109] 2 Tim 3:16. [110] 2 Cor 3:15. [111] 2 Cor 3:6. [112] PG 45:741-44; cf. NPNF 2 5:192. [113] PL 42:525.

its apparent triviality are ignoring the proper way in which the things written in Scripture are to be understood. For spiritual reflection, which is good and useful and enlightens the eyes of the mind, makes us understand the true meaning, enabling us to extract from the stories of Scripture whatever is useful for us, so that the divinely inspired text may appear to aid and help us. COMMENTARY ON ISAIAH 1.4.[114]

The Antiquity of the Scriptures

THE OLDEST AND MOST ACCURATE HISTORY IN EXISTENCE. THEOPHILUS OF ANTIOCH: I want to give you a more accurate account of the different historical periods, so that you may see that our teaching is not modern or fictitious but older and more true than the uncertain writings of poets and other authors who wrote in uncertainty. Some maintained that the world was never created and invented infinity [to explain it]. Others said it was created and came up with an age of 153,075 years for the earth. This is what Apollonius the Egyptian says. Even Plato . . . babbled nonsense in his *Laws* when he said, "If things had always been as they are now, when could anything new have been discovered? Ten thousand times ten thousand years have elapsed without any record, and one or two thousand years have gone by since Dedalus, Orpheus and Palamedes made their discoveries."[115] . . . He would have done better if he had become a scholar of God and allowed himself to be taught by the divine law. Did not Homer, Hesiod and Orpheus all claim to have been inspired by divine providence? It is said that among your writers there were prophets and fortune tellers who predicted things accurately. How much more then shall we know the truth, since we have been instructed by the holy prophets who were inspired by the Holy Spirit of God. For this reason all the prophets spoke harmoniously, in agreement with one another, and foretold what would come to pass in the world. The accuracy of what they said should be enough to confirm the truth of their account of the years before the flood, which shows just how ridiculous and untrue the statements of your pagan authors are. To AUTOLYCUS 3.16-17.[116]

ORTHODOXY EXISTED BEFORE HERESY. TERTULLIAN: I say that my gospel is the true one and that Marcion's is false. He claims the opposite. How can one decide which of us is right? The only answer is that of time—authority lies with the teaching that can be shown to be most ancient. It assumes that corruption belongs to the view that can be shown to be of more recent origin. If error is the falsification of truth, then it is evident that truth must have come first. With regard to Luke's Gospel, which we hold in common with Marcion, it is evident that the parts of it that we alone accept are so much older than Marcion, and indeed that Marcion himself accepted the whole thing in the days when he still belonged to the church, before he invented his heresy. AGAINST MARCION 4.4.[117]

APOSTOLIC TRUTH IS MORE ANCIENT THAN HERESY. TERTULLIAN: "The hope that is laid up for you in heaven, of which you have heard before in the word of the truth of the gospel, has come to you just as it has to all the world."[118] Now, if it is our gospel that has spread everywhere and not Marcion's, then it will be obvious that it is our gospel that is the true one. But even if Marcion's Gospel did spread all over the world, it would still not be apostolic, because that word can be applied only to the truth that filled the world first. AGAINST MARCION 5.19.[119]

---

[114]PG 70:192. [115]Plato *Laws* 3.376. Theophilus mistakenly ascribes the quote to Plato's *Republic*. [116]PG 6:1144-45; cf. ANF 2:116. [117]PL 2:365; cf. ANF 3:348-49. [118]Col 1:5-6. [119]PL 2:519; cf. ANF 3:470.

The Authority and Sufficiency of the Scriptures

ONLY CHRISTIANS ARE RIGHTFUL HEIRS OF SCRIPTURE. TERTULLIAN: Since heretics are not Christians, they have acquired no right to the Christian Scriptures. Thus it is fair for us to say to them, "Who are you? When did you arrive on the scene, and from where did you come? Since you do not belong to what is mine, what have you to do with that which is mine? Indeed, Marcion, by what right do you hew my wood? By whose permission, Valentinus, are you diverting the streams of my fountain? By what power, Apelles, are you removing my landmarks? This is my property. . . . I hold sure title-deeds from the original owners themselves, to whom the estate belonged. I am the heir of the apostles. Just as they carefully prepared their will and testament, and committed it to a trust, . . . even so do I hold it now.". PRE-SCRIPTIONS AGAINST HERETICS 37.[120]

PAUL SPOKE WITH DIVINE AUTHORITY. TERTULLIAN: Although Paul did not have a specific commandment from the Lord, he was accustomed to give counsel and dictate matters on his own authority, because he possessed the Spirit of God, who guides us into all truth. For this reason, his advice is equivalent to a divine command. THE CHAPLET 4.[121]

EVERYTHING NECESSARY FOR SALVATION. TERTULLIAN: Heretics usually tell us that the apostles did not know everything. By saying this, they are blaming Christ for having sent out apostles who were either too ignorant or too confused. But what sane person could possibly think that they were ignorant of anything, once the Lord had ordained them to be teachers? . . . Was anything withheld from Peter, who was called to be the rock on which the church would be built? After all, he also received the keys of the kingdom of heaven, so that he had the power both to bind and to loose—in heaven as well as on earth. And was anything hidden from John, the beloved disciple who leaned on the Lord's breast? . . .

"When the Spirit of truth comes, he will lead you into all truth."[122] This shows that there was nothing of which the apostles were ignorant, because Jesus promised them that they would receive all truth with the help of the Spirit of truth. PRESCRIPTIONS AGAINST HERETICS 22.[123]

MINOR DISCREPANCIES DO NOT INVALI-DATE THE SCRIPTURES. TERTULLIAN: The apostles Matthew and John instill faith in us, and this is backed up by those apostolic helpers, Mark and Luke. All four of them start with the same basic principles of the faith, in so far as it relates to the one and only Creator God and his Christ, who was born of a virgin and came to earth in order to fulfill the Law and the Prophets. Never mind if there are variations in the order of the Gospel narratives. What matters is that there is agreement in the essential doctrine of the faith. AGAINST MARCION 4.2.[124]

CORRUPT TEXTS OF SCRIPTURE ARE THE WORK OF HERETICS. TERTULLIAN: Where diversity of doctrine is found there must be corruption both of the Scriptures and the expositions of it. Those who wanted to teach something different had to arrange the texts of doctrine in a different way. They could not possibly have achieved their diversity of teaching by any other means. Corruption in doctrine could not have succeeded unless the texts that convey it were also corrupted, just as we could not have maintained the integrity of our doctrine without maintaining the integrity of our texts. What is there in our Scriptures that goes against what we teach? What have we

---

[120]ANF 3:261. [121]PL 2:81-82; cf. ANF 3:95. [122]Jn 16:13.
[123]PL 2:34; cf. ANF 3:253. [124]PL 2:363; cf. ANF 3:347.

introduced that comes from us and not from them? We are what the Scriptures are, and have been since the beginning. We came into being as a result of them, before any other way had appeared and before they were interpolated by you heretics. All interpolation is a later process because it derives from rivalry that can never precede what it emulates.[125] It is obvious that we, who have existed from the beginning, cannot have interpolated anything into the Scriptures, since those interpolations came later. One person perverts the Scriptures by altering the text, and another does it by changing the interpretation. Valentinus, for example, seems to make use of the entire volume but has laid violent hands on the truth by using his cunning mind and skill even more than Marcion. Marcion used the knife, not the pen, in that he abbreviated the Scriptures to suit his teaching. Valentinus avoided such excision. He did not invent Scriptures to fit his doctrine but adapted his doctrine to the existing texts. Yet he managed to take away more from them than Marcion did, and he added more too, because he removed the proper meaning of every particular word and added fantastic constructions of things that have no real existence. PRESCRIPTIONS AGAINST HERETICS 38.[126]

THE TEACHING OF THE APOSTOLIC CHURCHES.
TERTULLIAN: No doubt, after the time of the apostles, the truth about belief in God suffered corruption, but it is equally certain that during their lifetime their teaching on this great subject did not suffer at all. Therefore, only the teaching that is currently given in the churches of apostolic foundation can rightly be called apostolic. AGAINST MARCION 1.21.[127]

NOVEL PRACTICES ARE UNLAWFUL.
TERTULLIAN: The church lays down the rule that our faith has ceremonies appointed either by the Scriptures or by ancestral tradition. No addi-

tion can now be made to this deposit, because innovation is unlawful. ON FASTING 13.[128]

OUR AUTHORITY IN ALL THINGS.
ORIGEN: In order that I may not appear to be building my assertions on subjects of such importance and difficulty on mere inference or to be requiring your assent to what is only a matter of conjecture, let us see whether we can find any declarations of holy Scripture, by the authority of which my position can be more credibly defended. I shall mention first what holy Scripture says about evil powers and then go on to examine the rest, as the Lord may be pleased to enlighten us, so that we may find out what is closest to the truth or what we ought to believe in accordance with the standard of truth. ON FIRST PRINCIPLES 1.5.4.[129]

THE ONLY AUTHORITY FOR CHRISTIAN TEACHING.
HEGEMONIUS: Those who set up some new teaching have a way of twisting the Scriptures to make them fit whatever it is they want them to say. The apostolic word says, "If anyone preaches any gospel to you other than that which you have received, let him be anathema."[130] Therefore a disciple of Christ should accept no new teaching beyond what has once been committed to us by the apostles. DISPUTATION OF ARCHELAUS AND MANES 40.[131]

FAULTY MANUSCRIPTS MUST BE CORRECTED.
JEROME: Some of my enemies have accused me of trying to correct passages in the Gospels. . . . I am not so stupid or ignorant as to suppose that any of the Lord's Word is in need of correction or is not divinely inspired,

---

[125]The frequency of Tertullian's use of these rhetorical questions suggests that this may have been a hymn or a common apologetic formula. [126]PL 2:51-52; cf. ANF 3:261-62. [127]PL 2:270; cf. ANF 3:286. [128]PL 2:971; cf. ANF 4:111. Tertullian quotes this as a saying of his opponents, which he wishes to refute. The context, however, indicates that the principle was one that was generally held at the time. [129]PG 11:160; cf. ANF 4:258. [130]Gal 1:9. [131]PG 10:1492; cf. ANF 6:213-14.

but the Latin manuscripts of the Scriptures are evidently faulty because of the variations that they all exhibit, and my intention has been to restore them to the form of the Greek original. LETTERS 27.1.[132]

THE AUTHORITY OF SCRIPTURE. AUGUSTINE: The authority of Scripture has come down to us from the apostles through the succession of bishops and the spread of the church, and from a position of lofty supremacy, it claims the submission of every faithful and pious mind. AGAINST FAUSTUS, A MANICHAEAN 11.5.[133]

HOW THE AUTHORSHIP OF BIBLICAL BOOKS HAS BEEN DETERMINED. AUGUSTINE: You are so hardened in your errors against the testimonies of Scripture that nothing can be done with you. Whenever anything is quoted against you, you have the temerity to say that it is written not by the apostle but by some pretender under his name. . . . How do we know the authorship of the works of Plato, Aristotle, Cicero, Varro and other similar writers, except by the unbroken chain of evidence? So it is with the numerous commentaries on the ecclesiastical books that have no canonical authority and yet show a desire to be useful and a spirit of inquiry. How is the authorship ascertained in each case, except by the author's having brought his work to public notice as much as possible in his own lifetime and, by the transmission of the information from one to another in continuous succession, the belief becoming more certain as it becomes more general, up to our own day? AGAINST FAUSTUS, A MANICHAEAN 33.6.[134]

THERE CAN BE NO FALSE STATEMENT IN HOLY SCRIPTURE. AUGUSTINE (TO JEROME): It seems to me that the most disastrous consequences will follow if we believe that there is anything false to be found in our sacred books, that is to say, if we believe that the men

by whom the Scriptures have been given to us and committed to writing put anything false in them. It is one question to ask whether a good person might occasionally have a duty to deceive others, but quite another to ask whether the same applies to a writer of holy Scripture. . . . Once you admit that a false statement has been made out of a sense of duty, there will not be a single sentence in the entire Bible that will be free of such suspicion if it seems difficult in practice or hard to believe. In such circumstances it would be all too easy to explain the passage away by saying that the writer deceived his readers out of a sense of duty. LETTER 28.3.[135]

FAULTY TRANSMISSION OR POOR UNDERSTANDING. AUGUSTINE (TO JEROME): Of all the books in the world, I believe that only the authors of holy Scripture were totally free from error, and if I am puzzled by anything in them that seems to go against the truth, I do not hesitate to suppose that either the manuscript is faulty or the translator has not caught the sense of what was said, or I have failed to understand it myself. As for other writings, however superior their authors may be to me in holiness and learning, I do not accept their teaching as true because it is what they thought but only because they have succeeded in convincing my judgment, either by arguments that appeal to these canonical writings or by the force of reason. I believe, my brother, that you share my opinion about this. LETTER 82.3.[136]

THERE IS NO AUTHORITY OUTSIDE SCRIPTURE. AUGUSTINE: Where do you find any authority apart from the gospel and the apostolic writings? How can we be sure of the authorship of any book if we doubt the apostolic origin of those books that are attributed to

---

[132]PL 22:431; cf. NPNF 2 6:44. [133]PL 42:249; cf. NPNF 1 4:180. [134]PL 42:514-15; cf. NPNF 1 4:343. [135]PL 33:112-13; cf. NPNF 1 1:251-52. [136]PL 33:277; cf. NPNF 1 1:350.

the apostles by the churches that the apostles themselves founded? AGAINST FAUSTUS, A MANICHAEAN 33.6.[137]

THE SCRIPTURES ARE NECESSARY BECAUSE OF OUR SINFULNESS.

CHRYSOSTOM: Consider what a great evil it is for us, who in theory ought to be able to live in such purity that we should have no need of any written words, but only to offer up ourselves as books to the Spirit, now that we have lost that honor and stand in need of written instruction, to fail once more by neglecting this second chance to put matters right. We ought to be blamed for standing in need of written words, but think how guilty we would become if we failed to pay attention to them when they have been given to help us, and rather than use them properly, we should neglect what is written as if it had no purpose. HOMILIES ON THE GOSPEL OF MATTHEW 1.2.[138]

THE DIVINE AUTHOR IS SUFFICIENT.

THEODORET OF CYR: Some have said that not all the psalms come from David, but that some are the work of others. I have no opinion on this matter either way. What difference does it make to me whether they are all David's or whether some are the compositions of others, when it is clear that they are all the fruit of the Holy Spirit's inspiration? PREFACE TO THE PSALMS.[139]

GOD IS THE TRUE AUTHOR OF JOB.

GREGORY THE GREAT: It is pointless to ask who wrote the book of Job, since the Holy Spirit is rightly believed to have been its author. In other words, the one who wrote it is the one who dictated what was to be written. He is both the author and the inspirer of the work, and through the voice of a scribe he has transmitted the matters that we are called on to imitate. If we get some letters and in them read the words of some great person and then ask who actually did the writing, it would be absurd to recognize the author and understand his meaning but then fret over whose pen put the words on paper. Therefore, since we recognize the substance and hold that the Holy Spirit is its author, why should we bother about the writer? What would that mean except that we would be putting form before substance? MORALS ON THE BOOK OF JOB, PREFACE 1.2.[140]

The Canon of Scripture

THE CHRISTIAN SCRIPTURES.

ATHANASIUS: In proceeding to make mention of these things, I shall adopt as my guide the pattern of Luke the Evangelist and adapt his words as follows: Forasmuch as some have taken in hand[141] to reduce to order for themselves the books termed apocryphal and to mix them up with the divinely inspired Scripture, concerning which we have been fully persuaded, as they who from the beginning were eyewitnesses and ministers of the Word delivered to the Fathers; it seemed good to me also, having been encouraged in this by true brethren and having learned from the beginning, to set before you the books included in the canon and handed down, and accredited as divine, so that anyone who has fallen into error may condemn those who have led him astray and that the one who has continued steadfast in purity may once again rejoice to have these things brought to his remembrance.

The Old Testament contains twenty-two books, being the same number as the letters of the Hebrew alphabet. . . . The books of the New Testament are the four Gospels according to Matthew, Mark, Luke and John; the Acts of the Apostles, the seven Catholic Epistles (James, 1 and 2 Peter, 1, 2 and 3 John and Jude); the fourteen epistles of Paul . . . and the Revelation of John. These are fountains of

---

[137]PL 42:514; cf. NPNF 1 4:343. [138]PG 57:14-15; cf. NPNF 1 10:1. [139]PG 80:861. [140]PL 75:517. [141]Lk 1:1.

salvation, where those who thirst may be satisfied with the living words that they contain. In them alone is the doctrine of godliness proclaimed. No one must add to these, nor should anyone take anything away from them. For it was concerning them that the Lord put the Sadducees to shame when he said, "You err, not knowing the Scriptures"[142] and reproved the Jews, saying, "Search the Scriptures, for they bear witness of me."[143] FESTAL LETTER 39.3-6.[144]

THE AUGUSTINIAN CANON. AUGUSTINE: The canon of Scripture is contained in the following books: five books of Moses, that is, Genesis, Exodus, Leviticus, Numbers and Deuteronomy. One book of Joshua the son of Nun. One of Judges, one short book called Ruth, which seems to belong to the beginning of Kings, four books of Kings,[145] and two of Chronicles—these last not following one another but running parallel, so to speak, and going over the same ground. The books now mentioned are history, which contains a connected narrative of the times and follows the order of events. There are other books that seem to follow no regular order, such as Job, Tobit and Esther, Judith, the two books of the Maccabees and the two of Ezra,[146] the last of which look more like a sequel to the history contained in Kings and Chronicles. Next are the prophets, in which there is one book of the psalms of David and three books of Solomon—Proverbs, Song of Songs and Ecclesiastes. Two other books, one called Wisdom and the other Ecclesiasticus, are attributed to Solomon but seem rather (on grounds of style) to come from Jesus the son of Sirach. Still, they are to be reckoned among the books of the prophets since they have attained recognition as being authoritative. The remainder are the books that are strictly called the Prophets. Twelve separate books of the prophets that are connected with one another and, having never been disjoined, are considered to be a single

book; the names of these prophets are Hosea, Joel, Amos, Obadiah, Jonah, Micah, Nahum, Habakkuk, Zephaniah, Haggai, Zechariah and Malachi. Then there are the four greater prophets, Isaiah, Jeremiah, Daniel and Ezekiel. The authority of the Old Testament is contained within the limits of these forty-four books.

That of the New Testament is contained within the following: four books of the Gospel, according to Matthew, Mark, Luke and John; fourteen epistles of the apostle Paul—one to the Romans, two to the Corinthians, one to the Galatians, one to the Ephesians, one to the Philippians, two to the Thessalonians, one to the Colossians, two to Timothy, one to Titus, one to Philemon and one to the Hebrews. There are two epistles of Peter, three of John, one of Jude and one of James. Also there is a book of the Acts of the Apostles and the Revelation of John. CHRISTIAN INSTRUCTION 2.8.12.[147]

THE OLD TESTAMENT CANON. MELITO OF SARDIS: You have often expressed a wish to have extracts made from the Old Testament concerning the Savior. I have made an inventory of the books concerned and am sending you the list as follows. The five books of Moses, Joshua, Judges, Ruth, the four books of Kings, the two books of Chronicles, the psalms of David, the proverbs of Solomon, Wisdom, Ecclesiastes, the Song of Songs, Job, the prophets Isaiah and Jeremiah, the twelve prophets, Daniel, Ezekiel and Ezra. I have made six books of extracts from them. FRAGMENT 4.[148]

THE BOOKS OF THE OLD TESTAMENT. VICTORINUS OF PETOVIUM: The twenty-four elders are the twenty-four books of the Law

---

[142]Mt 22:29. [143]Jn 5:39. [144]PG 26:1176-77; cf. NPNF 2 4:551-52. [145]What we now call 1 and 2 Samuel plus 1 and 2 Kings. [146]The second being what we now call Nehemiah. [147]PL 34:41; cf. NPNF 1 2:538-39. [148]PG 5:1213-16; cf. ANF 8:759.

and the Prophets, which give testimonies of the judgment. There are twenty-four Old Testament books that we accept as canonical. COMMENTARY ON THE APOCALYPSE 4:7-10.[149]

READ ONLY THE HEBREW CANON OF THE OLD TESTAMENT. CYRIL OF JERUSALEM:
Of the books [contained in the Septuagint] read only the twenty-two [contained in the Hebrew canon] and have nothing to do with the apocryphal writings. Study earnestly only those that we read openly in the church. The apostles and bishops of old, the presidents of the church who handed down these books to us, were far wiser and more pious than you are. As a child of the church, therefore, do not go against its rules. Of the Old Testament, as we have said, study the twenty-two books that, if you want to learn them, try to commit their names to memory as I recite them:

Of the Law, the books of Moses are the first five: Genesis, Exodus, Leviticus, Numbers, Deuteronomy.

Next, Joshua, the son of Nun[150] and the book of Judges (including Ruth) counted as the seventh book.

Of the other historical books, the first and second books of Samuel[151] are regarded as one book by the Jews, as are the first and second books of Kings.[152]

Similarly, first and second Chronicles are one book to the Jews, as are Ezra and Nehemiah.[153] Esther is the twelfth book, which completes the historical writings.

Those books that are written in poetry are five in number: Job, Psalms, Proverbs, Ecclesiastes and the Song of Solomon, which is the seventeenth book.

After these come the five prophetic books: the Twelve Prophets in one book, followed by Isaiah, Jeremiah (including Baruch, Lamentations and the Letter),[154]

Ezekiel and Daniel, the twenty-second book of the Old Testament. CATECHETICAL LECTURES 4.35.[155]

THE SOLOMONIC CORPUS. JEROME: This includes the most excellent book of Jesus the son of Sirach and another pseudepigraphal work called the Wisdom of Solomon. Of these, I have found the first in Hebrew, though it is not Ecclesiasticus (as it is among the Latins) but Proverbs, to which were joined Ecclesiastes and the Song of Songs, so as to resemble Solomon not only in the number of books but also in the type of literature. The second book [Wisdom] does not exist in Hebrew. It is purely Greek in style, and some ancient writers think that it comes from Philo Judaeus. Therefore, just as the church reads the books of Judith, Tobit and the Maccabees without accepting them as canonical, so it should read these two volumes for the edification of the people but not for the purpose of supporting the authority of church doctrines. PREFACE TO THE BOOKS OF SOLOMON.[156]

THE BOOKS OF THE NEW TESTAMENT. EUSEBIUS OF CAESAREA: The books of the New Testament are as follows: the holy foursome of the Gospels and following them the Acts of the Apostles. Next come the epistles of Paul, then the first epistle of John and the first epistle of Peter. After them . . . comes the Apocalypse of John. These are the accepted writings. The disputed writings, which are nevertheless accepted by many, are the epistles of James and Jude, the second epistle of Peter and the second and third epistles of John, whether they were written by the Evangelist or by someone

---

[149]PL Supp. 1:121-25; cf. ANF 7:348-49. [150]This is rendered "nave" in the text, following the usage of the Septuagint. [151]Given as Kings in the original, following Septuagint usage. [152]Given as 3 and 4 Kings in the original, following Septuagint usage. [153]Given as 1 and 2 Esdras in the original, following Septuagint usage. [154]Baruch and the Letter of Jeremiah are not in the Hebrew canon. [155]PG 33:497-500; cf. NPNF 2 7:27. [156]PL 28:1242.

else of the same name. Among the rejected writings must be reckoned the so-called Acts of Paul, the Shepherd of Hermas, the Apocalypse of Peter, the Epistle of Barnabas, the Didache and perhaps also the Apocalypse of John, which some reject but which others class among the accepted books. Some would also include the Gospel according to the Hebrews, a book that especially delights converted Jews. All these may be classified among the disputed books. ECCLESIASTICAL HISTORY 3.25.1-5.[157]

CLEMENT OF ALEXANDRIA'S CANON. EU-SEBIUS OF CAESAREA: In the *Hypotyposeis* [Clement of Alexandria] has made an abbreviated gloss of the whole of canonical Scripture, including the disputed books, namely, Jude and the other Catholic Epistles, Barnabas and the so-called Apocalypse of Peter. He also says that the epistle to the Hebrews was written by Paul and that it was written to the Hebrews in the Hebrew language, but that Luke translated it carefully and published it for the Greeks, which explains why the same style of expression is found both in this epistle and in the Acts of the Apostles. He also says that the words "Paul the Apostle" were probably not prefixed because, in sending it to the Hebrews who were prejudiced against him to begin with, he wisely did not want to put them off at the start by mentioning his name. Farther on he says, "But now, as the blessed elder said, since [Christ] the Lord, the apostle of the Almighty, was sent to the Hebrews and Paul was sent to the Gentiles, the latter, on account of his modesty, did not sign himself an apostle to the Hebrews out of respect for the Lord and because, as the apostle to the Gentiles, he wrote to the Hebrews as something above and beyond his duty."

Clement of Alexandria also wrote down the tradition he had received concerning the order in which the Gospels were written. First came the ones with the genealogies in them, and then Mark was composed in the follow-

ing circumstances. Peter preached the Word publicly at Rome, proclaiming the gospel in the power of the Holy Spirit. Many of the people present urged him to write it down, because he had been with Peter from very early on and remembered what had been said. Mark wrote his Gospel and gave it to the people who had urged him to write it, but when Peter heard of it he was indifferent to what Mark had written. When John saw that the Gospels described primarily natural events, he composed a spiritual Gospel under the inspiration of the Spirit and at the request of his friends. ECCLESIASTICAL HISTORY 6.14.[158]

CYRIL OF JERUSALEM'S CANON. CYRIL OF JERUSALEM: In the New Testament there are only four Gospels, for the rest have false titles and are deceptive. The Manichaeans also wrote a Gospel according to Thomas, which being scented with the fragrance of the evangelical title, corrupts simple-minded souls. Accept also the Acts of the Apostles, and in addition to these the seven catholic Epistles of James, Peter, John and Jude, and as a seal on them all, the last work of the disciples—the fourteen epistles of Paul.[159] Let all the rest be put aside as of secondary importance, and as I said before, do not read any books that are not read in the churches. CATECHETICAL LECTURES 4.36.[160]

THE ORIGINS OF THE GOSPELS. IRENAEUS: It is wrong to say that the apostles preached before they received perfect knowledge. . . . After the Lord rose from the dead, they were filled with power from on high—with the Holy Spirit. Because they were completely filled, they had perfect knowledge and went off to the ends of the earth, preaching the good news of the blessing we had received from God. . . . Matthew also issued a written Gospel

---

[157]PG 20:268-69; cf. NPNF 2 1:155-57. [158]PG 20:549-52; cf. NPNF 2 1:261. [159]Cyril evidently considered Hebrews to be Pauline. [160]PG 33:500-501; cf. NPNF 2 7:27-28.

among the Hebrews, in their own language, while Peter and Paul were preaching at Rome and laying the foundations of the church. After their departure, Mark, the disciple and interpreter of Peter, handed down in writing what Peter had preached. Luke, the companion of Paul, recorded in a book the gospel preached by him. Afterwards John, the disciple of the Lord who had leaned on his breast, also published a Gospel during his time of residence at Ephesus. AGAINST HERESIES 3.1.1.[161]

THE APOSTOLIC EPISTLES. ORIGEN: Paul, who was made fit to be a minister of the new covenant, not of the letter but of the spirit, who preached the gospel from Jerusalem to Illyricum, did not write epistles to all the churches he taught, and to those to which he did write, he sent only a few lines. Peter, on whom the church of Christ is built, against which the gates of hell shall not prevail,[162] left one genuine epistle, and perhaps two, though that is doubtful. And what about the disciple who leaned on Jesus' breast, John, who left only one Gospel, though he admitted that he could have made so many that the world would not have been able to contain them all?[163] He also wrote the Apocalypse, being commanded to be silent and not to write the voices of the seven thunders.[164] He also left an epistle of very few lines, and perhaps two others as well, though not everyone accepts those as genuine. But the last two together do not amount to a hundred lines! COMMENTARY ON THE GOSPEL OF JOHN 5.3.[165]

THE ORDER OF PAUL'S EPISTLES. MURATORIAN FRAGMENT: Paul wrote 1 Corinthians first in order to deal with the problem of heresy. Next he wrote to the Galatians in order to put a stop to circumcision. After that, he wrote to the Romans about the rule of the Old Testament to show them that Christ was the primary theme of the Scriptures.

Following the rule of his predecessor John,

the blessed apostle Paul wrote to only seven churches by name, in the following order: Corinth first, Ephesus second, Philippi third, Colossae fourth, Galatia fifth, Thessalonica sixth and Rome seventh. Although he wrote to Corinth and to Thessalonica twice, it is still true that this sevenfold pattern demonstrates that there is only one church spread throughout the world. . . . Paul also wrote a letter to Philemon, another to Titus and two to Timothy, in which he expresses simple love and affection. These are sanctified in the mind of the universal church and are used for the regulation of church discipline. MURATORIAN FRAGMENT 3.[166]

THE CATHOLIC EPISTLES. MURATORIAN FRAGMENT: The epistle of Jude and two belonging to John, or bearing his name, are numbered among the Catholic Epistles. So is the book of Wisdom, written by friends of Solomon to honor him. We also accept the revelation of John and the revelation of Peter, though there are some who will not allow the second of these to be read in church. MURATORIAN FRAGMENT 4.[167]

THE SPURIOUS TEACHING OF PETER. ORIGEN: If anyone quotes *The Teaching of Peter*, in which the Savior seems to say, "I am not an incorporeal demon," I can only say that it is not one of our canonical books. We can demonstrate that it was not written by Peter or by anyone who was inspired by God's Spirit. ON FIRST PRINCIPLES PREFACE 8.[168]

PETER'S WRITINGS. EUSEBIUS OF CAESAREA: One epistle of Peter is acknowledged as genuine, and the ancient elders used it freely in their own writings as an undisputed work. But we have learned that the second epistle does not

---

[161]PG 7:844-45; cf. ANF 1:414. [162]Mt 16:18. [163]See Jn 21:25. [164]Rev 10:4. [165]PG 14:188-89; cf. ANF 9:346-47. [166]PL 3:189-91; cf. ANF 5:603. [167]PL 3:192-96; cf. ANF 5:603-4. [168]PG 11:119-20; cf. ANF 4:241.

belong to the canon, although since many have found it profitable it has been included with the other Scriptures. . . . The so-called Acts of Peter, however, and the Gospel that bears his name, and the Preaching and the Apocalypse, as they are called, we know have not been universally accepted because no ecclesiastical writer, ancient or modern, has made use of them. Ecclesiastical History 3.3.1-2.[169]

Do Not Read the Spurious Books in Church. Apostolic Constitutions: If anyone publicly reads the spurious books of the ungodly in church, as if they were holy, in a way that might lead the people and clergy to ruin, let him be deprived of his office. Constitutions of the Holy Apostles 8.47.60.[170]

No More Canonical Books Will Be Discovered. Augustine: Any writings outside the canon of Scripture that are now produced, bearing the name of one of the ancient prophets, cannot serve as an aid to our knowledge, because it is uncertain whether they are genuine. On this account they are not trusted, particularly the ones in which are found things that contradict the canonical books, a fact that makes their inauthenticity obvious. City of God 18.38.[171]

Apocryphal Books Attributed to Andrew and John. Augustine: Our opponent has quoted evidence from apocryphal books that circulate under the names of the apostles Andrew and John. If they were genuine, they would have been accepted by the church, which has continued in an unbroken succession of bishops from their time up to the present. Against the Adversary of the Law and Prophets 1.20.39.[172]

The Translation of Scripture

How the Greek Translation of the Old Testament Was Made. Clement of

Alexandria: It is said that the Scriptures both of the Law and of the Prophets were translated from Hebrew into Greek in the reign of Ptolemy I, son of Lagos [305-282 b.c.], or according to others, in the reign of Ptolemy II Philadelphus [282-246 b.c.], when Demetrius Phalereus brought the greatest dedication to this task and employed the most painstaking accuracy on the materials used for the translation. The king wanted to adorn his library at Alexandria with all writings and asked the people of Jerusalem to translate the prophecies they possessed into Greek. They selected seventy elders of the highest character, well versed in the Scriptures and competent in Greek, and sent them to him with the divine books. Each of the seventy translated every prophetic book separately, and when the different versions were compared, they were found to be identical in both meaning and expression. It was the counsel of God carried out for the benefit of Greek ears. It was not alien to the inspiration of God, who gave the prophecies, to produce the translation also, and make it in effect a Greek prophecy. Stromateis 1.22.[173]

Easier to Check Translations from Greek Than from Hebrew. Augustine (to Jerome): I have heard that you have translated Job out of the original Hebrew, although in your own translation of the same prophet from the Greek tongue we already had a version of that book. In that earlier version you marked the words found in Hebrew but missing in Greek with asterisks, and the words found in Greek but missing in Hebrew with obelisks. This was done with such astonishing exactness that in some places every word is distinguished by a separate asterisk, as a sign that they are present in the Hebrew text but

---

[169]PG 20:216-17; cf. NPNF 1:133-34. [170]DCA 502; cf. ANF 7:503. [171]PL 41:598; cf. NPNF 1 2:383. [172]PL 42:626. [173]PG 8:889-93; cf. ANF 2:334.

not in the Greek one. But in this more recent version from the Hebrew, there is not the same scrupulous fidelity as to words, and the thoughtful reader is perplexed as to know why. I have not got the translation from the Hebrew at hand and so cannot furnish you with specific examples of what I mean, but I am sure you understand my point and can give me an answer without any difficulty.

For my part, I would much rather that you should furnish me with a translation of the Greek version of the canonical Scriptures, known as the Septuagint. For if your translation begins to be more generally read in many churches, it will be sad if, in the reading of Scripture, differences arise between the Latin and Greek churches that could have been avoided by referring to the Greek original, since it is such a well-known language. But if anyone is disturbed by something unusual in a translation made from the Hebrew and claims that the new translation is wrong, it will be difficult and perhaps impossible to get at the original text to check whether the translation in question is right or not. And who will accept that so many Latin and Greek authorities could have been wrong? Besides, if Jews are consulted about the meaning of the text, they may give an opinion that is different from yours, in which case your presence would be indispensable, since you are the only one who could refute their views. LETTER 71.3-4.[174]

THE PURPOSE OF THE LATIN TRANSLA-TION. JEROME (TO AUGUSTINE): You ask why a former translation that I made of some of the canonical books was carefully marked with asterisks and obelisks, whereas I afterwards published a translation without these. You must pardon my saying so, but it seems to me that you have not understood the matter at all. The former translation is from the Septuagint, and whenever there are obelisks, they are designed to indicate that the Seventy have said more than is in the Hebrew. The asterisks . . . indicate what has been added by Origen from the version of Theodotion. In that version, I was translating from the Greek, but in the later version I translated from the original Hebrew, giving what I took it to mean and being careful to preserve the exact sense of the text rather than the order of the words. I am surprised that you do not read the books of the Seventy translators in the genuine form in which they were originally given to the world but as they have been corrected (or rather, corrupted) by Origen, with his obelisks and asterisks, and that you refuse to follow the translation, however feeble, that has been made by a Christian—especially since Origen borrowed his additions from the edition of a man who was a Jew and a blasphemer who lived after the death of Christ [and rejected him]. Do you want to be a true admirer of the Seventy? Then do not read what you find under the asterisks but erase them from the volumes, so that you may indeed be a follower of the ancients. But if you do this, you will be compelled to find fault with all the libraries of the churches, for you will hardly find more than a single manuscript here and there that does not have these interpolations.

A few words now as to your remark that I ought not to have given a translation of my own, after so much labor had been expended by the ancients. . . . In my attempt to translate into Latin the corrected Greek version of the Scriptures, I have not tried to supersede what has long been esteemed but only to bring into prominence those things that have either been omitted or tampered with by the Jews, so that Latin readers may know what was in the original Hebrew. If anyone is averse to reading it, there is no one who will compel him to do so against his will. Let him drink the old wine with satisfaction and despise my new wine, if he so desires. LETTER 75.19-20.[175]

[174]PL 33:242; cf. NPNF 1 1:326-27.   [175]PL 33:261-62; cf. NPNF 1 1:341-42.

The Interpretation of Scripture

FAITH SAVES US, NOT OUR INTERPRETATIVE SKILL. TERTULLIAN: According to Jesus, it is your faith that has saved you,[176] not your skill in the Scriptures. Faith has been deposited in the rule; it has a law, and [by observing it, you can obtain] salvation. Skill, however, consists in obscure arts, whose glory is nothing but the expertise that comes from having the knack. Such obscure arts must give way to faith; such glory must yield to salvation. To know nothing other than the rule of faith is to know everything! PRESCRIPTIONS AGAINST HERETICS 14.[177]

READING AND APPLYING THE SCRIPTURES. CLEMENT OF ALEXANDRIA: The spiritual person is one who has reached maturity in his reading of the Scriptures, who maintains the orthodox doctrine of the apostles and the church and who lives in accordance with the gospel. STROMATEIS 7.16.[178]

THE OLD TESTAMENT IS NOT ALWAYS QUOTED EXACTLY IN THE NEW. JEROME: There are some people who claim that in almost all the quotations that are taken from the Old Testament, there are inaccuracies. Either the order of the words has been altered or the words themselves are different, and sometimes even the meaning has been changed. These people ascribe this to the fact that the apostles and Evangelists were not quoting directly from the texts themselves but from memory, which is sometimes fallible. COMMENTARY ON MICAH 2.5.2.[179]

GREATER WEIGHT MUST BE GIVEN TO THE BOOKS WIDELY RECEIVED AS CANONICAL. AUGUSTINE: The most skillful interpreter of the sacred writings will be the one who has read them all and memorized them, perhaps not with full understanding but with such knowledge as reading gives. He will confine himself to those books that are called canonical and will be better placed to read the rest once he has been built up in the truth, so that they will not take possession of a weak mind and fill it with prejudices that go against a sound understanding. . . .

Among the canonical Scriptures he will judge according to the following standard—he will prefer those that are received by all the churches to those that are received by only some of them. When dealing with the second category, he will give greater weight to those that are received by the larger number and less to those that are received by fewer. But if a book is received by only a minority of churches, yet those churches are ones of greater authority [because they were founded by the apostles], then equal weight must be given to them—though I must say that such a situation is most unlikely to occur. CHRISTIAN INSTRUCTION 2.8.12.[180]

MORE THAN ONE INTERPRETATION IS POSSIBLE. AUGUSTINE: It may be that one or two different interpretations are put on a passage of Scripture, even though the writer's intended meaning is obscure, but if so, there is no danger as long as there are other passages of Scripture to demonstrate that these interpretations are in line with the truth [of the gospel]. . . . What more liberal and fruitful provision could God have made with regard to the sacred Scriptures, than that the same words might be understood in several senses, all of which are sanctioned by the concurring testimony of other passages that are equally divine? CHRISTIAN INSTRUCTION 3.27.38.[181]

THE SPIRITUAL UNDERSTANDING INCREASED OVER TIME. GREGORY THE GREAT: We must also realize that the spiritual under-

---

[176]Lk 18:42. [177]PL 2:27; cf. ANF 3:250. [178]PG 9:544; cf. ANF 2:554. [179]PL 25:1197. [180]PL 34:40-41; cf. NPNF 1 2:538. [181]PL 34:80; cf. NPNF 1 2:567.

standing of the ancients increased over time. Moses knew more than Abraham, the prophets knew more than Moses, and the apostles were more learned in the knowledge of almighty God than the prophets. HOMILIES ON EZEKIEL 2.4.12.[182]

Scripture, Tradition and Faith

APOSTOLIC TRADITION. IRENAEUS: Apostolic tradition exists in the church and is a permanent feature among us. It is found in the Scriptures written by the apostles. We must look to them to discover their doctrine of God. AGAINST HERESIES 3.5.1.[183]

THE TRUTH PRESERVED BY A SUCCESSION OF FAITHFUL TEACHERS. IRENAEUS: True knowledge consists of the teaching of the apostles and the ancient practice of the church throughout the world. It also consists of the particular manifestations of the body of Christ according to the succession of bishops. It is they who have handed down the church to us. That church is protected and preserved by a complete system of doctrine, without any forging of sacred books. Nothing is either added to or taken away from the truth that the church believes. True knowledge also consists of reading the Word of God without distortion, following the correct and thorough exposition that is in harmony with the Scriptures as a whole. Above all, truth consists in the overarching gift of love, which is more precious than knowledge, more glorious than prophecy and more excellent than any other of God's gifts. AGAINST HERESIES 4.33.8.[184]

WE TEACH WHAT THE APOSTOLIC CHURCHES TEACH. TERTULLIAN: Since the Lord Jesus Christ sent his apostles to preach, our rule is that no one ought to be received as teachers except those whom Christ appointed. The Son does not seem to have revealed the Father to anyone other than the apostles.

What they preached was what he revealed to them, and nothing else. The only way to prove this is by looking to the churches that the apostles founded, by preaching the gospel directly to them, orally and later in their epistles. If that is the case, then it follows that all doctrine that agrees with the apostolic churches must be regarded as true. [By contrast], whatever does not agree with this must be considered false. We are in communion with the apostolic churches because our teaching is the same as theirs. This is how we bear witness to the truth. PRESCRIPTIONS AGAINST HERETICS 21.[185]

TRADITION AND CUSTOM MAY SUPPLEMENT THE TEACHING OF SCRIPTURE. TERTULLIAN: If no passage of Scripture has prescribed a certain practice, surely custom, which flows from tradition, confirms it. For how can anything come into general use if it has not been handed down? You claim that traditions must be based on written authority to be valid. Let us inquire, therefore, to see whether this is so or not. We shall certainly agree that a given practice should not be accepted if there are no similar cases of unwritten traditions relying on the sanction of custom alone that might offer us a precedent. To deal with this matter briefly, I shall begin with baptism. Just before we go into the water, we make a solemn profession in front of the congregation and at the direction of the president that we renounce the devil, his pomp and his angels. Then we are immersed three times, and we make a somewhat fuller pledge, which the Lord has appointed in the gospel. Then when we come up out of the water as newborn children, we taste a mixture of milk and honey first of all, and we give up bathing for a week. We also take the sacrament of the Eucharist before dawn, and from the hands of no one but

---

[182]PL 76:980. [183]PG 7:857; cf. ANF 1:417. [184]PG 7:1077-78; cf. ANF 1:508. [185]PL 2:33; cf. ANF 3:252-53.

the presidents, which the Lord commanded us to do at meal times and enjoined on all alike. Every year we commemorate the anniversary of this event by making offerings for the dead. We think it is unlawful to fast or to kneel in worship on the Lord's day. We rejoice in the same privilege from Easter to Pentecost. We get upset if any of the bread or wine should fall to the ground, even if it is our own. We make the sign [of the cross] on our foreheads every time we go in or out, when we get dressed, when we bathe, when we sit at table, when we light the lamps and when we go to bed.

If for these and other such rules you demand a scriptural injunction, you will find none. Tradition will be offered to you as their origin, custom as their confirmation and faith as their observer. That reason will support tradition, custom and faith, you will either perceive for yourself or learn from someone else who has perceived it. In the meantime, accept at least that there is some reason to which we ought to submit. . . . Among the Jews, for instance, it is usual for the women to be veiled, in order that they may be recognized. There is no law governing this, nor has the apostle spoken. If Rebecca drew down her veil when she saw her be-trothed approaching her in the distance, this modesty of a private individual could not have made a law, or perhaps it would have done so only for those who find themselves in the same position as she did. Let virgins alone be veiled, and this when they are com-ing to be married, and not until they have recognized their appointed husband! . . . There is no official dress code prescribed in the Law. It was a matter of tradition, sancti-fied by custom, that later found its autho-rization in the apostle's sanction, which he based on the true interpretation of reason. This will make it sufficiently clear to you that you can justify the keeping of unwrit-ten traditions established by custom. Even in civil matters custom is accepted as law when

positive legal enactment is wanting, and it makes no difference whether it is based on writing or on reason, since reason is the true basis of law. THE CHAPLET 3-4.[186]

LITURGICAL PRACTICES HAVE ONE OF TWO ORIGINS. BASIL THE GREAT: Some of the beliefs and practices that are generally re-ceived and enjoined by the church are derived from written teaching, but others we have received "in a mystery"[187] by the tradition of the apostles. Both of these have the same validity in relation to true religion. No one who knows anything about the church and its ways will dispute this. If we were to try to reject unwritten traditions in the church on the ground that they are of little importance, we would discover that we would be doing harm to the essence of the gospel. For exam-ple, who has told us in writing to sign newly baptized believers with the sign of the cross? What Scripture tells us to turn towards the east for prayer? Which of the saints has left us anything concerning the invocation used at the elevation of the bread and the cup at the Eucharist? It is well known that we do not restrict ourselves to the words recorded in the New Testament but add, both at the begin-ning and the end of the service, words of great importance to the validity of the ministry, which are derived from unwritten teaching. We bless the water of baptism and the oil of chrism, as well as the person being baptized. On what written authority do we do this? Is our authority not the silent and secret tradi-tion? What written text teaches the anointing with oil? Where does the custom of baptizing people three times come from? What Scrip-ture tells us to renounce the devil and his angels? Does this not come from that unpub-lished and secret teaching that our ancestors guarded in silence, out of the reach of curious meddling and inquisitive investigation? They

---

[186]PL 2:78-81; cf. ANF 3:94-95. [187]See 1 Cor 2:7.

had learned the lesson that the dignity of the mysteries is best preserved by silence. On the Holy Spirit 27.66.[188]

The Need to Respect Tradition. Epiphanius of Salamis: Not all the words of God need allegory for their interpretation. They must be read reflectively and according to their meaning for the force of their argument to be understood. But there is need also for tradition, since not everything can be found in Scripture. The holy apostles left some things in writing and others in [unwritten] traditions. Panarion 61.6.[189]

Many Things Were Passed on by Oral Tradition. Chrysostom: "So then, brothers, stand firm and hold to the teachings we passed on to you, whether by word of mouth or by letter."[190] From this it is clear that not everything was passed on by letter, but many things were communicated orally. Both sources are equally important. This is why we regard the tradition of the church as trustworthy. The fact that it is tradition is enough—there is no need to inquire beyond that. Homilies on 2 Thessalonians 2, Homily 4.2.14.[191]

Customs Have the Force of Divine Law. Jerome: Do you not know that it is the church's custom to lay hands on the newly baptized to invoke the Holy Spirit? Do you ask where this is written? In the Acts of the Apostles.[192] But even if there were no scriptural authority for the practice, the universal consensus of the entire church would take its place. For there are many other things as well that are observed in the churches for traditional reasons, and in these cases tradition has claimed for itself the authority of the written law. Dialogue Against the Luciferians 8.[193]

Authority in the Church. Augustine:

We retain many unwritten customs that are observed by the whole world. They are understood either to have been handed down from the apostles themselves or else to have been commanded and authorized by universal councils, which enjoy the highest authority in the church. Letters 54.1.1.[194]

What the Universal Church Holds. Augustine: Whatever the universal church holds and has always held, even without conciliar approval, is most rightly believed to have been handed down by apostolic authority. On Baptism, Against the Donatists 4.24.31.[195]

The Apostolic Succession. Theodoret of Cyr: We have preserved the doctrinal teaching of the apostles intact up to the present time. It is not only the apostles and prophets who have handed these things down to us but also those who have interpreted the texts—Ignatius, Eustathius, Athanasius, Basil the Great, Gregory [of Nazianzus?], John [Chrysostom?] and the other illuminators of the universe, not least the fathers of the council of Nicaea, whose confession of faith we hold undefiled as our paternal inheritance. Letters 89.[196]

The Rule of Catholicity. Vincent of Lérins: There is great need, on account of the many kinds of error that there are, for the standard of prophetic and apostolic interpretation to be guided by the tradition established by the universal understanding of the church. Therefore great care must be taken in the universal[197] church to ensure that we hold to everything that has been believed everywhere, always and by everyone. Commonitories 2.[198]

---

[188]PG 32:188; cf. NPNF 2 8:40-42. [189]PG 41:1048. [190]2 Thess 2:15. [191]PG 62:488; cf. NPNF 1 13:390. [192]See Acts 8:14-17. [193]PL 23:163-64. [194]PL 33:200. [195]PL 43:174. [196]PG 83:1284. [197]"Catholic." [198]PL 50:640.

IN ONE GOD

πιστεύομεν **εἰς ἕνα Θεὸν**	*Credo **in unum Deum***	*We believe **in one God,***
πατέρα, παντοκράτορα,	*Patrem omnipotentem;*	*the Father, the Almighty,*
ποιητὴν οὐρανοῦ καὶ γῆς,	*factorem coeli et terrae,*	*maker of heaven and earth,*
ὁρατῶν τε πάντων καὶ ἀοράτων.	*visibilium omnium et invisibilium.*	*of all that is, seen and unseen.*

HISTORICAL CONTEXT: Christians inherited their belief in one God from Judaism and were insistent on this throughout the patristic period. At the popular level, they had to defend their faith against the prevailing polytheism of the ancient world. Many early Christian texts contain examples of anti-polytheistic satire, but few of them mount a sustained attack on polytheism as a system of belief. The main reason for this is that Christians did not often have to fight this battle at the intellectual level, since many educated pagans were equally critical of polytheism and ridiculed the ancient myths every bit as much as Christians did. They preferred to believe in a perfect being out of which existing reality had been formed. Precisely how this had happened, however, was a matter for furious disagreement among the different philosophical schools of ancient Greece, and Christians were quick to point out the inconsistencies of the various theories that were put forward to explain what we call the creation.

There was nevertheless one belief that was constant in ancient pagan philosophies, and that was that evil was something opposed to the perfect being and in no way part of it. This caused problems for Christians, who could not accept that evil was a power outside the control of God. To protect the divine perfection and goodness, some heterodox Christians came up with the theory that the God of the Old Testament was an inferior deity who created the world as we know it. In their view the true God dwelt above and beyond this creator (demiurge) and was completely unknowable. Orthodox Christians insisted that the one true God was also the Creator, and that whatever evil was, it could not be completely independent of him or outside his control.

The early Christians also insisted that God is a personal being who establishes a relationship with human beings, who are created in his image and likeness. This relationship was initially given to the Jews, and in Christ it has been extended to others as well. God does not reabsorb us into his being but establishes a fellowship with us that will endure for eternity. It is this personal character of God that distinguishes Christian belief most obviously from any philosophical equivalent, and the insistence with which it was hammered home is a good indication of how difficult it was for the average pagan to embrace this concept.

It would be wrong to suggest that the doctrine of the one God developed in any significant way during the first Christian centuries, and the teaching of Augustine and John of Damascus can be found in the second century, with very little difference. However, Christian theologians had to explain how the one God was at the same time a Trinity of persons, a doctrine that did not contradict the monotheism of the Old Testament. Belief in a communion of three divine persons led to a growing understanding of God as love, a biblical idea that finds its greatest flowering in the works of Augustine. By stressing the concept of divine love, he was able to combine the unity of the three persons in one God and our union with him (and them) as the height of our spiritual experience and the ultimate goal of the divine plan of salvation.

OVERVIEW: God cannot be called by a proper name but was referred to inexplicably by Moses as "I am who am," in contrast with the gods that do not exist (JUSTIN MARTYR), yet this incomparable One is worshiped under many different names (ORIGEN). Some of these have been given to him by different peoples, and others depend on particular functions that belong to him (TERTULLIAN), though the most accurate name used for him is that of pure Being (EPHREM, BASIL, GREGORY OF NAZIANZUS, HILARY, AMBROSE, AUGUSTINE). Even so, there is no name that can describe him adequately (CYRIL OF ALEXANDRIA), and God is beyond even Being (PSEUDO-DIONYSIUS). The eternal God has no sex (ARNOBIUS, LACTANTIUS) but transcends everything else and is the absolute being (TERTULLIAN, GREGORY OF NAZIANZUS, HILARY, AUGUSTINE). There is nothing like him, and so he can only be defined as being himself (NOVATIAN, CYRIL OF JERUSALEM). Because of this, God can only be defined by what he is not (JOHN OF DAMASCUS), and only he is a fit object of human worship (AUGUSTINE). He does not compel but calls us to worship him (TERTULLIAN).

God is beyond our understanding (IRENAEUS, CHRYSOSTOM), beyond the power of human nature to comprehend, as if dwelling in impenetrable darkness (ORIGEN). Knowledge of him must therefore begin by confessing our ignorance of who or what he really is (CYRIL OF JERUSALEM). He is perfect and for that reason absolutely unique (AMBROSE, JOHN OF DAMASCUS). He is the supreme Being, which makes it absurd to suppose that there can be more than one of him (TERTULLIAN, EUSEBIUS, EPHREM). All three persons of the Trinity share this absolute oneness of the Godhead (ORIGEN, ATHANASIUS, BASIL, GREGORY OF NAZIANZUS) and may be addressed as three holies in the one divine holiness (AMBROSE). The God of the Old Testament and the God of the New are one and the same, though the Trinity is revealed more clearly in the New (GREGORY OF NYSSA, AUGUSTINE). However, it remains a fundamental belief of the Christian church that God is One, as he proclaimed to the ancient Israelites (GREGORY OF NYSSA, HILARY, EPIPHANIUS, AMBROSE, AUGUSTINE, FULGENTIUS).

God is eternal (CYRIL OF ALEXANDRIA) and sovereign and can do whatever he likes (MELITO). He knows the future (IRENAEUS, AUGUSTINE), but his foreknowledge is compatible with human free will (TATIAN, JUSTIN MARTYR). A distinction must be made between things that God actively wills, all of which are good, and things that he merely allows to happen, many of which may be evil (TERTULLIAN, CLEMENT OF ALEXANDRIA).

God is eternal (LACTANTIUS), knows everything (IRENAEUS) and is everywhere at the same time (MELITO, CYPRIAN, MINUCIUS FELIX, GREGORY THE GREAT). He has no body (GREGORY OF NAZIANZUS, CYRIL OF ALEXANDRIA) but is infinite and invisible spirit by nature (HILARY, LEO). He is simple in the sense that he is not compounded of different substances (DIDYMUS, CHRYSOSTOM, JOHN), and he cannot change (AUGUSTINE). God is greater than his attributes, each of which equals the sum of his being (AUGUSTINE, JOHN OF DAMASCUS), but no words can describe him adequately (HILARY). He is not the cause of evil, though he allows it to occur (CLEMENT OF ALEXANDRIA) and can even make use of it for his own good purposes (ORIGEN). But God has no experience of evil in himself, and in that sense may be said not to know it (BASIL), nor can he do things that contradict his nature (ORIGEN).

God's wrath is not a vice but a virtue (NOVATIAN). The term is a metaphor for his disciplining of the human race, because he cannot have human passions (ORIGEN, GREGORY THE GREAT). God's wrath is part of him and is therefore both righteous and eternal (LACTANTIUS).

God's goodness is made manifest by his

determination to punish evil (Lactantius). He desires our salvation (Chrysostom) which he planned before the foundation of the world (Augustine). From our point of view, union with God is the best thing we could ever have or desire (Augustine, Pseudo-Dionysius).

In sharp contrast to this, pagan idolatry is both foolish and absurd (Justin Martyr, Tatian). Pagan polytheism makes no sense, imagining that it is even possible to invent new gods (Theophilus). God cannot be depicted in material objects, and it is blasphemous to worship such things (Athenagoras, Tertullian, John of Damascus). He has no need of sacrifices either (Lactantius). Idolatry springs from evil (Athanasius), and the pagan gods are powerless to do what they are asked (Augustine).

God can be known by his works, but only partially (Athanasius, Pseudo-Dionysius), and the first step toward knowing him is to confess our ignorance of him (Cyril of Jerusalem). He is ultimately indefinable (Gregory of Elvira), and so we must do what we can to find words to describe him (Marius Victorinus), knowing all along that whatever we come up with will be inadequate (Basil, Gregory of Nyssa). Our knowledge of him may be compared with that of children (Chrysostom), but in truth, if we could understand him, he would not be God (Augustine).

Who God Is

God Has No Proper Name. Justin Martyr: God cannot be called by any proper name. Names are given to mark out and distinguish their subject matters because these are many and diverse, but no one existed before God who could give him a name, nor did he see any need to name himself, since he is one and unique, as he testifies by his own prophets, saying, "I am the first, and besides me there is no other God."[1] For this reason, when God

sent Moses to the Hebrews, he did not mention any name but taught the people by using a participle that he is the one and only true God. He says, "I am who am,"[2] obviously contrasting himself with the gods who do not exist. He did this so that those who had previously been deceived might see that they had been worshiping not beings but things that had no being. Hortatory Address to the Greeks 21.[3]

We Know God by His Works of Creation. Tatian: God alone is to be feared— he who is not visible to human eyes nor comes within the compass of human art. Only when I am commanded to deny him will I not obey, but will rather die than show myself false and ungrateful. Our God has no origin in time; he alone is without beginning, and he is the beginning of all things. "God is a spirit,"[4] not pervading matter but the maker of material spirits and of the forms that are in matter. He is invisible, impalpable, being himself the Father of both visible and invisible things. We know him from his creation and apprehend his invisible power by his works.[5] To the Greeks 4.[6]

The Difference Between "God" and "Lord." Tertullian: Hermogenes claims that because God was always God, there was never a time when he was not also Lord. But it was impossible for God to be regarded as Lord in eternity, since there has not always been something that he might be Lord of. Therefore, Hermogenes is forced to conclude that matter has always existed, so that God could be its eternal Lord. This is nonsense. . . . The name "God" always existed in him, but the title "Lord" is not eternal in origin. The reason for this is that they designate different things. "God" means the substance of his divinity, but "Lord" is the title given to his power. The sub-

[1]Is 44:6. [2]Exod 3:14. [3]PG 6:277; cf. ANF 1:281. [4]Jn 4:24. [5]See Rom 1:20. [6]PG 6:813; cf. ANF 2:66.

stance has always existed with its own name, but the title "Lord" was added after the creation of the things over which he is Lord. From the moment when those things over which God is Lord began to exist, God became Lord and received that particular name. In the same way, God is both Father and Judge, but he has not always had these titles, merely as a consequence of being God. He could not have been a Father prior to the existence of the Son, nor could he have been a Judge prior to the coming of sin. There was, however, a time when neither sin nor the [incarnate] Son existed.[7] In the same way, he was not Lord until the things over which he is Lord came into being. AGAINST HERMOGENES 3.[8]

GOD BESTOWS HIS BLESSINGS ON THE WICKED AND THE RIGHTEOUS. TERTULLIAN: We are worshipers of one God, of whose existence and character nature teaches all people, at whose lightnings and thunders you tremble, whose benefits minister to your happiness. You think that others are also gods, but we know that they are devils. Nevertheless, it is a fundamental human right, a privilege of nature, that everyone should worship according to his own convictions. One person's religion neither harms nor helps that of another. It is certainly no part of religion to compel religious observance. Free will and not force should lead us to that, for the sacrificial victims are demanded from a willing mind. You will render no real service to your gods by forcing us to sacrifice to them. They can have no desire to receive offerings from the unwilling, unless they are moved by a spirit of contention that is altogether ungodly. The true God bestows his blessings on wicked people just as much as on his chosen ones, which is why he has appointed an eternal judgment, when both the grateful and the ungrateful will have to stand before his bar. TO SCAPULA 2.[9]

THERE CANNOT BE MORE THAN ONE SUPREME GOD. TERTULLIAN: The main, indeed the entire contention, lies in the question of number—can we admit the existence of two gods, by poetic licence if necessary, or pictorial fantasy or by a third process that we have to call heretical depravity? Christianity has emphatically declared this principle: If God is not one, he does not exist, because we correctly believe that a thing has no existence if it is not what it is supposed to be. In order for you to know that God is one, ask where God is, and then you will see that that must be the case. In so far as a human being can form a definition of God, let me present one that the conscience of all people will acknowledge. God is the supreme Being, existing in eternity, unbegotten, not made, without beginning, without end. For such a condition as this must be ascribed to that eternity that makes God to be the supreme Being, because this very attribute exists in God for that purpose. So it is also with his other qualities, so that God is the supreme Being in form and reason, in might and power. Everyone agrees on this point, because nobody will deny that God is the supreme Being unless he wants to deny his divinity by robbing him of one of his divine attributes. If that is the case, what is his being like? Surely it must be that there is nothing equal to him, because if he had an equal he would no longer be the supreme Being. The supreme Being must by definition be unique. He will not exist otherwise than by the condition that gives him his being, which is his absolute uniqueness. Since God is the supreme Being, our Christian faith has rightly declared that if he is not one, he does not exist. We have never doubted his existence but rather have defined it in the way that makes him necessarily who he is—by

---

[7]Here Tertullian draws near to what would later become the Arian heresy. The passage is a reminder to us of how Christians before the time of Arius could dismiss the eternal generation of the Son in the Godhead without thereby denying his divine equality with the Father. As the bracketed "incarnate" suggests, he may have been referring to the time before the incarnation. [8]PL 2:199-200; cf. ANF 3:478. [9]PL 1:699; cf. ANF 3:105.

calling him the supreme Being. Moreover, this supreme Being must be unique. This unique being will therefore be God. Any other god you may introduce cannot be held to be divine in this way, since two supreme Beings cannot coexist. AGAINST MARCION 1.3.[10]

WHEN WE PRAY TO GOD. ORIGEN: In prayer, Christians do not use even the precise names that holy Scripture gives to God. The Greeks use Greek names, the Romans use Latin names, and everyone sings and prays to God as best he can in his own mother tongue. The Lord of all the languages of the earth hears those who pray to him in every different language. AGAINST CELSUS 8.37.[11]

WHY GOD MUST BE WHO HE IS. NOVATIAN: God is always like and equal to himself. What is not born cannot be changed, for the only things that undergo change are those that are made or begotten. . . . Things that have no birth or creation are incapable of change because they have no beginning, which is the cause of change. So God is proclaimed as the One who has no equal. Whatever can be God must necessarily be the highest, but whatever is highest must be so in a sense that does not admit the possibility of any equal. Therefore he must also be alone and without peer. There cannot be two infinites, as the very nature of infinity makes clear. Whatever is without beginning or end is infinite, and whatever has occupied the whole excludes the beginning of another. If God does not contain everything that is . . . he ceases to be God, since he will then be included in the power of another who is greater than he is. In that case, whatever contained him would claim to be God in his place. Thus it happens that God's own name cannot be declared, since he cannot be conceived. A name contains what can be comprehended from the nature of a thing, but as God is incomprehensible, he cannot have a name. ON THE TRINITY 4.[12]

GOD HAS NO SEX. ARNOBIUS OF SICCA: When we speak of God, we use a masculine word, but let no thoughtless person accuse us of saying that God, is a man. It is not gender that is expressed but rather his name, its customary meaning and the way in which we habitually use words. The deity is not male, even though his name is of the masculine gender. In contrast, [pagans] attribute gender to the gods, by calling them either "god" or "goddess." We cannot believe that God has a body, because if he did, he would have to be either male or female. AGAINST THE NATIONS 3.8.[13]

GOD HAS NO BODY OR SEX. LACTANTIUS: How can there be anything difficult or impossible for God, who by his providence designed, by his energy established and by his judgment completed those works so great and wonderful, which even now he sustains by his Spirit and governs by his power, being incomprehensible and inexplicable, fully known to no one but himself? Those who worship the gods sometimes appear so blind and incapable of reflection . . . as to believe that those who are born of the sexes have something of the divine majesty and influence, though even the Erythraean Sibyl said, "It is impossible for a god to be fashioned from the loins of a man and the womb of a woman." This is quite true, and it means that Hercules, Apollo, Bacchus, Mercury, Jupiter and the rest of them were but men, since they were born from the two sexes. But what is so far removed from the nature of God as that operation that he himself assigned to mortals for the propagation of their race and that cannot be effected without corporeal substance? If the gods are immortal and eternal, why do they need the other sex, when they do not need offspring to succeed them? . . . After all, there is no other

---

[10]PL 2:249-50; cf. ANF 3:273. [11]PG 11:1573; cf. ANF 4:653. [12]PL 3:892-94; cf. ANF 5:614-15. [13]PL 5:946-97; cf. ANF 6:466.

reason for having sex and procreation, and an immortal God does not need either. Divine Institutes 1.8.[14]

God Is Always Himself. Cyril of Jerusalem: For purposes of devotion it is enough to know that we have a God who is one, a living and ever-living God, always like himself. He has no Father, there is no one mightier than he is and no successor who might depose him from his kingdom. He has many names, his power is infinite, his substance is uniform. Although he is called good, just, Almighty and Sabaoth, he is not on that account diverse and various. Being one and the same, he sends forth countless operations of his godhead, neither overdoing nor underdoing it but remaining always just as he is in himself. He is not great in loving-kindness and small in wisdom but uses both of these in equal power. He is not partially blind but all-seeing. He is not partially ignorant but all-knowing. Anything else would be blasphemy and unworthy of the divine substance. He foreknows everything that will come to pass. He is holy, Almighty and excels everything else in goodness, majesty and wisdom. He has neither beginning nor form nor shape. Catechetical Lectures 6.7.[15]

The Name of God. Ephrem the Syrian: God revealed his name to Moses when he called himself "I am,"[16] which is the name of Being. He never called any other beings by this name in the way that he called many things by their names, so that by means of the one name that he revealed he might teach us that he is the only true Being and that there are no others. Sermons Against Heretics 53.[17]

The Glory of God's Being. Ephrem the Syrian: God is absolute Being. His Being is as glorious as his name. If his name is essentially different from all others, so his origin remains hidden to us all. He is so great that his

creatures struggle in vain to understand him, because there is nothing in him that resembles any creature. Sermons Against Rash Inquirers 27.[18]

God's Names Are of Different Kinds. Ephrem the Syrian: God has names that are perfect and true in themselves, but he also has names that apply only in special circumstances and that he puts on and takes off. Thus you have learned that he is righteous and good [in all circumstances], but he is also a begetter and creator [in particular cases]. Sermons Against Rash Inquirers 44.[19]

God's Unbegottenness Is Not the Same as His Essence. Basil the Great: Our mind does its best to find out whether God, who is over and above everything else, has something superior to him, and because it is unable to find anything, it calls his life unbegotten and lacking any source. . . . When Luke says that Adam comes from God,[20] our natural reaction is to ask where God comes from, and is it not the case that every one of us has a ready answer in mind—from nothing? Whatever is from nothing has no source, and whatever has no source is unbegotten. But just as the begottenness of human beings is not the same thing as their essence, so the fact that God is unbegotten and depends on nothing for his existence does not entitle us to say that unbegottenness is his essence. Against Eunomius 1.15.[21]

God Is One in Nature but Not in Number. Basil the Great: Against those who accuse us of tritheism, let us answer that we confess that there is only one God—not in number but in nature. For everything that is called one in nature is not one absolutely,

---

[14]PL 6:153-55; cf. ANF 7:18. [15]PG 33:548-59; cf. NPNF 2 7:35. [16]Exod 3:14. [17]ESOO 2:555. [18]ESOO 3:48. [19]ESOO 3:79. [20]Lk 3:38. [21]PG 29:545-48.

nor is it simple in nature. God, however, is universally confessed to be simple and not composite. Therefore he is not one in number. What I mean is this. We say that the world is one in number, but it is not one by nature, nor is it simple, for we divide it into its constituent elements—fire, water, air and earth. Again, a human is said to be one in number. We often speak of one person, but this person is a compound of body and soul, and not simple. Similarly we talk of one angel in number, but not one by nature and not simple, because we think of an angel as a being who also possesses sanctification. Therefore, if everything that is one in number is not one in nature, and that which is one and simple in nature is not one in number, and if we call God one in nature, how can the issue of number be raised against us, when we exclude it from that blessed and spiritual nature? Number relates to quantity and quantity only makes sense in terms of bodily nature. We believe that our Lord is the creator of bodies and therefore that every number refers to things that have received a material and finite nature. LETTER 8.2.[22]

GOD IS RIGHTEOUSNESS AND WISDOM. BASIL THE GREAT: God knows what is and does not know what is not. God, who is of his own nature righteousness and wisdom, knows what these things are but does not know unrighteousness or wickedness, because the God who made us is not himself unrighteousness or wickedness. LETTER 8.7.[23]

GOD'S BEING MUST BE DISTINGUISHED FROM HIS ATTRIBUTES. BASIL THE GREAT: The person who denies that he knows the essence of God does not thereby disclaim all understanding of him, because our idea of God is garnered from his attributes. He may reply that God is simple and therefore that his attributes, which I claim are knowable, in fact belong to his essence. This is absurd. When we list God's attributes—his greatness,

power, wisdom, goodness and righteousness—are these just names of his one essence? Are they indistinguishable from one another? If our opponents say that this is indeed the case, we should not ask them whether they know God's essence but whether they know that he is powerful, righteous or merciful. We say that we do indeed know these things, which means that there must be a distinction between the divine attributes and God's essence, which is unknowable. We know our God from his operations (energies) but do not attempt to approach his essence. His operations (energies) come down to us, but his essence remains beyond our reach. LETTER 234.1.[24]

GOD IS THE ONLY TRUE BEING. GREGORY OF NAZIANZUS: As far as we can tell, "He who is"[25] and "God" are the special names of the divine essence, particularly "He who is," both because this is the name that he revealed to Moses . . . and also the one that is most appropriate. . . . Here we are inquiring into a nature whose being is absolute and not into a being that is bound up with something else. In its proper sense, being is peculiar to God and belongs entirely to him. It is not limited to any before or after, because in him there is no past or future. ON THE SON, THEOLOGICAL ORATION 4(30).18.[26]

GOD'S BEING IS ETERNAL AND INFINITE. GREGORY OF NAZIANZUS: God always was and always is and always will be, or rather, God always is, for was and will be are fragments of our time and of changeable nature. But he is eternal being, and this is the name that he gives himself when speaking to Moses. In himself he sums up and contains all being, having neither beginning in the past nor end in the future. He is like some great sea of being, limitless and

---

[22]PG 32:248-49; cf. NPNF 2 8:116. [23]PG 32:257; cf. NPNF 2 8:119. [24]PG 32:869; cf. NPNF 2 8:274. [25]Exod 3:14. [26]PG 36:125-28; cf. NPNF 2 7:316.

unbounded, transcending all conception of time and nature, only sketched out by the mind, and that very dimly and scantily. On the Holy Spirit, Theological Orations 45.3.[27]

God Is Simple. Didymus the Blind: God is simple and of an uncompounded spiritual nature. He has no ears or vocal cords but remains a solitary and incomprehensible substance with no particular parts to him. The same must be said for the Son and the Holy Spirit. On the Holy Spirit 35.[28]

What It Means to Know God in Part. Chrysostom: The apostle Paul says that we know God in part.[29] . . . This cannot mean that we know one part of his substance but not another, because God is a simple being. Rather, it means that we know that God exists but do not know what his essence is. On the Incomprehensible Nature of God 1.5.[30]

What God Really Is in Himself. Chrysostom: Let us then call him the ineffable, unintelligible God, invisible, incomprehensible, surpassing the power of human language [to express], exceeding the comprehension of mortal mind, unexaminable by angels, invisible to the seraphim, unintelligible to the cherubim, undetectable by principalities, dominions and powers—in a word, by the whole creation—known only by the Son and the Holy Spirit. On the Incomprehensible Nature of God 3.1.[31]

Why the Angels Hide Their Faces. Chrysostom: "Above him were seraphs, each with six wings. With two wings they covered their faces, with two they covered their feet."[32] Why did they cover their faces with their wings? Why indeed, unless it was because they could not bear the brightness coming out from the throne or its rays? Yet they did not see the light itself or the pure substance of God without a protective filter, because what they

saw was modified in that way. What is this modification? It is when God appears not as he is but in a way which is designed to accommodate the weakness of those who want to see him. On the Incomprehensible Nature of God 3.3.[33]

God Can Never Be Known as He Is in Himself. Chrysostom: Why did John say, "No one has ever seen God"?[34] He was speaking here of perfect comprehension and clear understanding. For because everything that exists has been made in relative inferiority, and no one has ever seen God's pure substance, it is clear that each person has seen something different. God is simple, uncompounded and without form, but people in the past have seen various forms, . . . so that when you hear John's words, understand by them that there is no one who knows God perfectly in his own substance and being. . . . So that when the prophet says that he does not possess the strength needed to stand in the presence of God, even when God accommodates himself to the situation, he really means that he is unable to maintain a clear knowledge and accurate understanding of him, nor can he appreciate the pure and perfect divine substance, even when it is filtered through to him. On the Incomprehensible Nature of God 4.3.[35]

The Supreme Characteristic of God's Being. Hilary of Poitiers: I have found the following words in the Old Testament: "I am that I am," and again, "He who is has sent me to you."[36] I confess that I was amazed to find a description of God so exact that it expressed in the terms best adapted to human understanding an unattainable insight into the mystery of the divine nature. There is no comprehensible property of God more characteristic of him

---

[27]PG 36:625; cf. NPNF 2 7:423. [28]PG 39:1064. [29]1 Cor 13:12. [30]PG 48:706-7. [31]PG 48:720. [32]Is 6:2. [33]PG 48:721-22. [34]Jn 1:18. [35]PG 48:730-31. [36]Exod 3:14.

than existence, since absolute existence cannot be ascribed to something that will come to an end or to something that has had a beginning. The one who combines continuity of being with the possession of perfect happiness could not in the past, nor will be able in the future, to be nonexistent, for what is divine can neither be created nor destroyed. Since God's eternity is inseparable from himself, it was worthy of him to reveal this one thing, that he *is*, as an assurance of his absolute eternity. ON THE TRINITY 1.5.[37]

GOD IS SPIRIT. HILARY OF POITIERS: First of all it must be understood that God has no body and does not consist of the parts and functions that normally make up such a thing. For we read in the Gospel, "God is a Spirit,"[38] which means that he is an invisible, infinite, self-sufficient and eternal nature. It is also written, "A spirit does not have flesh and bones."[39] These make up a body, and so the substance of God does not have them. But at the same time God, who is everywhere and in everything, hears, sees, acts and sustains everything there is. HOMILIES ON THE PSALMS 129.3.[40]

GOD'S ONENESS IS ABSOLUTE. RUFINUS OF AQUILEIA: When the Eastern churches put "in one God" in their versions of the creed, the "one" is not to be understood numerically [as if there were also others], but absolutely. He is said to be one because there is no other. COMMENTARY ON THE APOSTLES' CREED 5.[41]

GOD'S BEING IS REVEALED IN HIS NAME. AMBROSE: Names are distinctive qualities of every individual, by means of which they may be understood. Thus I conclude that Moses wanted to know what the special quality of God was when he asked him, "What is your name?"[42] God knew what Moses was thinking and answered him not with his name but with the substance lying behind it, and said, "I

am who I am,"[43] because there is nothing more characteristic of God than his eternal Being. EXPOSITION OF THE TWELVE PSALMS 43.19.[44]

GOD AFFECTS THE WORLD BUT IS NOT AFFECTED BY IT. AMBROSE: God's nature is simple, not compound or conjoined with anything else. He is just what he is in his divine nature. He fills everything but is not mingled with anything. He penetrates everything but is not penetrated in return by anything else. He is fully present everywhere and at the same time—in heaven, on earth or in the depths of the sea. He is incomprehensible to the eye, inexplicable to the tongue, unfathomable to the mind. He is to be followed in faith and venerated in worship, so that whatever is thought to be deserving of worship reveals his glory, and whatever is deemed to be higher in virtue speaks of his power. ON THE CHRISTIAN FAITH 1.16.106.[45]

GOD'S BEING AND HIS ATTRIBUTES ARE THE SAME. AUGUSTINE: In God, to be is the same as to be strong or to be just or to be wise, or whatever is said of that simple multiplicity or multifold simplicity, whereby to indicate his substance. ON THE TRINITY 6.4.6.[46]

GOD IS NOT A SUBSTANCE BUT AN ESSENCE. AUGUSTINE: It is wrong to say that God subsists and is a subject in relation to his own goodness and that this goodness is not a substance or essence. This would mean that God is not his own goodness but that it subsists in him like a subject. Thus it is clear that it is not correct to call God a substance but much better to say that he is properly an essence, indeed, the only true essence. He is unique because he alone is unchangeable and declared that his name was being itself,

---

[37]PL 10:28; cf. NPNF 2 9:41. [38]Jn 4:24. [39]Lk 24:39. [40]PL 9:719-20. [41]PL 21:343; cf. NPNF 2 3:544-45. [42]Exod 3:13. [43]Exod 3:14. [44]PL 14:1100. [45]PL 16:552-53. [46]PL 42:927; cf. NPNF 1 3:100.

as when he said to Moses, "I am that I am."[47] . . . But whether we call God an essence or a substance, both terms describe him as he is in himself and do not refer to anything else. In God, to be is the same as to subsist, so that in effect essence and substance are one and the same thing in his case. ON THE TRINITY 7.5.10.[48]

WORSHIP IS DUE TO GOD ALONE. AUGUSTINE: What is properly divine worship, which the Greeks call *latria*, and for which there is no word in Latin, both in doctrine and in practice, we give only to God. To this worship belongs the offering of sacrifices, as we see by the word *idolatry*, which means the giving of this worship to idols. Accordingly, we never offer or require anyone to offer sacrifice to a martyr or to a holy soul or to any angel. Anyone falling into this error is instructed by doctrine, either in the way of correction or of caution. For holy beings themselves, whether saints or angels, refuse to accept what they know to be due to God alone. AGAINST FAUSTUS, A MANICHAEAN 20.21.[49]

GOD HAS NO ORIGIN. CYRIL OF ALEXANDRIA: God is the source of all things, but he himself has no origin. Everything that exists came into being through him, but he was not born of anyone—he is the one who is and who is to come. That is his name. COMMENTARY ON ISAIAH 4.2.[50]

GOD'S BODY PARTS. CYRIL OF ALEXANDRIA: When holy Scripture, which contains the Word of God, makes mention of his body parts, it must above all be understood that it does not expect the mind to be drawn toward visible things but by means of what is visible to be led upwards by analogy to contemplate the beauty of intelligible things, and from the form, size, shape, type and so on of these bodily things to arrive at some understanding of God. We speak about him in a human way

because there is no other means by which we can understand what is so far above us. EXPLANATION OF THE PSALMS 11(10.3).[51]

THE SIMPLICITY OF THE DIVINE NATURE. CYRIL OF ALEXANDRIA: The nature of the supreme Being is simple and not compound. In one sense, it extends through the properties of the [divine] hypostases and the differences of persons and names and goes into the holy Trinity, yet it also comes together through the unity of the nature and its perfect and universal sameness, which is called, and indeed is, God. DIALOGUE ON THE TRINITY 7.[52]

THE INVISIBILITY OF GOD. LEO THE GREAT: Let no one think that the divine substance of the Holy Spirit has ever appeared to human eyes. His nature is invisible and is common to that of the Father and the Son. He has revealed the nature of his office and work in his own chosen way but has retained the properties of his being within his divinity, because human sight cannot reach the Holy Spirit any more than it can see the Father or the Son. For in the divine Trinity there is nothing dissimilar or unequal, and nothing that can be thought about its substance varies in power, glory or eternity. Although the Father, Son and Holy Spirit differ in their personal properties, there is no difference in divinity, nor is their nature distinct in any way. SERMON 75.3.[53]

GOD IS EVERYWHERE. GREGORY THE GREAT: God dwells in everything, beyond everything, above everything and beneath everything. He is above everything in his power and beneath everything in his providence.[54] He is beyond everything because of his greatness and

---

[47]Exod 3:14. [48]PL 42:942-43; cf. NPNF 1 3:111. [49]PL 42:385; cf. NPNF 1 4:262. [50]PG 70:924. [51]PG 69:792-93. [52]PG 75:1092. [53]PL 54:401-2. [54]The idea is that he supports and sustains everything from below.

inside everything because of his subtle nature. He rules from above, sustains from below, surrounds from outside and penetrates inside, nor can it be said that he has one part above, another below, another outside and another inside. Rather, it is one and the same God who sustains by ruling and rules by sustaining, who penetrates by surrounding and who surrounds by penetrating. MORALS ON THE BOOK OF JOB 2.12.20.[55]

THE SUBJECT AND THE OBJECT OF LOVE AND DESIRE. PSEUDO-DIONYSIUS: Why is it that theologians sometimes say that God is the subject of desire and love but at other times they say that he is their object? The reason is that he is these things in himself, as well as being their author, creator and begetter. He moves in himself, but he also moves other things. He directs himself and also directs others to himself. Theologians therefore call him lovable and desirable, because he is beautiful and good, love and desire themselves. He is both the motivating force of the world and the one who draws all things to himself, because he alone truly exists as beautiful and good in himself. He manifests himself in and through himself, and as the blessed process of that sublime union and loving motion, he leads all things toward his own goodness. DIVINE NAMES 4.14.[56]

THE ATTRIBUTES OF GOD'S BEING. JOHN OF DAMASCUS: We believe in one God, one beginning who has no beginning, uncreated, unbegotten, imperishable, immortal, everlasting, infinite, unlimited, boundless, omnipotent, simple, uncompound, incorporeal, immoveable, impassible, unchangeable, unalterable, unseen, the fountain of goodness and justice, the light of the mind, inaccessible, a power known by no measure, measurable only by his own will, creator of all things visible and invisible, the maintainer and preserver of all, the provider, master, lord and king over all, whose kingdom is immortal and everlasting.

There is nothing that can encompass him, but everything is encompassed by him. He occupies all things and extends beyond them, being separate from all being, above all things and absolute God, absolute goodness and absolute fullness. He determines all sovereignties and ranks, being above them all himself, as well as above being, life, word and thought. He is himself light, goodness, life and being, because he does not derive his being from anyone else. Rather, he is the source of being for everything that exists, the source of life to all who are alive, the source of reason to all who are rational, the ultimate cause of good to all. He sees things before they come to pass, being one essence, one divinity, one power, one will, one energy, one beginning, one authority, one dominion and one sovereignty. He is made known in three perfect hypostases and is served by all rational creatures. ORTHODOX FAITH 1.8.[57]

THE DIFFERENCE BETWEEN VENERATION AND WORSHIP. JOHN OF DAMASCUS: Let us venerate and worship only God, who is by nature worthy of worship, as our creator and maker. Let us also venerate the holy Godbearer (*Theotokos*), not as God but as the mother of God according to the flesh. Let us also venerate the saints, as the chosen friends of God who have ready access to him. ON DIVINE IMAGES 3.41.[58]

Attacks on Pagan Idolatry

THE VANITY OF IDOLS. LETTER TO DIOGNETUS: Come and take a good look at those whom you claim are gods. Is not one of them a stone, just like the ones we walk on? Is not another brass, no different from those vessels that we use every day? Is not a third wood, and that

---

[55]PL 75:565. [56]PG 3:712. [57]PG 94:808-9; cf. NPNF 2 9.2:6. [58]PG 94:1357.

already rotten? Is not a fourth silver, which has to be guarded in case it is stolen? Is not a fifth iron, eaten away by rust? Is not a sixth earthenware, no more valuable than the cheapest cooking pot? Are these not all made of corruptible matter? Are they not fabricated by means of iron and fire? Did not the sculptor fashion one of them, the brazier a second, the silversmith a third and the potter a fourth? Was not each one of them, in its primitive state before the artisans got hold of them, subject to change? Would they not have become pots or whatever, if they had met with different artisans? Are they not all deaf, blind, lifeless, without feeling, motionless and corruptible? These are the things you call gods—you worship them, you serve them, and in the end you become altogether like them! LETTER TO DIOGNETUS 2.[59]

THE FOLLY OF IDOL WORSHIP. JUSTIN MARTYR: We do not honor with garlands of flowers such deities as human beings have created and set up in shrines. We see that they are lifeless and dead and that they do not have the form of God (who has no form) but rather have the names and forms of wicked demons. I do not have to tell you how the artisan makes them or how easy it is to change the shape of some cheap pot and turn it into something you would call a god. Not only do we think that this is senseless—we think that it is insulting to God, who thus gets his name attached to things that are corruptible and require constant maintenance. FIRST APOLOGY 9.[60]

THE ABSURDITY OF THE HEATHEN GODS. TATIAN: There are legends about the metamorphosis of human beings, but with you the gods too are metamorphosed. Rhea becomes a tree, Zeus a dragon (on account of Persephone), the sisters of Phaethon are changed into poplars, and Leto becomes a bird of little value. A god becomes a swan, or takes the form of an eagle or enters into a sordid relationship with Ganymede, having made him

his cupbearer. How can I reverence gods who are eager for presents and angry if they do not receive them? . . . You sacrifice sheep and worship the same animal. The Bull is in heaven, and you slaughter his image [on earth]. . . . The swan is noble because it was an adulterer, and the Dioscuri, who live on alternate days, are also noble even though they raped the daughter of Leucippus. To THE GREEKS 10.[61]

HOW MANY JUPITERS ARE THERE? THEOPHILUS OF ANTIOCH: Why should I say anything about all the animals that the Egyptians worship—reptiles, cattle, wild beasts, birds and fish? They even worship washpots and disgusting noises! The Greeks worship stones and wood and other kinds of material substances, including the images of dead people. Phidias can be found in Pisa, making the Olympian Jupiter, as well as Athena on the Acropolis at Athens. How many Jupiters are there? There is the Olympian one, then Jupiter Latiaris, Jupiter Cassius, Jupiter Tonans, Jupiter Propator, Jupiter Pannychius, Jupiter Poliuchus and Jupiter Capitolinus. Jupiter the son of Saturn was thought worthy of a tomb in Crete, but I suppose that the others did not make it to his level! These are not gods but idols, the work of human hands and unclean demons. To AUTOLYCUS 1.10.[62]

YOU CAN MAKE YOUR OWN GODS. THEOPHILUS OF ANTIOCH: It seems to me to be absurd that sculptors, carvers, painters or molders should make gods who are considered to be of no value until they are purchased by someone and placed in a so-called temple or in a house. Then, not only do those who bought them sacrifice to them, but also those who made and sold them come with much devotion to worship them. They think of them as gods, ignoring the fact that they are no different

---

[59]PG 1:1169; cf. ANF 1:25. [60]PG 6:340; cf. ANF 1:165. [61]PG 6:828; cf. ANF 2:69. [62]PG 6:1040; cf. ANF 2:92.

from when they originally made them of stone, brass or wood. TO AUTOLYCUS 2.2.[63]

GOD AND MATTER ARE POLAR OPPOSITES. ATHENAGORAS: Are we Christians expected to worship images just because the masses cannot distinguish matter from God and therefore pray to idols made of material things? If matter and God are really the same thing, then yes, we are indeed guilty of impiety. But if they are polar opposites, what are we guilty of? God is as different from matter as the potter is from the clay that he uses to work his art. Just as the clay cannot become anything without that art, so matter cannot become anything unless God gives it distinction, shape and order. We do not think that pottery is more valuable than the potter, and for the same reason we give glory to God, who made the world, and not to the matter out of which it has been made. If we were to regard the various forms of matter as gods, we would have no sense of the true God, because we would be putting perishable things on the same level as the eternal. A PLEA REGARDING CHRISTIANS 15.[64]

MAKING IDOLS IS FORBIDDEN. TERTULLIAN: God prohibits an idol to be made as well as to be worshiped. In so far as making an idol is prior to worshiping it, the prohibition to make them comes first. In order to prevent this, the divine law proclaims, "You shall make no idols."[65] ON IDOLATRY 4.[66]

GOD DOES NOT NEED PAGAN OFFERINGS. LACTANTIUS: Pagans sacrifice fine and fat victims to God as though he were hungry. They pour out wine to him as if he were thirsty. They kindle lights to him as if he were in darkness. If they were able to conceive in their minds what those heavenly goods are, the greatness of which we cannot imagine as long as we are still surrounded by an earthly body, they would immediately realize how foolish they are. If they contemplated that heavenly

light that we call the sun, they would at once see that God has no need of their candles when he has given so clear and bright a light for our use. DIVINE INSTITUTES 6.2.[67]

EVIL IS THE CAUSE OF IDOLATRY. ATHANASIUS: Evil is the cause of idolatry, for once people learned to contrive evil, which has no reality in itself, it was but a short step to create for themselves gods that have no real existence. Just as a person who dives deep into the sea leaves the light behind him and thinks that only the things which he can see in the depths have any reality, so the ancients, when they were plunged into the lusts and imaginations of carnal things, forgot the knowledge and glory of God and made gods for themselves, glorifying the creature rather than the Creator and deifying the works instead of God, their cause and maker. AGAINST THE HEATHEN 8.3.[68]

THE PAGAN GODS DID NOT PROTECT ROME. AUGUSTINE: Let us look at the disasters that have befallen Rome in the course of its history, disasters that pagans would happily blame on the Christian religion if the teaching of the gospel had then been proclaimed, with its sweeping condemnation of their false and deceiving gods. In mentioning these facts, I am dealing with the ignorant populace, whose stupidity has given rise to the saying "No rain? It's all the Christians' fault." The well-educated know better, but whenever they want to excite the mob against us, they ignore the facts and do their best to support the vulgar notion that the disasters that are bound to fall on the human race in any given time and place are to be blamed on Christianity, which is now being extended everywhere in opposition to their gods. So let us help them to recall the

---

[63]PG 6:1048; cf. ANF 2:94. [64]PG 6:920; cf. ANF 2:135. [65]Exod 20:4. [66]PL 1:665; cf. ANF 3:62. [67]PL 6:637-38; cf. ANF 7:163. [68]PG 25:117; cf. NPNF 2 4:8.

many and varied disasters that befell the Roman state before the coming of Christ. In the face of those facts, let the pagans defend their gods if they can, assuming that the reason they worship them is to avoid such calamities. Why did the gods allow catastrophes to fall on their worshipers before the proclamation of Christ's name offended them and put a stop to their sacrifices? CITY OF GOD 2.2-3.[69]

THE EVIL OF DIVINATION. AUGUSTINE: All arts of divination are vanities or else arise out of a malignant fellowship between human beings and devils. They are therefore to be avoided by the Christian as covenants of a false and treacherous friendship. The apostle Paul says, "It is not as if the idol were anything in itself, but the things that they sacrifice they sacrifice to demons and not to God, and I do not want you to have fellowship with demons."[70] What the apostle has said about idols and the sacrifices offered in their honor is something that we ought to feel in regard to all fancied signs that lead either to the worship of idols or to worshiping creation or its parts instead of God. CHRISTIAN INSTRUCTION 2.23.36.[71]

GOD CANNOT BE DEPICTED. JOHN OF DAMASCUS: If we make an image of the invisible God, we have really sinned, for it is impossible for the incorporeal, invisible, uncircumscribed and undefined to be depicted. And if we make pictures of people, call them gods and worship them as such, we have done something very wrong. But in fact we do neither of these things. ON DIVINE IMAGES 2.5.[72]

The Unknowable God

GOD IS BEYOND OUR COMPREHENSION. IRENAEUS: The Father of all is far above the tempers and passions that operate among human beings. He is a simple, uncompounded being, without different parts. He is everywhere just like himself and equal to himself,

since he is wholly understanding, wholly spirit, wholly thought, wholly intelligence, wholly reason, wholly hearing, wholly seeing, wholly light, wholly the source of all that is good—as the religious and pious habitually speak about him.

He is, however, above all these properties and therefore indescribable. He may well and properly be called an Understanding who comprehends all things, but that does not make him like the understanding of human beings. Likewise, he may most properly be called Light, but that does not mean that he is anything like the light with which we are familiar. And thus, in every other respect as well, the Father of all is quite unlike human weakness. He is spoken of in these terms according to the love we have for him, but as far as his greatness is concerned, our thoughts about him transcend these expressions. AGAINST HERESIES 2.13.3-4.[73]

GOD DWELLS IN IMPENETRABLE DARKNESS. ORIGEN: We must point out that darkness is not always intended in a bad sense in Scripture. Sometimes we should understand it as being something good. The heretics have failed to understand this, and as a result they have said the most shameful things about the Creator of the world. . . . We must therefore show how and when darkness is meant in a good sense. In Exodus it is said that darkness, tempest and clouds surround God,[74] and in Psalm 18, "He made darkness his secret place."[75] If we consider the amount of speculation and knowledge about God, which is beyond the power of human nature to take in, . . . we discover how he is surrounded by darkness. For he is beyond the power of human nature to comprehend. COMMENTARY ON THE GOSPEL OF JOHN 2.23.[76]

[69]PL 41:49; cf. NPNF 1 2:24. [70]1 Cor 10:19-20. [71]PL 34:53; cf. NPNF 1 2:547. [72]PG 94:1288. [73]PG 7:744; cf. ANF 1:374. [74]Exod 19:9-16. [75]Ps 18:11 (17:12 LXX). [76]PG 14:161-64; cf. ANF 9:339.

God Is Incomparably Superior. Origen: God cannot be understood or measured. Whatever knowledge we may be able to obtain about him, we must still believe that he is far better than what we perceive him to be. . . . What is there that is more superior to all intelligent and incorporeal beings than God, whose nature cannot be grasped or seen by the power of any human understanding, even the purest and the brightest? On First Principles 1.1.5.[77]

Impossible for Us to Understand God. Ephrem the Syrian: Our human habitation, which dwells within the confined limits of visible things, shows that the attempts of our understanding to grasp the Son [of God] are futile, because no one can comprehend his beginning or examine it. For his Father is in all things hidden from each one of us, and however far people might extend their own knowledge and reasoning, it is still impossible to find out how he exists or to understand how great he is. So marvel at creation and glorify the Creator, but do not try to understand a being who is more excellent than everything else. Sermons Against Rash Inquirers 47.[78]

To Try to Find Out What God Is Like. Ephrem the Syrian: It is an aberration if we try to examine what God is and what he is like. For how can we describe the image of his being in us, which is similar to the mind? We cannot examine his appearance in such a way as to describe it in our intellect. He hears but without ears, he speaks without a mouth, he works without hands, and he sees without eyes. Our mind cannot understand this, and for that reason it stops trying to do so. Nisibene Hymns 3.[79]

God Can Be Known Only by His Works. Athanasius: God is good and merciful, taking care of the souls that he has created. It is his nature that he cannot be seen or compre-

hended, and he transcends every created substance. It is therefore natural that the human race would not be able to come to a knowledge of him, because people are made out of nothing and God has no beginning. For that reason he made created nature by his Word capable only of perceiving him in and through his works, since he himself remains invisible by nature. Against the Heathen 35.[80]

Confessing Our Ignorance. Cyril of Jerusalem: When we speak of God, we do not say all that we might (for that is known to him only) but only what human nature is able to receive and our weakness can bear. We do not explain what God is but candidly confess that our knowledge of him is not exact. Where God is concerned, confessing our ignorance is the sign of greatest knowledge. Catechetical Lectures 6.2.[81]

God Is Defined As Indefinable. Gregory of Elvira: Whatever you say about God, you are only describing the effectiveness of his works and the dispensations of his acts of grace; you cannot explain what he is like or how great he is. God is defined as being indefinable; that is all there is to it. Origen's Tractates on the Books of Holy Scripture 1.[82]

We Try to Find Words to Describe God. Marius Victorinus: Since there is no way of finding a name that is truly worthy of God, we call him God on the basis of the limited knowledge that we have. . . . Thus we say that God is alive and that he is intelligent. On the basis of our own actions, we ascribe various activities to God and say that he exists above and beyond all other things. In fact, he does not really exist as such; we merely use words like "substance," "existence" and "essence" as

[77]PG 11:124; cf. ANF 4:243. [78]ESOO 3:85. [79]ESCN 78. [80]PG 25:69. [81]PG 33:540-41; cf. NPNF 2 7:33. [82]TOSS 11.

ways of describing him, since all these things are ultimately created and therefore quite different from what he is in himself. ON THE GENERATION OF THE DIVINE WORD 28.[83]

NO ONE NAME CAN DESCRIBE GOD ADEQUATELY. BASIL THE GREAT: There is no one name that is adequate to give a complete description of God. Rather, there are many names for him, each of which has its own particular meaning. . . . Taken together they afford us only a small and unclear knowledge of God's nature, but this is still adequate enough for our purposes. AGAINST EUNOMIUS 1.10.[84]

THE PARADOX OF GOD'S UNKNOWABILITY. GREGORY OF NYSSA: The mind advances to ever greater and more perfect attentiveness and so comes to understand what the understanding is. . . . The closer it comes to the vision of God, the more it realizes just how invisible he is. The true vision of the seeker is that the invisible is seen, because the quest goes beyond what is visible and is enclosed on all sides by incomprehension, which is a kind of sacred darkness. LIFE OF MOSES.[85]

DIFFERENT ENDS IN VIEW. GREGORY OF NYSSA: We teach that we have only a confused and paltry perception of the divine nature by our own processes of reasoning, yet by means of the names that are rightly used to describe that nature, we come to some understanding of God, however inadequate it may be. We proclaim that not all the names of God have the same meaning. Some tell us what God is, and others tell us what he is not. So when we say that he is both righteous and incorruptible, we claim that righteousness is something that he has in himself, whereas corruptibility is something that he lacks. AGAINST EUNOMIUS 12.[86]

USING ANALOGIES. GREGORY OF NYSSA: Humans possesses power, life and wisdom,

but no one believes that these human attributes give us any clue as to what the power, life and wisdom of God are like. We can only speak of those things by using analogies taken from our own experience. Our nature, after all, is corruptible and weak, our life is short, our strength is uncertain and our reasoning unreliable. We can see something of the same qualities in the supreme Being, but we must expound them in relation to the magnitude of the one whom we are contemplating [and not within the limitations of our own being]. ADDRESS ON RELIGIOUS INSTRUCTION 1.[87]

OUR KNOWLEDGE OF GOD IS LIKE THAT OF CHILDREN. CHRYSOSTOM: After saying "When I was a child," the apostle Paul goes on to add, "Now we see through a glass darkly."[88] Here is the second proof of our present weakness, in that our knowledge is imperfect. And the third proof is found in the word *darkly.* A little child sees, hears and says many things but does not understand anything in an analytical manner. The child knows something at one level but knows nothing properly. In the same way, I know many things in one way, but at another level I do not know them at all. I know that God is everywhere and that all of him is everywhere, but I do not know how this is possible. I know that he is without beginning, unbegotten and eternal, but again I do not know how this can be. The human mind is unable to understand how something that does not owe its origin either to itself or to anything else can be called a substance. I know that he has begotten the Son, but I do not know how. I also know that the Spirit comes from him, but again I have no idea how. ON THE INCOMPREHENSIBLE NATURE OF GOD 1.3.[89]

A GODLY CONFESSION OF IGNORANCE. AUGUSTINE: We are talking about God, so

[83]PL 8:1033-34. [84]PG 29:533. [85]PG 44:376-77. [86]PG 45:953. [87]PG 45:13. [88]1 Cor 13:11-12. [89]PG 48:704.

why are you surprised if you do not understand him? If you understood him, he would not be God. A godly confession of ignorance is better than an audacious claim to knowledge. To arrive at some knowledge of God is a great blessing, but to understand him completely is quite impossible. SERMONS 117.3.5.[90]

THE PEACE OF GOD THAT PASSES UNDERSTANDING. AUGUSTINE: The apostle Paul says that the peace of God passes all understanding,[91] by which I presume he means that even the angels do not understand it. . . . In fact, it passes all understanding but God's own, though one day, we shall be called to share in it. . . . In this sense, both angels and humans understand God's peace according to the measure of knowledge that has been given to them, however little it may be. CITY OF GOD 22.29.1.[92]

THE NAMES OF GOD. CYRIL OF ALEXANDRIA: We see that there are many names ascribed to God, but none of them describes what he is in his essential being. Either they say what he is not, or else they describe how he is related to other things. For example, the words *incorruptible* and *immortal* tell us what he is not, while "Father" and "uncreated" tell us that he is the begetter of a Son and that he has not been created. Yet none of these terms explains what his essence is—they only indicate something that relates to it. THESAURUS ON THE TRINITY 31.[93]

EVEN THE ANGELS CANNOT UNDERSTAND GOD. THEODORET OF CYR: But since the bridegroom[94] is by nature incomprehensible even to the holy angels, they have not given any answer to my request, declaring by their silence that he cannot be understood by me because the uncreated cannot be understood by his creatures. For this reason I have abandoned my quest for him. COMMENTARY ON THE SONG OF SONGS BOOK 2, SONG OF SONGS 3:3-4.[95]

HOW WE MAY KNOW GOD. PSEUDO-DIONYSIUS: We must inquire how we may know God, who is perceived neither by sense nor by intellect and cannot be identified with any existing thing. Rather, we must say that God is not known by his nature (because he is by nature unknowable and transcends all reason and thought). We know him from the order of all things, both because it was laid out by him and because it contains images and likenesses of certain divine qualities that enable us, according to the measure of our strength, to rise to an understanding of the greatest good and the height of all goodness, by transcending the intermediate steps along the way to that goal. DIVINE NAMES 7.3.[96]

HOW TO INTERPRET THE DIVINE EMOTIONS. GREGORY THE GREAT: God is said to be jealous, to be angry, to be repentant, to be merciful and to be prescient—how? He is jealous because he keeps a watch over the purity of the soul of every one of us, which from a human point of view looks like a form of jealousy, although it does not affect him in that way. He is said to be angry because he punishes sins, although he is not at all disturbed in his own mind by that. And because he is immutable in himself but can change whatever he likes, he is said to repent, although what happens is that he changes the thing concerned, not his own mind. And when he comes to aid us in our misery he is called merciful, although in fact he is helping us in our misery, not sharing in it himself. And because he sees things that to us are still future, though they are ever-present to him, he is said to be prescient, although in reality he sees no future events because they are all present to him. All these descriptions therefore refer not to God as he is in his own eternal self but to the way in which he is

---

[90]PL 38:663. [91]Phil 4:7. [92]PL 41:796-97; cf. NPNF 1 2:507. [93]PG 75:452. [94]This is meant to be a reference to God, as the author is commenting on the Song of Songs. [95]PG 81:116. [96]PG 3:869-72.

revealed among us. MORALS ON THE BOOK OF JOB 20.32.63.[97]

The Unity of God's Being

WHY WE BELIEVE THERE IS ONLY ONE GOD. EUSEBIUS OF CAESAREA: Necessity forces us to say that there is a supreme Being who is divine, ineffable, good, simple, uncompounded, uniform and above and beyond everything else. . . . This something is God, who is mind, reason, wisdom, light, life, beauty, goodness and whatever other supreme virtue you can think of. . . . Moreover, he is above and beyond every thought, inquiry and discussion. ON THE THEOLOGY OF THE CHURCH 2.14.[98]

THE TRINITARIAN CHARACTER OF GOD'S UNITY. ATHANASIUS: He who worships and honors the Son worships and honors the Father in the Son, since the Godhead is one and therefore the worship and honor paid to the Father in and through the Son is one also. DISCOURSES AGAINST THE ARIANS 3.6.[99]

THE THREEFOLD SANCTUS GLORIFIES THE TRINITY. ATHANASIUS: When the seraphim glorify God by singing three times "holy, holy, holy, Lord God of hosts,"[100] they glorify the Father, the Son and the Holy Spirit. In the same way, when we are baptized in the name of the Father and of the Son and of the Holy Spirit,[101] we are made children of God, not of the gods. For the Father, the Son and the Holy Spirit is the Lord God of hosts. There is one divinity and one God, in three hypostases. ON THE INCARNATION AND AGAINST THE ARIANS 10.[102]

THERE CANNOT BE MORE THAN ONE GOD. EPHREM THE SYRIAN: There cannot be two gods, since the name of God who is to be worshiped is one. If God is not one, he is not God. But he is not one unless he is also supreme and above everything else. For it is impossible for him to be supreme or above everything else if there is something equal to him. And if there are not many gods, then there are not many supreme Beings. For the name of both these is one, and the glory of the supreme Being and of God is also one, for that is the name of God. He is an essence that has no beginning, a substance that is before and above all others. SERMONS AGAINST HERETICS 3.[103]

THE GODHEAD IS ONE. GREGORY OF NAZIANZUS: To us there is only one God because the Godhead is one, and everything that proceeds from him is referred to one, even though we believe in three persons. For no one of them is more or less God than the others, nor does one of them have priority over the others, nor are they divided in will or parted in power. When we look at the Godhead, or the first cause or the monarchy, what we conceive is one, but when we look at the persons in whom the Godhead dwells and at those who eternally and with equal glory have their being from the first cause, there are three whom we worship. ON THE HOLY SPIRIT, THEOLOGICAL ORATION 5(31).14.[104]

UNITED IN DIVERSITY. GREGORY OF NAZIANZUS: When I speak of God, you must be illumined at once by one flash of light and by three. Three in individuality, hypostasis or person—choose whatever name you like—but one in respect of the substance, which is the Godhead. They are divided without division, so to speak, and they are united in diversity. The Godhead is one in three, and the three are one. ON THE HOLY LIGHTS, ORATION 39.11.[105]

THE LORD GOD IS ONE. GREGORY OF NYSSA: Scripture says, "The Lord God is one

---

[97]PL 76:175-76. [98]PG 24:928-29. [99]PG 26:333; cf. NPNF 2 4:397. [100]Is 6:3. [101]See Mt 28:19. [102]PG 26:1000. [103]ESOO 2:443. [104]PG 36:148-49; cf. NPNF 2 7:322. [105]PG 36:345-48; cf. NPNF 2 7:355-56.

Lord."[106] By the word *Godhead* it proclaims too the only-begotten God and does not divide the unity into a duality so as to call the Father and the Son two gods, although each is called God by holy writers. On Not Three Gods.[107]

Thomas's Confession Explained. Hilary of Poitiers: Let us see whether the confession of the apostle Thomas agrees with this teaching of the Evangelist, when he says, "My Lord and my God."[108] He is therefore his God whom he acknowledges as God. And certainly he was aware that the Lord had said, "Hear, O Israel, the Lord your God is one."[109] And how did the faith of the apostle become unmindful of the first commandment, so that he confessed Christ as God, since we are to live in the confession of the one God? The apostle, who perceived the faith of the entire mystery through the power of the resurrection, after he had often heard "I and the Father are One,"[110] and "All things that the Father has are mine,"[111] and "I in the Father and the Father in me"[112] now confessed the name of the nature without endangering the faith. On the Trinity 7.12.[113]

The Law Proclaims God's Unity. Epiphanius of Salamis: The law of God given to the Jews prescribed . . . that they should acknowledge and worship only one God. His name is predicated in unity, . . . the Trinity is proclaimed as one, and this is what was always believed by the best of them, the prophets and the saints. Panarion 8.5.[114]

God Is Always the Same. Ambrose: Such too was the teaching of the Law: "Hear, O Israel, the Lord your God is one Lord,"[115] that is, unchangeable, always abiding in unity of power, always the same and not altered by any accession or diminution. Therefore Moses called him One. On the Holy Spirit 3.15.105.[116]

Three Holies in One Holiness. Ambrose: The Father is holy, the Son is holy, and the Spirit is holy, but they are not three holies, for there is one holy God, one Lord. For the true holiness is one, as the true Godhead is one, as that true holiness belonging to the divine nature is one. Everything that we think of as being holy proclaims that one holiness. Cherubim and seraphim, with unwearied voices, praise God and say, "Holy, holy, holy is the Lord God of hosts."[117] They say it not once, in case you should believe that there is only one [person], nor twice, in case you should exclude the Spirit, not in the plural, in case you should imagine that there is more than one God, but three times in the singular, so that you may understand the distinction of persons in the Trinity but also the oneness of the Godhead. There is no better word than "holy" to describe what God is like. Anything else merely diminishes his glory. On the Holy Spirit 3.16.109-11.[118]

One God. Augustine: Let us believe that the Father, the Son and the Holy Spirit is one God, the Creator and Ruler of the universe, and that the Father is not the Son, nor the Holy Spirit either the Father or the Son, but a Trinity of persons mutually interrelated and a unity of an equal essence. On the Trinity 9.1.1.[119]

The One God of Israel. Augustine: That Trinity is one God. Not that Father, Son and Holy Spirit are identical. The Father is Father, the Son is Son and the Holy Spirit is Holy Spirit, and this Trinity is one God, as it is written, "Hear, O Israel, the Lord your God is one God."[120] On Faith and the Creed 9.16.[121]

---

[106]Deut 6:4. [107]PG 45:132-33; cf. NPNF 2 5:336. [108]Jn 20:28. [109]Deut 6:4. [110]Jn 10:30. [111]Jn 16:15. [112]Jn 14:11. [113]PL 10:209; cf. NPNF 2 9:122. [114]PG 41:212. [115]Deut 6:4. [116]PL 16:801; cf. NPNF 2 10:150. [117]Is 6:3. [118]PL 16:802-3; cf. NPNF 2 10:150-51. [119]PL 42:961; cf. NPNF 1 3:125. [120]Deut 6:4. [121]PL 40:189; cf. NPNF 1 3:327.

THERE IS ONLY ONE GOD. AUGUSTINE:
Consider the passages of Scripture that
force us to confess that the Lord is one God,
whether we are asked about the Father alone,
or the Son alone, or the Holy Spirit alone or
about the Father, Son and Holy Spirit together. Certainly it is written, "Hear, O Israel,
the Lord your God is one Lord." Of whom do
you think that this is said? If it is said only of
the Father, then our Lord Jesus Christ is not
God. Why did those words come to Thomas
when he touched Christ and cried out, "My
Lord and my God,"[122] which Christ did not re-
prove but approved, saying, "Because you have
seen, you have believed."[123] LETTERS 238.[124]

THE TRINITY IS ONE GOD. FULGENTIUS OF
RUSPE: The holy and ineffable Trinity is by
nature one God, of whom it is said, "Hear, O
Israel, the Lord your God is one God"[125] and
"You shall worship the Lord your God, and
him alone shall you serve."[126] Indeed, since we
have said that this one God, who is the only
true God by nature, is not the Father only, nor
the Son only nor the Holy Spirit only, but is at
one and the same time Father, Son and Holy
Spirit, we must be wary that while we say that
Father, Son and Holy Spirit are one God in
unity of nature, we dare not say or believe that
they are all identical with each other, something that is quite blasphemous. To PETER, ON
THE FAITH 1.3.[127]

GOD'S UNITY IS BEYOND ESSENCE. PSEUDO-
DIONYSIUS: In the divine union and super-
essentiality there is something united and
common, which is supremely the superessen-
tial existence of the one Trinity. His divinity
is beyond the divine. . . . It is both ineffability
and multivocity, both incomprehensibility and
perfect intelligibility, the presence of everything and the absence of everything, beyond
all presence or absence of the divine persons
in themselves, if we can speak in this way. The
persons share a common home and dwelling

place; they are perfectly joined together in one
yet not confused in any way. DIVINE NAMES
2.4.[128]

GOD IS PERFECT IN EVERY RESPECT.
JOHN OF DAMASCUS: God is perfect, without blemish in goodness, wisdom and power,
without beginning or end, everlasting, uncircumscribed and perfect in everything. If
we want to say that there are many gods, we
must recognize the differences among them,
because if there is no such difference they are
not many but only one. But if there are differences among them, what becomes of their
perfection? That which falls short in goodness, power, wisdom, time or place cannot
be God. It is this very identity in all respects
that proves that there can be only one God,
not many. ORTHODOX FAITH 1.5.[129]

The Sovereign Freedom of God

**GOD DENIED HIS OWN NATURE FOR OUR
SAKE.** MELITO OF SARDIS: The whole creation
saw clearly that for humanity's sake the judge
was condemned, the invisible was seen, the
unlimited was circumscribed, the impassible
suffered, the immortal died and the heavenly
one was laid in a grave. For our Lord, when he
was born as man, was condemned in order that
he might show mercy, was bound in order that
he might set free, was seized in order that he
might release, suffered in order that he might
give life, was laid in the grave that he might
rise from the dead. FRAGMENT OF A DIS-
COURSE ON THE SOUL AND THE BODY.[130]

GOD KNOWS THE FUTURE. IRENAEUS: God
knows what is hidden, including all future
events. AGAINST HERESIES 4.21.2.[131]

---

[122]Jn 20:28. [123]Jn 20:29. [124]PL 33:1045; FC 32:201. [125]Deut
6:4. [126]Deut 6:13. [127]PL 65:673; FC 95:61. [128]PG 3:641.
[129]PG 94:801; cf. NPNF 2 9.2:4. [130]ANF 8:756. [131]PG
7:1044-45; cf. ANF 1:493.

HARDENING PHARAOH'S HEART. TERTULLIAN: God hardened the heart of Pharaoh but he deserved it because he had already denied God. AGAINST MARCION 2.14.[132]

GOD KNOWS EVERYTHING. CLEMENT OF ALEXANDRIA: God knows everything, both present and future. He knows how each and every thing will come to be. STROMATEIS 6.17.[133]

GOD NOT RESPONSIBLE FOR EVIL. ORIGEN: God preserves the free will of each individual, but he may make use of the evil deeds of wicked people in his administration of the world. . . . Nevertheless, such people still deserve to be condemned. AGAINST CELSUS 4.70.[134]

GOD KNOWS EVERYTHING THAT WILL HAPPEN. AUGUSTINE: Against the sacrilegious and impious speculations of reason, we say that God knows everything that will come to pass and also that we do by our own free will whatever we know and feel to be done by us only because we will it. But we do not say that all things come to pass by fate, which is a meaningless word. An order of causes in which the highest is attributed to God is not fate, unless we choose to derive this word from "fari" ("to speak"), because we cannot deny that Scripture says, "God has spoken once, and twice have I heard the same, that power belongs to God."[135] CITY OF GOD 5.9.[136]

The Divine Will

WHAT GOD WILLS AND PERMITS. TERTULLIAN: Some things appear to reflect the will of God in that they are allowed by him. But it does not necessarily follow that everything that he permits proceeds out of God's unqualified and absolute will. . . . If we thought that, . . . we would have every reason to excuse our sins, and that would be the ruin of the Christian life. . . . In fact there are some things

that he forbids, and even rewards with eternal punishment, and those things must certainly be against his will. EXHORTATION TO CHASTITY 2-3.[137]

NOTHING HAPPENS APART FROM GOD'S WILL. CLEMENT OF ALEXANDRIA: Nothing happens without the will of the Lord of the universe. Nevertheless, bad things happen because God permits them, not because he actively causes them. Only by saying this can we preserve both the providence and the goodness of God. We must not therefore think that God actively produces afflictions, but we must be persuaded that he does not prevent those who cause them. At the same time, he overrules the crimes committed by his enemies. STROMATEIS 4.12.[138]

The Divine Attributes

GOD CANNOT LIE. CLEMENT OF ROME: Nothing is impossible with God, except lying. . . . Everything is plain to him, and nothing can be hidden from his counsel. 1 CLEMENT 27.[139]

ABOVE AND BEYOND EVERY KIND OF LIMITATION. ARISTIDES: God possesses neither anger nor indignation, because there is nothing that can stand against him. . . . God is not born or made. His nature always stays the same and has no beginning or end. God is immortal, perfect and incomprehensible. When I say that God is perfect, I mean that there is no defect in him and that he has no need of anything. On the contrary, everything else needs him! . . . He has no name, because everything that has a name is a creature. He has no form or body parts and is neither male nor female. APOLOGY 1.[140]

---

[132]PG 2:301; cf. ANF 3:308. [133]PG 9:388; cf. ANF 2:517. [134]PG 11:1140; cf. ANF 4:528. [135]Ps 62:11 (61:12 LXX). [136]PL 41:150; cf. NPNF 1 2:91. [137]PL 2:915-17; cf. ANF 4:50. [138]PG 8:1296; cf. ANF 2:424. [139]PG 1:268; cf. ANF 1:12. [140]ANF 10:263-64.

God Cares About Human Choices.
Justin Martyr: God knows in advance
that some will be saved by repentance, even
though they may not yet be born. In the
beginning he made the human race with the
power of thought, of choosing the truth and
of doing right, so that no one has any excuse
before God, for they have been born with
reason and the power to reflect. If anyone
refuses to believe that God cares for these
things, he is either insinuating that God does
not exist or else asserting that he delights in
vice or is like a stone, indifferent to virtue
or vice, which mean nothing to him but only
to human beings. To say that would be the
greatest profanity and wickedness. First
Apology 28.[141]

**God Is Everywhere and Knows Every-
thing.** Melito of Sardis: God is never
absent, and nothing happens that he does not
know about. Discourse to Antoninus Caesar (fragment).[142]

**God Has No Beginning and Does Not
Change.** Theophilus of Antioch: He is
without beginning because he is unbegotten,
and he is unchangeable because he is immortal.
To Autolycus 1.4.[143]

**God Has Perfect Knowledge of Every-
thing.** Irenaeus: Not a single thing that has
been made or that will be made escapes the
knowledge of God. Through his providence,
every single thing has obtained its nature,
rank, number and special quantity. Nothing
has been produced or is produced in vain or by
accident. On the contrary, everything has been
made with exact suitability by the exercise of
transcendent knowledge. Against Heresies
2.26.3.[144]

God Gains Nothing from Our Worship.
Irenaeus: Service to God adds nothing to

him, and he has no need of human obedience.
On the contrary, he grants life, incorruptibility
and eternal glory to those who follow and serve
him. He bestows benefits on those who serve
him just because they serve him and on his
followers just because they follow him, but he
does not receive any benefit from them because
he is rich, perfect and in need of nothing. God
demands service from us not because he needs it
but because he is good and merciful and wants
to benefit those who continue in his service.
Against Heresies 4.14.1.[145]

God Is Beyond Space and Time. Clement
of Alexandria: God is above both space and
time, which is why he is never in any particular
place at any particular time.... "What house
will you build for me?" says the Lord.[146] He
has not even built one for himself, because he
cannot be contained by anything. Even though
heaven is called his throne, he is not contained
by it but rests, delighted in his creation. Stromateis 2.2.[147]

When God Rested on the Seventh Day.
Clement of Alexandria: When God rested,
he did not stop acting, as some people think.
God is good, and if he should ever stop doing,
he would cease to be God. Stromateis 6.16.[148]

God Has Chosen to Be Good. Clement
of Alexandria: God is not involuntarily
good the way a fire is involuntarily hot. In him,
the distribution of good things is entirely voluntary.... God does not do good by necessity
but blesses others by his free choice. Stromateis 7.7.[149]

**God Cannot Do Things That Contra-
dict His Nature.** Origen: We do not back

[141]PG 6:372; cf. ANF 1:172. [142]PG 5:1230; cf. ANF 8:755.
[143]PG 6:1029; cf. ANF 2:90. [144]PG 7:801; cf. ANF 1:398. [145]PG
7:1010; cf. ANF 1:478. [146]Is 66:1. [147]PG 8:937; cf. ANF 2:348.
[148]PG 9:369; cf. ANF 2:513. [149]PG 9:457-60; cf. ANF 2:534.

ourselves into a corner by saying that God can do everything. He cannot do things that are nonexistent or inconceivable. He cannot do what is disgraceful, because in that case he would cease to be God. Against Celsus 5.23.[150]

God's Nature Is Shared by Father and Son. Origen: Any property of a physical body cannot be ascribed to the Father or to the Son. What belongs to the nature of deity is common to the Father and the Son. On First Principles 1.1.8.[151]

God Is Fully Present Everywhere. Cyprian: God cannot be seen—he is too bright for our vision. He cannot be comprehended, because he is too pure for our discernment. He cannot be measured, because he is too great for our minds to perceive. What temple can God have when his temple is the whole world? While people live all over the place, how can I shut God up into one small space? He must be dedicated in our mind and consecrated in our breast. Nor should you ask God's name. God is his name. Where there are a great number of things that have to be distinguished from one another, names are appropriate. But God is unique and comprehends the entire designation "God." Therefore he is one and is present everywhere in his entirety. The Vanity of Idols 9.[152]

God's Presence in Us. Minucius Felix: How can God be far away when everything in heaven and on earth is known to him and full of him? Not only is he everywhere very near to us, but he is infused into us as well. Octavius 32.[153]

The "Ancient of Days." Lactantius: The most high God is called the "ancient of days"[154] because his age and origin cannot be comprehended. He alone was from generations and will always be to generations. Divine Institutes 4.12.[155]

The Secrets of Our Hearts. Pseudo-Clement of Rome: God knows everything beforehand and is well aware of what is in our hearts. 2 Clement 9.[156]

God Does Not Have a Body. Gregory of Nazianzus: God is not a body, . . . and we are forced to conceive of him as incorporeal. But even this does not fully describe his essence, any more than the words "unbegotten," "unoriginate," "unchanging," or "uncorruptible" or any other predicate that is used to describe God. For what difference does it make to his being that he has no beginning and is unable to change? On Theology, Theological Orations 2(28).9.[157]

God's Essence Is Unknown and Unknowable. Gregory of Nazianzus: What God is in nature and essence no one has ever yet discovered or can discover. Whether it will ever be discovered is a question that anyone who wants to may examine and decide. In my opinion it will be discovered when that within us that is godlike and divine, I mean our mind and reason, mingles with its like and the image ascends to its archetype, which it now longs for. This, I think, is the solution to the vexed problem of "We shall know even as we are known."[158] But in our present life all that comes to us is a little ray from a great light. If anyone has known God or has had the witness of Scripture to his knowledge of God, we are to understand that such a person has possessed a degree of knowledge that has given him the appearance of being more fully enlightened than others, but this is merely a matter of degree. On Theology, Theological Orations 2(28).17.[159]

---

[150]PG 11:1216; cf. ANF 4:553. [151]PG 11:129; cf. ANF 4:245. [152]PL 4:576-77; cf. ANF 5:467. [153]PL 3:341; cf. ANF 4:193. [154]Dan 7:13. [155]PL 6:481; cf. ANF 7:111. [156]PG 1:344; cf. ANF 7:519. [157]PG 36:36-37; cf. NPNF 2 7:291. [158]1 Cor 13:12. [159]PG 36:48-49; cf. NPNF 2 7:294.

GOD IS INFINITE BY NATURE. HILARY OF POITIERS: It is the Father to whom all existence owes its origin. In Christ and through Christ he is the source of all things. In contrast to everything else, he is self-existent. He does not draw his being from outside himself but possesses it from himself and in himself. He is infinite, for nothing contains him, and he contains everything. He is eternally unconditioned by space, because he is illimitable; he is eternally anterior to time, because time is his creation. Let your imagination extend to what you suppose is God's utmost limit and you will find him present there; strain as you will, there is always a further horizon toward which to strain. Infinity is his property. ON THE TRINITY 2.6.[160]

GOD'S PERFECTION IS OF A DIFFERENT ORDER FROM OURS. AMBROSE: Words often have to be understood in different senses according to context. For we say that God is good in one way, and humans in another way. We call God righteous in one sense, and humans in another sense. Likewise, we differentiate the wisdom of God from the wisdom of people. . . . There is in effect a double form of perfection, one of fractions and the other of full numbers, one here the other there, one measured by human capacities and the other by the perfection of the future age. God is righteous through everything, wise above everything and perfect in everything. DUTIES OF THE CLERGY 3.2.11.[161]

WORDS CANNOT DESCRIBE GOD. HILARY OF POITIERS: No words are adequate to describe the Father's attributes. We must feel that he is invisible, incomprehensible and eternal. But to say that he is self-existent, self-originating and self-sustained, that he is invisible, incomprehensible and immortal—all this is an acknowledgment of his glory, a hint of our meaning, a sketch of our thoughts, but speech is powerless to tell us what God is; words can-

not express the reality. ON THE TRINITY 2.7.[162]

GOD'S IMMORTALITY CANNOT CHANGE. AUGUSTINE: Holy Scripture would not say "who only has immortality"[163] of God unless it meant the term "immortality" to be understood in some special sense. Since the soul is also in some sense immortal, Scripture would not say "only has" of God unless it is because true immortality is unchangeableness, which no creature can possess because it belongs to the Creator alone. ON THE TRINITY 1.1.2.[164]

GOD IS GREATER THAN HIS ATTRIBUTES. AUGUSTINE: As far as we can, we should think of God as good but without quality, great but without quantity, a creator even though he lacks nothing, a ruler with no position, the sustainer of all things without having them, fully present everywhere but with no place of his own, eternal but without time, making things that are changeable but without change or passion in himself. Anyone who thinks about God like this, even though he cannot discover everything there is to know about him, nevertheless is careful not to think anything about him that is not true. ON THE TRINITY 5.1.2.[165]

GOD'S ATTRIBUTES ENCOMPASS EACH OTHER. AUGUSTINE: There are many ways in which God is rightly called great, good, wise, blessed, true and so on, but his greatness is the same as his wisdom, for he is not great by size but by power. Likewise, his goodness is the same as his wisdom and greatness, and his truth is the same as all those things, so that in him it is not one thing to be blessed and quite another thing to be great, wise, true or good. ON THE TRINITY 6.7.8.[166]

---

[160]PL 10:54-55; cf. NPNF 2 9:53. [161]PL 16:148. [162]PL 10:56; cf. NPNF 2 9:54. [163]1 Tim 6:16. [164]PL 42:821; cf. NPNF 1 3:18. [165]PL 42:929; cf. NPNF 1 3:88. [166]PL 42:919; cf. NPNF 1 3:101.

GOD IS SIMPLE AND UNCOMPOUNDED. JOHN OF DAMASCUS: God is simple and uncompound. Something that is composed of different elements is a compound. If we speak of God as uncreated, without beginning, incorporeal, immortal and everlasting, good, creative and so on, and make these things essential attributes of his being, then God would be composed of so many different qualities that he would be highly compound, which is nonsense, to put it mildly! Each of these affirmations about God must be understood not as referring to something concrete in him but rather to something that cannot be properly explained or as contrasts to things that exist in creation or as some kind of energy. ORTHODOX FAITH 1.9.[167]

THE DIVINE ATTRIBUTES. JOHN OF DAMASCUS: The divine attributes must be understood as common to the deity as a whole and as containing the notions of sameness, simplicity, indivisibility and union, while the names Father, Son and Holy Spirit, causeless and caused, unbegotten and begotten, and procession all contain the idea of separation, for these terms do not explain God's essence but the mutual relationship and manner of existence [of the three persons]. ORTHODOX FAITH 1.10.[168]

The Wrath of God

GOD'S WRATH REFERS TO HIS DISCIPLINE. ORIGEN: God's wrath does not indicate any passion on his part. It is something that he took on himself in order to administer strict discipline to sinners who have committed many serious sins. What is called God's wrath and his anger is . . . a means of discipline, as is clear from Psalm 6: "O Lord, do not rebuke me in your anger or chasten me in your hot displeasure,"[169] and in Jeremiah: "O Lord, correct me, but with judgment, not in your anger, lest you bring me to nothing."[170] Moreover, anyone who reads about the wrath of God in 2 Samuel, which induced David

to number the people, and then finds from 1 Chronicles that it was the devil who suggested this measure, will, when he compares the two statements, easily see why the word *wrath* was mentioned.[171] It is the same wrath that the apostle Paul talks about when he says, "We were by nature children of wrath, just as others were."[172] Wrath is not a passion on the part of God, but something that every one of us brings on ourselves by our sins. AGAINST CELSUS 4.72.[173]

GOD CANNOT HAVE HUMAN PASSIONS. ORIGEN: God is completely impassible and free from all affections of this kind. It is true that holy Scripture speaks of his wrath in both the Old Testament and in the Gospels, but we do not take such expressions literally. Rather, we try to think of God as he ought to be thought of. ON FIRST PRINCIPLES 2.4.4.[174]

GOD'S WRATH IS NOT A VICE BUT A VIRTUE. NOVATIAN: If we read of God's wrath and consider certain descriptions of his indignation and learn that hatred is asserted of him, we must not understand them to be asserted of God as they are of human beings. Anger and indignation can corrupt human beings, but not God. Human beings may be corrupted by such things because they are corruptible, but God cannot be because he is incorruptible. His anger arose out of wisdom, not out of vice. He is angry for our benefit. He is merciful even when he threatens, because it is by these threats that people are called back to the right path. Fear is necessary for those who need to be motivated to live a virtuous life, so that those who have abandoned reason may at least be moved by terror. ON THE TRINITY 5.[175]

---

[167]PG 94:833-36; cf. NPNF 2 9.2:12. [168]PG 94:837; cf. NPNF 2 9.2:12. [169]Ps 6:1. [170]Jer 10:24. [171]2 Sam 24:1; 1 Chron 21:1. [172]Eph 2:3. [173]PG 11:1141; cf. ANF 4:529. [174]PG 11:203; cf. ANF 4:277-78. [175]PL 3:894-95; cf. ANF 5:615.

God's Anger Is Righteous. Lactantius: God cannot have any unjust anger, because he cannot be harmed by anyone. However, there is also a righteous anger, which is necessary if wickedness is ever to be corrected. God must have this kind of anger, because he sets an example for us and restrains everyone's wicked behavior. On the Wrath of God 17.[176]

God's Anger Is Eternal. Lactantius: God is eternal, and so his anger must be eternal also. But God keeps his anger under control and regulates it according to his word. If it were absolutely eternal, satisfaction for sin and reconciliation to God would obviously be impossible. In fact, his anger remains active against those who go on sinning, but those who stop sinning extinguish God's anger toward them. On the Wrath of God 21.[177]

God's Goodness and Love

God Hates Unrighteousness. Lactantius: God is moved and is indignant when he sees unrighteousness at work. On the Wrath of God 12.[178]

God Punishes the Unrepentant. Lactantius: God is very patient, but even so, he punishes the guilty and does not allow them to carry on any further, once he sees that they will never change. On the Wrath of God 20.[179]

God Desires Our Salvation. Chrysostom: God earnestly desires our salvation. Where does such love, such affection for us come from? It comes from his goodness alone, for grace itself is the fruit of goodness. For this reason, says Paul, God has predestined us to the adoption of children, it being his will and the object of his earnest desire that the glory of his grace may be displayed.[180] Homilies on Ephesians 1.5.[181]

Before the Foundation of the World. Augustine: When a righteous person begins to be a friend of God, he is changed, but far be it from us to say that God, loves anyone in the realm of time with a new love that was not there in him before. God loved all his saints before the foundation of the world, when he predestined them, but when they are converted and find him, then it is said that they begin to be loved by him, so that we may understand what God is like by an analogy with human affections. On the Trinity 5.16.17.[182]

We Must Love God as the Only True Good. Augustine: We cannot honestly say that one thing is better than another unless we have some conception of what is good impressed on us, which we can use as a means of approving some things as good and preferring one form of good to another. God is to be loved, not this or that form of good, but Good itself. For the good that must be sought for the soul is not something that it can judge from the standpoint of its own superiority, but something to which it can cling in and by love. What can this be except God? On the Trinity 8.3.4.[183]

Our Good Is to Be United to God. Augustine: God is the fountain of our happiness and the goal of all our desires. Being attached to him, or rather reattached (for we had detached ourselves and lost hold of him), we incline toward him in love in order that we may rest in him and find our blessedness in attaining that end. For our good, about which philosophers have so keenly disputed, is nothing else than to be united to God. It is by embracing him spiritually that the rational soul is filled and impregnated with true virtues. City of God 10.3.[184]

---

[176]PL 7:131; cf. ANF 7:274. [177]PL 7:140; cf. ANF 7:277-78. [178]PL 7:115; cf. ANF 7:269. [179]PL 7:139; cf. ANF 7:277. [180]Eph 1:5-6. [181]PG 62:13; cf. NPNF 1 13:52. [182]PL 42:924; cf. NPNF 1 3:96. [183]PL 42:949; cf. NPNF 1 3:117. [184]PL 41:280-81; cf. NPNF 1 2:182

THE FATHER

πιστεύομεν εἰς ἕνα Θεὸν	*Credo in unum Deum*	*We believe in one God,*
πατέρα, παντοκράτορα,	***Patrem** omnipotentem;*	***the Father,** the Almighty,*
ποιητὴν οὐρανοῦ καὶ γῆς,	*factorem coeli et terrae,*	*maker of heaven and earth,*
ὁρατῶν τε πάντων καὶ ἀοράτων.	*visibilium omnium et invisibilium.*	*of all that is, seen and unseen.*

HISTORICAL CONTEXT: If faith in one God is part of the Christian church's Jewish inheritance, then confessing him as Father probably ought to be regarded as a specifically Christian contribution to that belief. It is not that Jews were totally unacquainted with the notion that God is a Father to his people,[1] and the concept of divine fatherhood was quite acceptable in Hellenistic circles, where "Father" and "Creator" were often used synonymously. The apostle Paul recognized this in his preaching ministry,[2] and the early Christians did not hesitate to follow his example. In the first two centuries of the Christian church, this use of the term "Father" for God was very common, because it provided a ready link between biblical and educated pagan notions of God. Christian writers therefore used it as a way of showing their pagan counterparts that the latter also recognized the God of the Bible, though without fully realizing what that meant. Whether this form of evangelism was effective or not, it was gradually understood that this interpretation was not the principal use of the term "Father" in the New Testament. Indeed, by the time Cyril of Jerusalem wrote his *Catechetical Lectures* (about 350), he was able to state quite categorically that it was erroneous! In the New Testament, said Cyril, God was first and foremost the Father of the Son Jesus Christ, and it is in that perspective that we must interpret the meaning of the term "Father."

Was Cyril right? Practically everyone now agrees that calling God "Father" was a particular hallmark of the ministry of Jesus, underlined in the New Testament by the preservation of the original Aramaic word *Abba*.[3] Jews did not normally refer to God in this way, and the evidence of the Gospels suggests that they were scandalized by Jesus' use of the term, because to them it implied that he was making himself equal to God.[4] That was in fact the case, and from the beginning Christians were aware that to call God Father implied that he had a Son—Jesus Christ himself. On balance, therefore, it seems that Cyril was justified in his insistence on the trinitarian context of the term "Father," although the more general use of the term cannot be excluded.

The precise relationship between Father and Son was difficult to define, since it implied both an equality of nature and a distinction of persons, concepts that were difficult to reconcile with the traditional Judeo-Christian belief in the absolute oneness of God. Much of the discussion that took place in the early church revolved around ways of solving this intellectual problem. Inevitably, many of the proposed solutions were later shown to be inadequate, but this must not detract from the central fact that all Christians regarded the issue as one that had to be resolved without denying either the specific identities of the Father and the Son or the unity of the Godhead.

One of the earliest, and crudest, attempts to solve the Father-Son puzzle was that which

---

[1]See Is 1:2. [2]Acts 17:28-29. [3]Mk 14:36; Rom 8:15; Gal 4:6. [4]Jn 5:18.

came to be associated with a certain Sabellius. He is completely unknown to us but was held to have been the author of the heresy now known as modalism, or more precisely as monarchian modalism. This was the belief that there is only one God, who is the sole source (monarch) of all that exists. The Son and the Holy Spirit are not separate beings but different ways (modes) in which the Father appears to us in his revelation. The heresy was based on such biblical statements as "I and the Father are one,"[5] but its opponents had little difficulty in demonstrating that this verse could not be interpreted in the way in which the modalists wished. It was all too obvious from the rest of John's Gospel (to go no further) that the Father and Son were frequently in dialogue with one another, which would hardly have been possible if they were one and the same person.

Modalism was therefore relatively easy to refute, but it provoked orthodox defenders of the faith to come up with a better way of safeguarding the identities of the three persons of the Trinity without losing sight of the divine unity (monarchy). This led to a two-tier understanding of God, in which it was stated that at the level of being (substance or nature) God was one, and everything said about him applied equally to all three persons without distinction. But at the level of personhood, or identity, God appears as three—Father, Son and Holy Spirit. They are distinguished from each other by certain incommunicable attributes, but each of them participates equally in the underlying divine nature. What to call these different levels of perception was undecided for a very long time, and there were various alternatives doing the rounds as late as the fifth century. But at the council of Chalcedon in 451 it was finally agreed that "person" should be used to describe the three-ness of God and "substance" or "essence" used to describe his oneness. These terms were not new—they could be traced back to Tertullian

(about 200)—but experience and controversy had refined them to the point where they could accommodate all the many nuances of the distinction that had to be maintained.

Christians called God "Father" not in imitation of Jesus but in union with him. In other words, God is our Father not because we are divine but because we have been united to him in the Son, Jesus Christ. What Jesus is by eternal right and nature, we have become by grace and adoption. To call God "Father" is therefore to participate in the inner life of the Trinity, a point that is underlined by the sending of the Paraclete (Holy Spirit), who comes from the Father and the Son in order to make fellowship with them a reality of our spiritual experience. Outside the trinitarian context, the designation of God as Father loses its relational dimension, and it was for this reason that from the time of Cyril of Jerusalem onwards, the fatherhood of God came to be interpreted in an almost exclusively trinitarian way.

In the centuries before Christianity became a legal religion, it was customary for Christians to say that while Father and Son were identical in nature, they differed in rank or status. However this was put, the Son derived his being from the Father and was therefore in some sense inferior to him. For example, it was often said that the Father was like the sun and that the Son was like one of the sun's rays. The substance is the same, but the Son is presented to us in a more manageable, or as we would say today, a more user-friendly form. This was believed to be necessary because otherwise it would be impossible for us, mere creatures that we are, to relate to the divine being, just as it is impossible for us to gaze directly at the sun. In this sense, therefore, the Son and the Holy Spirit represent an accommodation of the divine being to the limitations of human perception, enabling us thereby to have access to God.

---

[5]Jn 10:30.

In ancient times, views of this kind were usually stated hesitantly, because the Fathers had a clear sense that the truth of the matter was really beyond human understanding. Their innate reluctance to probe more deeply into the mysteries of the Godhead might have continued indefinitely had it not been for the heresy of Arius, which appeared at Alexandria around 318 and soon rocked the Christian world to its foundations. Arius denied that the Son and the Holy Spirit were coeternal with the Father and insisted that only the last of these was truly God in the absolute sense. Most of the ensuing controversy was primarily concerned with the identity of Jesus Christ as both God and man, but the trinitarian dimension of that problem could hardly be ignored. To defend the equality of the three persons in the Godhead, opponents of Arius had to stress as never before that the Son has the same substance and nature as the Father—an identity of being that is implied by the terminology used and that finds an exact parallel in human experience. There was still a lingering tendency to regard the Son and the Holy Spirit as somehow derivative and therefore subordinate to the Father, but as the implications of Arianism sank in, the inadequacy of this approach became more glaringly obvious. Nevertheless, it was very difficult for the church to avoid this subordinationist tendency altogether, not least because so many of its traditional formulations of the Trinity had taken something of this kind for granted and expressed themselves accordingly. A good example of this is the fact that although the word *Almighty* was attached to the Father as early as the second century, it was never formally extended to the Son and the Holy Spirit, even though fourth- and fifth-century theologians were quite prepared to say that both the second and the third persons of the Trinity were also almighty God.

When looking at texts that speak of God the Father, we must therefore be prepared to meet a certain tension between the traditional, basically subordinationist language and the insistence that all three persons are co-eternal and equal in every respect. The difficulty was compounded by a persistent tendency to think of God primarily as a substance, which inevitably led people to conclude that the persons were somehow derived from and dependent on it. The substance might be identified as the Father, but that was a form of latent Arianism, because the Son and the Spirit could only be parts or portions of the substance that dwelt fully (and uniquely) in the invisible, absolute and almighty Father alone. In the end, a way to resolve this problem was opened up by the council of Chalcedon, which produced a doctrine of Christ that insisted that it was his divine person, the Son of God, that possessed two natures, thereby making the concept of "person" an independent agent. Once it was accepted that the Son of God possessed his divine nature but was not bound by it (to the extent that he could acquire a second nature alongside it), it became possible to see the entire Trinity in this way—as a fellowship of persons who possess a common nature, rather than as a substance somehow divided up into three parts. The patristic era provided the theological concepts that would be needed in order to elaborate this transformation of our perception of God, but it would be many centuries before it would come to fruition. The fathers of the church pointed the way, but they did not develop the implications of their theology, and to that degree they left important unfinished business for future generations to wrestle with.

OVERVIEW: The name "Father" is given to the Creator of the universe and is used by Christians to show that we love God and do his will (CLEMENT OF ROME, MELITO, LACTANTIUS). The Father is the source of all things (THEOPHILUS) and it is to him that we pray, having been commanded by Jesus to do so (TERTULLIAN, CYPRIAN). The Father is uniquely eternal and unbegotten (Justin Martyr, Theophilus, Novatian, Hilary) and is also uniquely invisible (Tertullian). To call God "Father" is to name the fullness his essence, not one of his attributes (Athanasius), but it also points us to the first person of a Trinity that includes the Son and the Holy Spirit (Cyril of Jerusalem, Rufinus). The Father has always been the Father, which is one reason why the Son must be regarded as eternal (Tertullian, Origen, Alexander, Basil, Gregory of Nyssa). However, the Father is unbegotten, whereas the Son is begotten from him (Novatian, Cyril of Jerusalem, Epiphanius, Hilary). Jesus Christ has revealed the Father to us (Irenaeus, Clement of Alexandria, Hippolytus), because the Father is invisible in himself (Tertullian). This is because the Father sent the Son into the world (Epistle to Diognetus). The Father is not identical to the Son (Justin Martyr, Tertullian) although they are united to one another (Novatian, Hilary) and cannot exist without each other (Tertullian). They work together in harmony (Hippolytus, Hilary), sharing the divine monarchy (Irenaeus, Tertullian) and creating the universe together (Athanasius, Basil), but are not interchangeable (Athanasius, Ambrose) because each person of the Godhead has his own unique properties (John of Damascus).

When God is mentioned without further qualification, it is the Father who is intended (Tertullian), and it is he who is the ultimate giver of grace (Cyril of Jerusalem). The Father is greater than the Son (Tertullian, Origen, Alexander), but nevertheless, the Father and the Son are equal (Clement of Alexandria) because they share the same substance (Lactantius, Dionysius). The difference between them is one of order or relationship, not one of nature (Basil), and none of the persons in God is anything other than fully divine and eternal (Origen, Athanasius). The Son is the Father's image

(Origen), and we human beings are the image of the Trinity (Tertullian, Augustine). The Son is eternally present in the Father (Novatian, Athanasius), and they are inseparable (Dionysius, Hilary, Ambrose), although the Father did not die alongside the Son on the cross (Tertullian). It is through the Son that we come to know the Father (Clement of Alexandria, Hippolytus).

The Trinity is the one true God (Justin, Athenagoras, Irenaeus) in three persons (Tertullian, Novatian, Hippolytus, Marius Victorinus, Jerome), though this term is a convenient description and not a definition of God (Basil, Augustine). It is an article of faith, not a deduction of human reason (Hilary), though the existence of each individual person implies that of the others (Didymus). Images of trinitarian relationships can be found in nature, but the true wonder of them surpasses human understanding (Ephrem). The oneness of God does not exclude the presence of more than one person in him (Chrysostom, Hilary), nor can the persons be identified with specific divine attributes that might then be detached from the whole (Augustine, Cyril of Alexandria). The charge of atheism that pagans level against Christians is absurd, particularly since we know God in a Trinity of persons (Justin Martyr, Athenagoras). Our baptism is trinitarian (Justin Martyr, Tertullian, Athanasius), and we experience all three persons in our spiritual life (Origen, Didymus) because each person has its own distinctive powers and gifts (Hilary). The Trinity works together in creating the universe (Irenaeus, Basil), and we have been created in its image (Tertullian, Augustine). The doctrine of the Trinity is found in the Bible and is intended for our enjoyment as believers (Augustine). God has inner relationships that are neither substances nor mere accidents, and the Trinity is not a compound of three distinct elements (Augustine).

The attributes of God do not belong to

each of the persons of the Trinity individually but are part of the divine unity (Augustine). Although they are distinct, the three persons constitute only one God (Leo), and they are distinguished from each other by their own peculiar properties, which do not affect their unity (John of Damascus).

The Name of Father

The Blessings of Our Father and Creator. Clement of Rome: Let us look steadfastly to the Father and Creator of the universe and cling to his magnificent and excellent gifts and blessings of peace. Let us contemplate him with our understanding and look with the eyes of our soul to his longsuffering will. Let us reflect how free from wrath he is towards all his creation. 1 Clement 19.[6]

Praying to the Father. Clement of Rome: Let us draw near to him with holiness of spirit, lifting up pure and undefiled hands to him, loving our gracious and merciful Father, who has made us partakers in the blessings of his chosen ones. 1 Clement 29.[7]

Doing the Father's Will. Pseudo-Clement of Rome: By doing the will of the Father, and keeping our flesh holy and observing the commandments of the Lord, we shall obtain eternal life. . . . Therefore, brethren, let us do the will of the Father who has called us, so that we may live. . . . If we do the will of God our Father, we shall be of the first church, which is spiritual and was created before the sun and the moon,[8] but if we do not do the Lord's will, we shall be of the church of which the Scripture says, "My house was made a den of thieves."[9] 2 Clement 8, 10, 14.[10]

There Is Only One Father. Pseudo-Ignatius: There is only one God and Father, and not two or three, one who is, and there is no one besides him, the only true God. For Scripture says, "The Lord your God is one Lord."[11] And again, "Has not one God created us? Do we not all have the same Father?"[12] Epistle of Ignatius to the Philippians 2.[13]

Those Who Love God Call Him Father. Melito of Sardis: No eye can see him, nor thought apprehend him nor language describe him. Those who love him speak of him as Father and God of truth. Discourse to Antoninus Caesar (fragment).[14]

Prophecies Given by the Father. Justin Martyr: The person of the Father spoke the following words through Isaiah the prophet: "The ox knows his owner and the donkey his master's stall, but Israel does not know, and my people have not understood. Woe to you, sinful nation, a people full of sins, a wicked seed, children who are transgressors and who have forsaken the Lord."[15] Elsewhere the person of the Father speaks through the same prophet as follows: "Where is the house you will build for me? Heaven is my throne, and the earth is my footstool."[16] From this you can see what kinds of things the Father spoke through the prophets. First Apology 37.[17]

No Name Is Given to the Father. Justin Martyr: To the Father of all, who is unbegotten, there is no name given. For anyone who is called by a name is dependent on the person who gives him that name. These words, Father, God, Creator, Lord and Master, are not names

---

[6]PG 1:248; cf. ANF 1:10. [7]PG 1:269; cf. ANF 1:12. [8]See Ps 72:5, 17 (71:5, 17 LXX). [9]Jer 7:11; cf. Mt 21:13; Mk 11:17; Lk 19:46. [10]PG 1:341, 344; AF 47-50; 114, 121; cf. ANF 7:519-21. [11]Deut 6:4. [12]Mal 2:10. [13]PG 5:921; cf. ANF 1:116. [14]PG 5:1226; cf. ANF 9:751. [15]Is 1:3-4. [16]Is 66:1. [17]PG 6:385; cf. ANF 1:175. Note that this section is followed by one giving prophecies uttered by the Son and by another that gives prophecies uttered by the Holy Spirit.

but titles derived from his good deeds and functions. SECOND APOLOGY 6.[18]

THE FATHER HAS NO ORIGIN. JUSTIN MARTYR: You must not imagine that the unbegotten God himself descended or ascended to or from anywhere. The ineffable Father and Lord of everything has not come to any place, does not walk, sleep or get up, but rather stays where he is. He is not moved, nor is he confined to one particular location, . . . for he existed before the world was made. DIALOGUE WITH TRYPHO 127.[19]

THE SOURCE OF ALL THINGS. THEOPHILUS OF ANTIOCH: If I call him Father, I am claiming that everything comes from him. . . . He is called Father because he comes before everything else. TO AUTOLYCUS 1.3-4.[20]

CHRIST REVEALED GOD AS FATHER. IRENAEUS: He whom the Law proclaimed as God, Christ revealed as Father, and the disciples of Christ must obey him alone. By means of the statements of the Law Christ put our adversary to utter confusion,[21] and the Law directs us to praise God the creator and to serve him alone. Since this is the case, we must not look for another Father besides him or above him, since it is the same God who justifies the circumcision by faith and the uncircumcision through faith.[22] If there were any other perfect Father greater than he, Christ would not have overthrown Satan by his words and commandments. He did not overcome the adversary by someone else's sayings but by those belonging to his own Father. AGAINST HERESIES 5.22.1.[23]

GOD IS FATHER AND MASTER. TERTULLIAN: God is a perfect Father and a perfect Master. He is a Father in his mercy but a Master in his discipline. He is a Father in the mildness of his power but a Master in its severity. He is a Father who must be loved

with dutiful affection, but he is also a Master to be feared. He is to be loved because he prefers mercy to sacrifice[24] and feared because he dislikes sin. He is to be loved because he prefers the sinner's repentance to his death[25] and feared because he dislikes sinners who do not repent. Scripture says that the obedient person must love God[26] and that the transgressor must fear him. AGAINST MARCION 2.13.[27]

THE MEANING OF THE LORD'S PRAYER. TERTULLIAN: The Lord's Prayer begins with a witness to God and with the reward of faith when we say, "Our Father, who is in heaven,"[28] for in saying this we both pray to God and commend faith, whose reward this address to God is. For it is written, "To them who believed in him he gave power to be called children of God."[29] Our Lord very often told us that God is our Father and even said that we should call no one on earth father, except the Father we have in heaven.[30] Happy are those who recognize their Father! This is precisely the reproach that is made against Israel, to which the Spirit calls forth the heavens and the earth as witness: "I have begotten children, and they have not recognized me."[31] Moreover, in saying "Father," we also call him God. That name is both one of filial duty and of power. Once again, the Son is invoked in the Father, for he said, "I and the Father are one."[32] Nor is our mother the church passed over, if the mother, from whom the Father and the Son both arise, is recognized in them. In one word, therefore, we both honor God and are mindful of the precept, and we set a mark on those who have forgotten their Father. ON PRAYER 2.[33]

---

[18]PG 6:453; cf. ANF 1:190. [19]PG 6:772-73; cf. ANF 1:263. [20]PG 6:1028-29; cf. ANF 2:90. [21]A reference to the temptations of Jesus (Mt 4). [22]Rom 3:30. [23]PG 7:1183; cf. ANF 1:550. [24]Hos 6:6. [25]Ezek 33:11. [26]Mt 22:37. [27]PL 2:300; cf. ANF 3:308. [28]Mt 6:9. [29]Jn 1:12. [30]Mt 23:9. [31]Is 1:2. [32]Jn 10:30. [33]PL 1:1153-55; cf. ANF 3:682.

WHEN WE CALL GOD FATHER. CYPRIAN: How great is the Lord's indulgence! How great is his condescension and plenteousness of goodness toward us, seeing that he has desired us to pray in the sight of God in such a way as to call God Father and to call ourselves sons of God, even as Christ is the Son of God— something that none of us would dare to do in prayer, unless he had encouraged us to do so. We ought, therefore, beloved brethren, to remember and to know that when we call God Father, we should act as God's children, so that just as we find pleasure in thinking of God as a Father, he might also be able to find pleasure in us. THE LORD'S PRAYER 11.[34]

FINDING THE FATHER IS DIFFICULT. CLEMENT OF ALEXANDRIA: It is a difficult task to discover the Father and maker of the universe, but having found him, it is impossible to explain him to everyone because his being is beyond all human forms of expression. STROMATEIS 5.12.[35]

WE LOVE GOD AS OUR FATHER. LACTANTIUS: We are bound to love him because he is our Father and revere him because he is our Lord. We must honor him for his generosity and fear him because he is strict. Each quality in him is worthy of reverence. ON THE WRATH OF GOD 23.[36]

THE FATHER IS THE FATHER OF THE SON. CYRIL OF JERUSALEM: The name of the Father, with the very utterance of the title, suggests the thought of the Son, just as one who names the Son thinks immediately of the Father. For if God is a Father, he must be the Father of a Son, and if he is a Son, he must be the Son of a Father. . . . God may be regarded as the Father of many, but this is a misinterpretation. In reality he is the Father of one only, the only-begotten Son, our Lord Jesus Christ. He did not become a Father at some point in time but was eternally the Father of the Only-begotten.

CATECHETICAL LECTURES 7.4-7.5.[37]

THE FATHER IS THE GIVER OF ALL GRACE. CYRIL OF JERUSALEM: The Father, through the Son, with the Holy Spirit, is the giver of all grace; the gifts of the Father are none other than those of the Son and those of the Holy Spirit, for there is one salvation, one power and one faith; one God, the Father, one Lord, his only-begotten Son, and one Holy Spirit, the comforter. It is enough for us to know these things; do not inquire into his nature or substance, for had it been written we would have spoken about it. What is not written, let us not venture on. It is enough for our salvation to know that there is Father, Son and Holy Spirit. CATECHETICAL LECTURES 16.24.[38]

GOD IS THE FATHER FROM ETERNITY. BASIL THE GREAT: The God of all is the Father from infinity, and there was no point in time when he became the Father. He is not hindered from doing his will by any lack of power, nor did he have to wait for the right moment to give birth, in the way that human beings and animals have to. He could do whatever he wanted when he wanted to do it, and his paternity is co-extensive with his eternity. AGAINST EUNOMIUS 2.12.[39]

THE FATHER HAS NO BEGINNING. GREGORY OF NYSSA: The Father is without beginning and is unbegotten, and he has always been regarded as the Father. AGAINST EUNOMIUS 1.[40]

THE FATHER IS INCOMPREHENSIBLE. EPIPHANIUS OF SALAMIS: The Father is unbegotten, uncreated and incomprehensible. The Son is begotten, but he is also uncreated and incomprehensible. The Holy Spirit is not begotten or created. He is not the Son's twin

[34]PL 4:526; cf. ANF 5:450. [35]PG 9:116; cf. ANF 2:462. [36]PL 7:146; cf. ANF 7:279. [37]PG 33:608-9; cf. NPNF 2 7:44-45. [38]PG 33:953; cf. NPNF 2 7:121. [39]PG 29:593. [40]PG 45:369.

brother, nor his uncle, nor his grandfather nor his grandson, but the Holy Spirit, of the same substance as the Father and the Son, for "God is a Spirit."[41] ANCORATUS 7.[42]

THE MEANING OF THE TERM "FATHER." RU-FINUS OF AQUILEIA: *God* is the name of that nature or substance that is above everything else. *Father* is a word that expresses a secret and ineffable mystery. When you hear the word *God*, you must understand thereby a substance without beginning, without end, simple, uncompounded, invisible, incorporeal, ineffable, inappreciable, that has nothing in it which has been added or created. The cause of all things does not himself have any cause. When you hear the word *Father*, you must understand by this the Father of a Son, which Son is the image of the aforesaid substance. Just as no one is called *lord* unless he has possessions or servants, and no one is a *master* unless he has disciples, so it is that no one can possibly be a *father* unless he has a son. Therefore, the name *Father* demonstrates that there is a Son also. COMMENTARY ON THE APOSTLES' CREED 4.[43]

The Father-Son Relationship

GOD SENT HIS WORD DOWN TO EARTH. LETTER TO DIOGNETUS: God who is Almighty and the creator of everything, and who is also invisible, has sent the One who is the truth, the holy and incomprehensible Word, down from heaven to dwell among people. . . . God did not send us merely a servant, an angel or a governor, as we might have expected, but instead he sent the Creator and Designer of all things, the one through whom he made the heavens. . . . As a king sends his son, who is also a king, so God sent him. He sent him as God. LETTER TO DIOGNETUS 7.[44]

THE SON OF THE TRUE GOD. JUSTIN MARTYR: It is logical for us to worship Jesus

Christ, . . . knowing that he is the Son of the true God himself, and we hold him in second place. FIRST APOLOGY 13.[45]

THE FATHER IS NOT THE SAME AS THE SON. JUSTIN MARTYR: Those who say that the Father and the Son are identical[46] obviously do not know the Father. The Father of the universe has a Son, who is God because he is the first-begotten Word of God. FIRST APOLOGY 63.[47]

THE SON OF GOD WAS PROPHESIED IN THE OLD TESTAMENT. JUSTIN MARTYR: If the Jews had understood what was written by the prophets, they would not have denied that he was God, the Son of the only, unbegotten, ineffable God. DIALOGUE WITH TRYPHO 126.[48]

THE FATHER AND HIS SON THE LOGOS. ATHENAGORAS: There is one God and the Logos, who proceeds from him, the Son. We know that the Son cannot be separated from God. A PLEA REGARDING CHRISTIANS 18.[49]

THE FATHER ANOINTS THE SON AS KING. IRENAEUS: "Your throne, O God, is for ever and ever; the scepter of your kingdom is a right scepter. You have loved righteousness and hated iniquity. Therefore God, your God, has anointed you."[50] The Spirit gives the name of God both to the one who is anointed as Son and to the one who anoints, that is, the Father. AGAINST HERESIES 3.6.1.[51]

JESUS IS THE ONLY MAN WHO IS ALSO ALMIGHTY GOD. IRENAEUS: Those who claim that Jesus was a mere man . . . have not yet

[41]Jn 4:24. [42]PG 43:28-29. [43]PL 21:341; cf. NPNF 2 3:543-54. [44]PG 2:1176-77; cf. ANF 1:27. [45]PG 6:345-48; cf. ANF 1:166-67. [46]These were the Sabellians, or modalists, who claimed that "Father" and "Son" were names for different modes (or roles) of the one God. [47]PG 6:425; cf. ANF 1:184. [48]PG 6:769; cf. ANF 1:263. [49]PG 6:925; cf. ANF 2:137. [50]Ps. 45:6-7 (44:7-8 LXX). [51]PG 7:860-61; cf. ANF 1:419.

been joined to the Word of God the Father. I
have demonstrated from the Scriptures that
there is not one son of Adam who is called
God or Lord in an absolute and universal
sense. But Jesus is God himself, by his own
right, beyond any human being who has ever
lived. He is the Lord, the eternal king . . . and
the incarnate Word. . . . He is the holy Lord,
the wonderful, the counselor, the one who
is beautiful in appearance and the almighty
God.[52] AGAINST HERESIES 3.19.2.[53]

CONFERRING INCORRUPTION. IRENAEUS:
The Spirit prepares a person in the Son of
God, and the Son leads him to the Father. It is
the Father who confers on him the incorrup-
tion needed for eternal life. AGAINST HER-
ESIES 4.20.5.[54]

**FATHER AND SON SHARE THE DIVINE
MONARCHY.** TERTULLIAN: I derive the Son
from no other source but the substance of the
Father and represent him as doing nothing
apart from the Father's will and as having
received all power from the Father. How then
can I possibly be destroying the monarchy,
when I preserve it in the Son just as it was
committed to him by the Father? The Son
does not destroy the monarchy but rather
administers it. In his possession it remains
the same as it always was, and that is how the
Son will restore it to the Father.[55] We have
proved that the Father and the Son are two,
not only by the mention of their individual
names as Father and Son but also by the fact
that he who delivered up the kingdom and he
to whom it has been delivered up must necessarily be two different persons. AGAINST
PRAXEAS 4.[56]

FATHER AND SON NEED EACH OTHER.
TERTULLIAN: A father must have a son in
order to be a father. Likewise, a son must have
a father in order to be a son. But it is one thing
to have and quite another thing to be. For

example, in order to be a husband, I must have
a wife, though I can never be my own wife.
Likewise, in order to be a father I must have
a son, because I can never be a son to myself.
AGAINST PRAXEAS 10.[57]

**GOD BY HIMSELF IS UNDERSTOOD TO BE
THE FATHER.** TERTULLIAN: The Father is
named without the Son whenever he is defined
as the principle in the character of its first
person. In such cases, he has to be mentioned
before the name of the Son, for it is the Father
who is acknowledged in the first place. "There
is one God," that is, the Father, "and without
him there is no one else."[58] If you look carefully at the contexts that follow statements like
this, you will find that they nearly always have
particular reference to idolaters and suggest
that the multitude of gods will be expelled by
the unity of the Godhead, who nevertheless
has a Son. In so far as this Son is undivided
and inseparable from the Father, he is to be
reckoned as being in the Father, even when he
is not named. AGAINST PRAXEAS 18.[59]

**THE FATHER DID NOT SUFFER ALONG
WITH THE SON.** TERTULLIAN: The Father
did not suffer alongside the Son. The heretics,
who do not want to be accused of blaspheming
the Father, try to say that Father and Son are
distinct enough for it to be the Son who suffers, while the Father merely suffers along with
him! What does this mean? Either the Father
is capable of suffering or else he is not. The Father can no more be a fellow sufferer alongside
the Son than the Son can suffer in his divine
nature. So how is it that the Son suffered but
the Father did not suffer with him? The Father
is separate from the Son, though not separated
from him as God. For example, a river flows

---

[52]Is 9:6. [53]PG 7:938-41; cf. ANF 1:448-49. [54]PG 7:1035;
cf. ANF 1:489. [55]See 1 Cor 15:27-28. [56]PL 2:159; cf. ANF
3:599-600. [57]PL 2:165; cf. ANF 3:604. [58]Is 45:5. [59]PL 2:177;
cf. ANF 3:613.

from its source, which has exactly the same nature as it has. But if the river is polluted with soil or mud, this does not affect the purity of the source. It is of course the same water that suffers downstream, but because it is not affected at its source, the source itself does not suffer. AGAINST PRAXEAS 29.[60]

THE SON REVEALS THE FATHER TO US.

CLEMENT OF ALEXANDRIA: From the Son, we learn about the hidden cause of the universe—the Father. He is the most ancient and the most beneficent of all. He is ineffable, but he is to be worshiped with reverence, silence and holy awe and is to be venerated above everything else. He was proclaimed by the Lord as far as those who learned were able to understand, and he was understood by those whom the Lord chose to acknowledge him. STROMATEIS 7.1.[61]

FATHER AND SON ARE EQUAL IN NATURE.

CLEMENT OF ALEXANDRIA: The Son of God is one with the Father by equality of nature. He orders all things in accordance with the Father's will and governs the universe in the best way, with unwearied and tireless power working all things in which it operates, keeping its hidden designs in view. STROMATEIS 7.2.[62]

GOD HAS ALWAYS BEEN A FATHER. ORIGEN:
Who can have a reverential attitude toward God and suppose that the Father existed, even for a moment of time, without having generated his Wisdom? In that case, he would have to say either that God was unable to generate Wisdom before he produced it, so that he later called into being something that had not previously existed, or that he possessed the power to do this but was unwilling to exercise it—both of which options are equally absurd and ungodly. What they amount to is the belief that God either progressed from being unable to do something to being able to do it, or else that he concealed his power and delayed the

generation of his Wisdom. Therefore we have always held that God is the Father of his only-begotten Son, who was indeed born of him and who derives his being from him, yet he has no beginning either in time or in logic. Thus we must also believe that Wisdom was generated before there was any beginning that can be understood or expressed. Since all the creative power of the future creation was included in the existence of Wisdom, Wisdom says (in the words of Solomon) that it was created "the beginning of the ways of God."[63] This is because it contained within itself the beginnings, forms and species of all creation. ON FIRST PRINCIPLES 1.2.2.[64]

DENYING THE ETERNITY OF THE FATHER.

ORIGEN: Whoever assigns a beginning to the Word or Wisdom of God must be careful not to become guilty of impiety toward the unbegotten Father. For whoever does this denies that there has always been a Father, who had always generated the Word and had possessed Wisdom from eternity. ON FIRST PRINCIPLES 1.2.3.[65]

THE IMAGE OF THE FATHER'S GREATNESS.

ORIGEN: The God and Father of all things is not the only being who is great in our judgment. He has imparted himself and his greatness to his only-begotten and firstborn of every creature, in order that he, being the image of the invisible God, might preserve the image of the Father in his greatness. There could not have been a well-proportioned and beautiful image of the invisible God unless it also preserved the image of his greatness. AGAINST CELSUS 6.69.[66]

THE FATHER IS GREATER THAN THE SON.

ORIGEN: John [1:4-9] speaks of Christ as the

---

[60]PL 2:194; cf. ANF 3:626. [61]PG 9:404-5; cf. ANF 2:523. [62]PG 9:408; cf. ANF 2:524. [63]Prov 8:22. [64]PG 11:131; cf. ANF 4:246. [65]PG 11:132; cf. ANF 4:246. [66]PG 11:140-41; cf. ANF 4:605.

light of life and as the "true light" that shines on everyone who comes into the world. Some have understood this to mean that the Son has the same substance as the Father. But those who are of sounder judgment have noted that the light that shines in the darkness is not necessarily the same as the light in which there is no darkness at all. The light that shines in the darkness is pursued by it but not overtaken, whereas the light in which there is no darkness does not confront it at all. . . . God is the Father of truth, which makes him greater than the truth. He is the Father of wisdom, which makes him greater and more excellent than wisdom. Likewise, as the Father of the true light, he is greater than the true light itself. COMMENTARY ON THE GOSPEL OF JOHN 2.18.[67]

WE KNOW THE FATHER THROUGH THE SON. HIPPOLYTUS: When Jesus said, "He who has seen me has seen the Father,"[68] he meant that if we have seen him, we may come to know the Father through him. This is because the Father is readily made known through his image [the Son]. Likewise the Son, who was sent and was not known by those who are in the world, confessed that he was in the Father in power and disposition. The Son is the Father's mind. We who have the Father's mind believe this, but those who do not have it have denied the Son. AGAINST NOETUS 7.[69]

THE SON IS ETERNALLY IN THE FATHER. NOVATIAN: God the Father, the founder and creator of all things, who alone knows no beginning, invisible, infinite, immortal, eternal, is one God. To his greatness, majesty and power I would say that not only can nothing be preferred, but nothing can be compared. When he willed it, he gave birth to his Son the Word, . . . who is acknowledged in the substance of the power put forth by God. No one . . . has learned the secrets of his sacred and divine nativity, which are known to the Son alone, because he knows the secrets of the Father.

Because he was begotten of the Father, the Son is always in the Father. I do not mean that he was unborn but that he was always born. Still, the one who was before all time must be said to have been in the Father eternally, because no time can be assigned to the one who is before all time. He must have been always in the Father, since otherwise the Father would not have been Father. But the Father also precedes the Son in some sense, for he has to exist first in order to become a father. Logically, the one who has no beginning must precede one who has a beginning. Likewise, the Son is less than the Father because he has an origin—birth from the Father. He shares the Father's nature because of his birth, but at the same time he has a beginning that the Father does not have. When the Father desired it, the Son proceeded from him. . . . I am speaking of the divine substance called the Word. ON THE TRINITY 31.[70]

THE SON IS DIFFERENT FROM THE FATHER. NOVATIAN: God proceeded from God, making a person second to the Father—the Son. The Son does not deprive the Father of his quality of being the one God. For if the Son had not been born—in contrast to the Father, who is unborn—they would be identical. The addition of the Son would have made two unborn beings, which in turn would have made two gods. ON THE TRINITY 31.[71]

GOD IS THE FATHER OF THE SON. DIONYSIUS OF ALEXANDRIA: I do not think that the Word was something made, which is why I do not say that God was his maker but rather his Father. But if at some point I may have said in passing that God was his maker, this manner of speaking would not be indefensible because Greek sophists say that they are the makers of the books as well as their fathers. LETTER

---

[67]PG 14:154-55; cf. ANF 10:336. [68]Jn 14:9. [69]PG 10:813-16; cf. ANF 5:226. [70]PL 3:949-50; cf. ANF 5:643. [71]PL 3:950; cf. ANF 5:643.

to Dionysius of Rome 2.11 (fragment).[72]

The Father Has His Son in Eternity.

Alexander of Alexandria: The Father is
always the Father. He is the Father because
the Son is always with him, which is why he is
called the Father. Therefore, because the Son
is always with the Father, he is always complete in himself, lacking nothing that is good.
He generated his only-begotten Son, not in
time nor after an interval or out of nothing.
How wicked it is, then, to say that the Wisdom or power of God did not always exist!
. . . It is therefore perfectly clear that the sonship of our Savior is quite different from any
other kind of sonship. Epistle on the Arian
Heresy 1.7.[73]

The Father Is Greater Than the Son.

Alexander of Alexandria: We must
maintain the dignity proper to the unbegotten Father by saying that there is no cause of
his being. . . . By all means let us ascribe to the
Son the honor that is due to him, recognizing that he was begotten of the Father before
all ages and worshiping him accordingly as
the only one who was always in existence. We
must not deny the Son's divinity but recognize
in him the exact likeness of the Father's image
and character in every respect. Nevertheless,
we also believe that it is the Father's unique
property to be unbegotten, for the Savior
himself said, "The Father is greater than I."[74]
Epistle on the Arian Heresy 12.[75]

The Father and the Son Have One Sub-
stance. Lactantius: Someone might ask
how we can claim to be monotheists when we
say that there are two Gods—God the Father
and God the Son. This misunderstanding has
been the downfall of many. When we speak of
God the Father and of God the Son, we do not
think of them as different beings, nor do we
separate them. The Father cannot exist without the Son, nor can the Son exist without the

Father. The reason for this is that the name
Father has no meaning apart from the Son, nor
can the Son have been begotten without the
Father. Since the Father makes the Son and
the Son makes the Father, they both have one
mind, one spirit and one substance. The Father
is like an overflowing fountain, and the Son is
a stream flowing from it. The Father is like the
sun, and the Son is like a ray coming from it.
Divine Institutes 4.29.[76]

The Mysterious Generation of the
Son. Eusebius of Caesarea: The theology
offered to us is beyond all compare. It bears
no relation to anything material but presents
the most brilliant mind with an only-begotten
Son, who was not missing at some point in order to be produced later on[77] but who existed
before all ages. The Son was always present
with the Father and not in an unbegotten state
either. He was always begotten from the unbegotten Father, the Only-begotten, the Word
and God from God, and this not by division or
subtraction or separation from the substance
of the Father. On the contrary, he teaches us
that he was begotten in a way that surpasses all
speech and reasoning, from eternity, beyond
the beginning of all ages, from the ineffable
and incomprehensible will and power of the
Father. Proof of the Gospel 4.3.[78]

God Was on Earth and in Heaven at
the Same Time. Ephrem the Syrian:
When the Lord came down to earth, he did
not relinquish his heavenly throne, and when
he dwelled in the womb of Mary he did not
leave heaven. The one who was asleep in
the boat was the same one who empowered
the winds;[79] and when he turned water into
wine,[80] the Word was not separated from the
body, but rather by all these things he dem-

---

[72]PL 5:126; cf. ANF 6:93. [73]PG 18:557; cf. ANF 6:293. [74]Jn
14:28. [75]PG 18:565. [76]PL 6:538-39; cf. ANF 7:132. [77]The idea
that there was a time when the Son did not exist was attributed
to Arius. [78]PG 22:257. [79]See Mt 8:23-27. [80]See Jn 2:1-11.

onstrated that he was truly God. SCATTERED HYMNS 15.1.[81]

THE SON IS IN THE FATHER. ATHANASIUS: The Son is in the Father because his whole being is proper to the Father's essence, . . . so that whoever sees the Son sees what belongs to the Father and understands that the Son's being, because it comes from the Father, is therefore in the Father. The Father is in the Son, because the Son is what is from the Father and belongs to him. They relate to one another as the radiance to the sun, the word to the thought expressed and the stream to the fountain. Whoever contemplates the Son like this contemplates what belongs to the Father's essence and knows that the Father is in the Son. DISCOURSES AGAINST THE ARIANS 3.23.3.[82]

SECOND IN ORDER BUT EQUAL IN NATURE. BASIL THE GREAT: The Son is second to the Father in order, because he comes from the Father, and also in rank, because the Father is his source and cause, but he is not second to him in nature, because the godhead of each person is one and the same. AGAINST EUNOMIUS 3.1.[83]

THE FATHER BROUGHT FORTH THE SON. HILARY OF POITIERS: The Unbegotten one brought forth a Son from himself before time began, not from any preexistent matter (for all things have come into being through the Son), not from nothing (for the Son is from the Father's being) nor by way of childbirth (for in God there is neither change or void.) The Son was not a piece of the Unbegotten who was somehow torn off or stretched out, for God is impassible and bodiless, and only a passible and embodied being could be so treated. As the apostle says, "In Christ the fullness of the Godhead dwelt bodily."[84] Incomprehensibly, ineffably, before time or worlds existed, he brought forth the Only-begotten from his own unbegotten substance, bestowing his whole

divinity on that birth through his love and power. ON THE TRINITY 3.3.[85]

FATHER AND SON ARE INSEPARABLE. HILARY OF POITIERS: Does the Son's birth demonstrate that his divinity is not his by nature and by right? Each is in the other; the birth of the Son is from the Father only, and no extraneous or dissimilar nature has been raised to deity and now subsists as God. Talk about two gods if you can, separate the Son from the Father as much as possible, yet still the Father is in the Son and the Son in the Father, and this is not by some exchange of emanations but by the perfect birth of a living nature. You cannot add together God the Father and God the Son and reckon them as two gods, for they are one God. You cannot merge them into one, because they are not one person. ON THE TRINITY 7.31.[86]

TO RECOGNIZE THE SON IS TO RECOGNIZE THE FATHER. HILARY OF POITIERS: God was recognized in Christ by those who recognized Christ as the Son on the evidence of the powers of his divine nature, and a recognition of God the Son produces a recognition of God the Father. For the Son is the image in such a way as to be one in kind with the Father and yet to indicate that the Father is his origin. ON THE TRINITY 7.37.[87]

A HARMONIOUS UNITY. HILARY OF POITIERS: We do not deny a unanimity between the Father and the Son, and the heretics are wrong when they accuse us of creating a division between them by refusing to accept their mutual harmony as itself the bond of unity between them. . . . The Father and the Son are one in nature, honor and power, and the same nature cannot will things that contradict each

---

[81]*ESHS* 4:730-31. [82]PG 26:328; cf. NPNF 2 4:395. [83]PG 29:656. [84]Col 2:9. [85]PL 10:77; cf. NPNF 2 9:62. [86]PL 10:226; cf. NPNF 2 9:131-32. [87]PL 10:230; cf. NPNF 2 9:134.

other. The Son describes the nature of his unity with the Father as follows: "When the Comforter comes, whom I shall send to you from the Father, the Spirit of truth who proceeds from the Father, he will testify of me."[88] ON THE TRINITY 8.19.[89]

HOW THE FATHER IS GREATER THAN THE SON.

HILARY OF POITIERS: The Father is greater than the Son, but in the way that a father is greater than his son—by generation, not in kind. The Son is a son and has come out of the Father. But even if the name Father is unique [to the first person of the Godhead], his nature is the same, because God born from God does not differ from the substance that brought him forth. HOMILIES ON THE PSALMS 138(139).17.[90]

FATHER AND SON SHARE A COMMON LIFE.

AMBROSE: Does not our Lord Jesus plainly appear to say that just as the Father is a living Father, so too the Son also lives? Who can fail to see that here we have a reference to unity of life, forasmuch as the same life is the life of the Father and the life of the Son? "For as the Father has life in himself, so has he given it to the Son to have life in himself."[91] He has given this because the Son is one with him. He has given it not to take away the Son's glory but that he may be glorified in the Son. He has given it not in order to keep a guard over it but so that the Son might have it in possession. ON THE CHRISTIAN FAITH 4.10.132.[92]

THE ONENESS OF GOD.

CHRYSOSTOM: When Paul called the one God the Father,[93] he did not mean to eject the Son from the Godhead, just as when he called the Son Lord he was not trying to depose the Father from his authority. His purpose was to strengthen the Corinthians in their weakness and take away any excuse they might have had [to resist him]. What

was at issue was why the Son of God was not clearly and openly revealed to the Jews, but only obscurely and rarely. For the Jews had only recently been rescued from the error of polytheism, and if they heard that there were two gods, they might easily fall back into that illness. Therefore the prophets often said, "There is one God, and beside him there is no other,"[94] not in order to deny the Son (which God forbid!) but in order to cure them of their weakness and persuade them to abandon their belief in many gods, who in reality do not exist. ON THE INCOMPREHENSIBLE NATURE OF GOD 5.3.[95]

GOD CANNOT BE MINDLESS OR POWERLESS.

CYRIL OF ALEXANDRIA: If a creature made out of nothing is transposed to the realm of being—for example, if Christ, who is the wisdom and power of God,[96] was a creature, as some would have it, we would have to confess that God is ignorant and powerless, only acquiring these qualities later on when Christ was created for that very purpose. This is the nature of created things, but it is both absurd and blasphemous to think that way about God. THESAURUS ON THE TRINITY 32.[97]

Father, Son and Holy Spirit

WE WORSHIP THE TRUE GOD.

JUSTIN MARTYR: The Greeks call us atheists, and so we are, with respect to their gods, though not when it comes to the most true God, who is the Father of righteousness. We worship and adore him, the Son who came forth from him and taught us these things, and the prophetic Spirit. FIRST APOLOGY 6.[98]

BAPTISM IN THE NAME OF THE THREE PERSONS.

JUSTIN MARTYR: In the name of God,

---

[88]Jn 15:26. [89]PL 10:250; cf. NPNF 2 9:142. [90]PL 9:801. [91]Jn 5:26. [92]PL 16:642; cf. NPNF 2 10:279. [93]1 Cor 8:6. [94]Deut 4:35. [95]PG 48:740. [96]1 Cor 1:24. [97]PG 75:484. [98]PG 6:336-37; cf. ANF 1:164.

the Father and lord of the universe, and of our Savior Jesus Christ and of the Holy Spirit, they receive the washing with water. FIRST APOLOGY 61.[99]

CHRISTIANS ARE NOT ATHEISTS. ATHENAGORAS: Who would not be astonished to hear people called atheists when they profess belief in God the Father, God the Son and God the Holy Spirit and who declare both their power in union and their distinction in order? A PLEA REGARDING CHRISTIANS 10.[100]

THE INNER UNITY OF THE TRINITY. ATHENAGORAS: Christians know God and his Word. They also know what the oneness of the Son with the Father is like and what kind of fellowship the Father has with the Son. Furthermore, they understand what the Spirit is and how all three are both distinct and united: the Spirit, the Son and the Father. A PLEA REGARDING CHRISTIANS 12.[101]

THE TRINITY IS UNITED BY ANOINTING. IRENAEUS: It is the Father who anoints and the Son who is anointed by the Spirit. The Spirit is the unction. This is made clear by the prophet Isaiah, who says, "The Spirit of the Lord is on me, because he has anointed me,"[102] pointing out both the anointing Father, the anointed Son and the unction, which is the Spirit. AGAINST HERESIES 3.18.3.[103]

THE TRINITY WORKS TOGETHER. IRENAEUS: The Father plans everything well and gives his commands, the Son executes them and performs the work of creation, and the Spirit nourishes them and gives them increase. AGAINST HERESIES 4.38.3.[104]

ONE GOD IN THREE PERSONS. TERTULLIAN: We believe that there is only one God, but in the following dispensation. The one and only God has a Son who proceeded from himself, by whom all things were made and without

whom nothing was made. We believe that the Father sent him from heaven into the womb of a virgin, of whom he was born as both man and God. . . . The Son also sent from heaven, from the Father, the Holy Spirit, the Paraclete, the sanctifier of the faith of those who believe in the Father, the Son and the Holy Spirit. . . . The mystery of the dispensation distributes the divine unity into a Trinity, placing the three persons in their order—the Father, the Son and the Holy Spirit. They are three not in condition but in rank, not in substance but in form, not in power but in aspect. They are one in condition, one in substance and one in aspect because he is only one God, from whom these ranks and forms and aspects are reckoned under the names of Father, Son and Holy Spirit. AGAINST PRAXEAS 2.[105]

GOD CANNOT BE SEPARATED FROM HIS OWN SUBSTANCE. TERTULLIAN: How can God be said to suffer division and separation from the Son and the Holy Spirit, when they hold the second and third places and are so closely united to the Father in substance? . . . Do you really believe that those who are naturally parts of God's own substance, pledges of his love and instruments of his might, are also the means by which those things are overthrown and destroyed? AGAINST PRAXEAS 3.[106]

HOW THE FATHER IS GREATER THAN THE SON. TERTULLIAN: The Father, the Son and the Spirit are inseparable from each other. The Father is one, the Son is one, and the Spirit is one, but they are all distinct from each other. This statement is taken in a wrong sense by uneducated and antagonistic people, as if it spoke of a diversity that would imply a separation between the Father, the Son and the

---

[99]PG 6: 420; cf. ANF 1:183. [100]PG 6:909; cf. ANF 2:133. [101]PG 6:913; cf. ANF 2:134. [102]Is 61:1. [103]PG 7:934; cf. ANF 1:446. [104]PG 7:1108; cf. ANF 1:521-52. [105]PL 2:156-57; cf. ANF 3:598. [106]PL 2:158-59; cf. ANF 3:599.

Holy Spirit. I have to say this, because they promote the divine monarchy at the expense of the divine dispensation and contend for the identity of Father, Son and Holy Spirit. The Father is not the same as the Son, who differ from each other in the mode of their being. The Father is the entire substance, but the Son is a derivation and portion of the whole, as he himself acknowledges: "My Father is greater than I."[107] . . . The Father is greater than the Son inasmuch as he who begets is one and he who is begotten is another. Likewise, he who sends is one, and he who is sent is another; he who makes is one and he through whom things are made is another. The Lord himself uses the term "Paraclete" to signify not a division in the Godhead but a disposition of mutual relations, for he says, "I will pray the Father, and he will send you another Comforter, the Spirit of truth."[108] The Paraclete is thus distinct from himself, a third degree in the divine economy, just as we believe the Son is the second degree. AGAINST PRAXEAS 9.[109]

THE TRINITY CREATED US IN HIS IMAGE.

TERTULLIAN: If the number of the Trinity offends you, let me ask you how it is possible for a being who is absolutely and only one to speak in the plural and say, "Let us make humankind in our image"[110] . . . and "Behold, the man is become like one of us."[111] Was he speaking to the angels, as the Jews interpret the passage, because they do not recognize the Son? Or was it because he was the Father, Son and Holy Spirit that he spoke to himself in the plural? It is obvious that he adopted the plural form because he already had his Son, his own Word, at his side as a second person, and a third person also, the Spirit in the Word. . . . In whose image did God make us, after all, if not in the image of the one who would one day put on human nature? AGAINST PRAXEAS 12.[112]

THE FATHER ALONE IS INVISIBLE.

TERTULLIAN: The one who is invisible is the Father in the fullness of his majesty. At the same time, we recognize that the Son is visible because of the dispensation of his derived existence. We cannot contemplate the sun in the full power of his substance, which is in the heavens, for our eyes can only endure one of its rays, which is filtered from the sun down to the earth. Now someone might want to say that the Son is also invisible because he is the Word, and also the Spirit, and then go on to say that because Father and Son have the same nature, they must be one and the same person. But Scripture maintains a distinction between them by saying that the Father is invisible and the Son is visible. AGAINST PRAXEAS 14.[113]

THE THREE PERSONS ARE DISTINCT.

TERTULLIAN: The link between the Father and the Son and between the Son and the Paraclete produces three coherent persons who are distinct from one another. These three are all one in essence but not one in person. When Jesus said, "I and the Father are one,"[114] he meant in unity of substance, not of person. Go through the whole Gospel and you will find that the one whom you believe to be the Father . . . is recognized by the Son as being in heaven, because "he lifted up his eyes" and commended his disciples to the Father's safekeeping.[115] Moreover, in another Gospel we have a clear revelation of the Son's distinction from the Father: "My God, why have you forsaken me?"[116] and again in Luke: "Father, into

---

[107]Jn 14:28. Tertullian is groping here for a way to express the nature of the Son's relationship to the Father. Later generations would come to see words like "derivation" and "portion" as suggestive of Arianism, but he did not mean it that way. To him, the Son was derived from the Father in the same way as a human child is derived from its parents. Children are equal to their parents in terms of being or substance but inferior in terms of precedence and honor. The Son is equal to his Father (and therefore fully God), but there is nevertheless an order in the Godhead, and in that order, the Father comes first.   [108]Jn 14:16-17.   [109]PL 2:164; cf. ANF 3:603-4.   [110]Gen 1:26.   [111]Gen 3:22.   [112]PL 2:167-88; cf. ANF 3:606-7.   [113]PL 2:171; cf. ANF 3:609.   [114]Jn 10:30.   [115]Jn 17:1, 11.   [116]Mt 27:46.

your hands I commend my spirit."[117] AGAINST
PRAXEAS 25.[118]

BAPTISM IS TRINITARIAN. TERTULLIAN:
Jesus commanded his disciples to baptize into
the Father, Son and Holy Spirit, not into a
one-person God. Indeed, it is not once only
but three times that we are immersed into the
three persons, once when each of their names
is mentioned. AGAINST PRAXEAS 26.[119]

THREE BEINGS WHO ARE CALLED GOD.
ORIGEN: There is one God who created and
arranged all things and who called everything into being out of nothing. . . . Second,
Jesus Christ was born of the Father before all
creatures, and after having been the Father's
servant in the work of creation, . . . he became
a man. But although he was incarnate, he was
still God. . . . Third, the apostles related that
the Holy Spirit was associated in honor and
dignity with the Father and the Son, but in his
case it is not clear whether he is to be regarded
as born or unborn, a Son of God or not. ON
FIRST PRINCIPLES, PREFACE 4.[120]

**WE EXPERIENCE EACH OF THE PERSONS
IN OUR SPIRITUAL LIFE.** ORIGEN: God the
Father bestows existence on all. Participation
in Christ, as the Word of reason, makes people
rational beings. It follows from this that we are
worthy of either praise or blame because we
are capable of both virtue and vice. The Holy
Spirit is therefore present among us so that
those who are not holy by nature can become
holy by participating in him. We derive our existence from God the Father and our rational
nature from the Word. Third, we derive our
holiness from the Holy Spirit. Those who have
been sanctified by him are enabled to receive
Christ, the righteousness of God, and those
who have reached this level by the sanctification of the Holy Spirit will obtain the gift of
wisdom according to the power and working of
the same Spirit. ON FIRST PRINCIPLES 1.3.8.[121]

**THE FATHER BRINGS FORTH THE OTHER
PERSONS IN ETERNITY.** ORIGEN: The Father
generates an uncreated Son and brings forth a
Holy Spirit, not as if he had no previous existence, but because the Father is the origin and
source of the Son and the Holy Spirit, and no
"before" or "after" can be understood as existing in them. ON FIRST PRINCIPLES 2.2.1.[122]

**ONLY THE TRINITY KNOWS THE SECRETS
OF GOD.** ORIGEN: How God orders everything
is known only to him, to his only-begotten
Son, through whom all things were created
and restored, and to the Holy Spirit, through
whom all things are sanctified. The Holy
Spirit proceeds from the Father,[123] to whom be
glory for ever and ever. ON FIRST PRINCIPLES
3.5.8.[124]

ONLY THE TRINITY IS UNCREATED. ORI-
GEN: Everything that exists was made by God,
except for the nature of the Father, the Son
and the Holy Spirit. . . . For the Father alone
knows the Son, and the Son alone knows the
Father, and the Holy Spirit alone searches the
deep things of God. ON FIRST PRINCIPLES
4.1.35.[125]

**FATHER AND SON ARE UNITED BUT RE-
MAIN DISTINCT PERSONS.** NOVATIAN: Heretics frequently quote the passage where
Jesus says, "I and the Father are one,"[126] . . . but
this does not mean that they are one person.
. . . Immediately afterwards he goes on to say,
"I and the Father," thereby severing the suposed
identity between them. If he really thought of
himself as the Father, he could have said, "I the
Father" and continued accordingly. . . . Moreover, the word *one* is used in the neuter gender
and refers to a social, not a personal, unity. It

---

[117]Lk 23:46. [118]PL 2:188; cf. ANF 3:621. [119]PL 2:190; cf. ANF
3:623. [120]PG 11:117-18; cf. ANF 4:240. [121]PG 11:154; cf.
ANF 4:255. [122]PG 11:186; cf. ANF 4:270. [123]Jn 15:26. [124]PG
11:333; cf. ANF 4:344. [125]PG 11:409; cf. ANF 4:380. [126]Jn
10:30.

refers to agreement, to identity of judgment and to the loving association between them. ON THE TRINITY 27.[127]

HOW GOD IS BOTH THREE AND ONE. HIPPOLYTUS: A person is compelled to recognize God the Father Almighty and Christ Jesus the Son of God, who became man and to whom the Father made all things subject apart from himself, and the Holy Spirit—three [persons]. But if he wants to know why we believe that there is still only one God, let him know that it is because the divine power is one. As regards his power, therefore, God is one. . . . There is one God in whom we must believe—unoriginated, impassible, immortal, doing all things as he wills, in the way he wills and when he wills. AGAINST NOETUS 8.[128]

IN HARMONY WITH EACH OTHER. HIPPOLYTUS: The Father is one, but there are two persons because there is also the Son, and then again, there is the Holy Spirit too. The Father decrees, the Word executes [the decree], and the Son is manifested [by the Spirit], through whom we come to believe in the Father. The dispensation of harmony leads straight back to one God, for God is one. It is the Father who commands, the Son who obeys and the Holy Spirit who gives understanding. The Father is above all, the Son is through all, and the Holy Spirit is in all. We cannot think of God in any other way than as Father, Son and Holy Spirit. AGAINST NOETUS 14.[129]

THE UNITY OF GOD MUST NOT BE DIVIDED. DIONYSIUS OF ROME: The admirable and divine unity must not be separated into three divinities. Nor must the dignity and eminent greatness of the Lord be diminished by introducing an element of creation. Instead, we must believe in God the Father Almighty, in Christ Jesus his Son and in the Holy Spirit. The Word is united to the God of all because he says, "I and the Father are one"[130] and "I am in the Father and the Father in me."[131] Thus will the doctrine of the Trinity be maintained in its integrity, and also the sacred revelation of the monarchy [of the one God]. AGAINST THE SABELLIANS 3.[132]

HOW THE PERSONS ARE INTERNALLY RELATED. EPHREM THE SYRIAN: The Father is the begetter, and the Son is begotten from his bosom. The Holy Spirit proceeds from the Father and the Son. The Father is the maker who made the world from nothing; the Son is the Creator who founded the universe along with his begetter. The Holy Spirit is the Paraclete and comforter, in whom everything that was and will be and is, is brought to perfection. The Father is the mind, the Son is the word, the Spirit is the voice; three names, one will, one voice. HYMN ON THE DEAD AND THE TRINITY.[133]

IMAGES OF THE ONE IN THREE AND THREE IN ONE. EPHREM THE SYRIAN: You have the sun as a type of the Father, its brilliance as a type of the Son and its warmth as a type of the Holy Spirit. Yet the three are one, and the Trinity reveals itself in the sun. Who can explain what is incomprehensible? One is many, one is three, and three are one. The mystery is great, the wonder self-evident. The sun is distinct from its brilliance; the two things are different but equal, and the brilliance of the sun is the sun itself. No one says that there are two suns, though as far as the lower creatures are concerned, it is the sun's brilliance that is the sun itself. Similarly, we do not say that there are two gods, and our Lord is God above the creatures. SERMONS AGAINST RASH INQUIRERS 1.73.[134]

RESORT TO SILENCE! EPHREM THE SYRIAN:

---

[127]PL 3:938; cf. ANF 5:637. [128]PG 10:816; cf. ANF 5:226. [129]PG 10:821; cf. ANF 5:228. [130]Jn 10:30. [131]Jn 14:11. [132]In Athanasius *De Decretis Nicaenae Synodi* 26 (PG 25:465); cf. ANF 7:365-66. [133]*ESHS* 3:241-43. [134]*ESOO* 3:137.

Believe in the Father, but do not believe that he is comprehensible. Believe that there is a Son, but do not believe that he can be understood. Believe that there is a Holy Spirit, but do not believe that he can be investigated. Believe that they are one, but do not doubt that they are three. Their will is one in agreement; there is no confusion in their conjunction. There is a great order here. You must not think that there is some confusion in their conjunction, nor must you think that because they are different, there must be some division among them. They are conjoined but not confused, different but not divided. Their conjunction is not confused, nor is their difference divided. Who would mix up their differences? Who would divide their conjunctions? Resort to silence, poor soul! Sermons Against Rash Inquirers 2.2.[135]

The Holy and Perfect Trinity. Athanasius: The Trinity is holy and perfect, contemplated in the Father, the Son and the Holy Spirit. It has nothing extraneous to itself or mixed in with it, nor does it depend on any creator or maker, since it is in itself the creator and maker of all things. It is one and indivisible by nature, and its actions are also one and the same. For the Father has made everything through the Word and the Holy Spirit, and thus the unity of the holy Trinity is maintained. . . . There is a Trinity not merely in words or in fantasy but in truth and reality. For just as the Father is the one who is, so too is the Son. The Holy Spirit also exists as a real person. Four Letters to Serapion 1.28.[136]

The Unity of the Trinity Seen in Baptism. Athanasius: When the Holy Spirit comes to us, the Son and the Father also come to dwell with us.[137] The Trinity is undivided, and the Godhead is one. There is one God over all things, through all things and in all things. This is the faith of the universal church, for the Lord has rooted and grounded

it in the Trinity, saying to his disciples, "Go and teach all nations, baptizing them in the name of the Father, and of the Son and of the Holy Spirit."[138] If the Holy Spirit were a creature, the Lord would not have linked him to the Father, because that would have led to an imbalance in the Trinity. Four Letters to Serapion 3.6.[139]

No Division Is Conceivable. Basil the Great: No division or separation is conceivable in the Godhead. The Son cannot be understood apart from the Father, nor can the Spirit be divorced from the Son. In them there is some ineffable and incomprehensible fellowship as well as difference, but the distinction of hypostases does not erase the conjunction of nature, nor does the community of essence blur the individuality of each hypostasis. Letter 38.4.[140]

The Works of God Are Those of the Trinity. Basil the Great: The Father, the Son and the Holy Spirit all hallow, quicken, enlighten and give comfort. No one will attribute a special and peculiar operation of hallowing to the work of the Spirit after hearing the Savior in the Gospel saying to the Father (about the disciples), "Sanctify them in my name."[141] In like manner all other operations are equally performed in all who are worthy of them, by the Father and by the Son and by the Holy Spirit—every grace and virtue, guidance, life, consolation, change into the immortal, the passage into freedom and all other good things that come down to us. . . . Even the heavenly dispensation is constituted only in relation to the Father, Son and Holy Spirit, each of them helping in proportion to his dignity and need. Identity of operation by the Father, Son and Holy Spirit proves that

---

[135]ESOO 3:194. [136]PG 26:596. [137]See Jn 14:23. [138]Mt 28:19. [139]PG 26:633-36. [140]PG 32:332-33; cf. NPNF 2 8:139. [141]Jn 17:11, 17.

they have the same nature. LETTER 189.7.[142]

THE DIFFERENCE BETWEEN "ESSENCE" AND "HYPOSTASIS."

BASIL THE GREAT: The difference between "essence" (*ousia*) and "hypostasis" is the same as that between the general and the particular. . . . In the case of the Godhead, we confess that there is one essence or substance, so as not to give a different definition of existence, but we confess particular hypostases, so that our conception of the Father, the Son and the Holy Spirit may be clear and without confusion. If we have no distinct perception of their separate characteristics, namely, fatherhood, sonship and sanctification, but take our conception of God from the general idea of existence, we cannot possibly give a sound account of our faith. We must therefore confess the faith by adding the particular to the common. The Godhead is common; the fatherhood is particular. We must therefore combine the two and say, "I believe in God the Father." The same course must be pursued when confessing the Son. We must combine the particular with the common and say, "I believe in God the Son." So also in the case of the Holy Spirit, we must make out utterance conform to the designation and say, "In God the Holy Spirit." The result of this is a satisfactory preservation of the unity by confessing the one Godhead, while in the distinction of the individual properties perceived in each there is a confession of the peculiar properties of the hypostases. Those who fail to distinguish between essence and hypostasis are compelled to confess only three "persons"[143] and in their hesitation to speak of the three hypostases are guilty of the error of Sabellius, who asserted that the same hypostasis changed its form to meet the needs of the moment. LETTER 236.6.[144]

THE WAY OF THE KNOWLEDGE OF GOD.

BASIL THE GREAT: The Holy Spirit shows the glory of the Only-begotten, who in turn bestows on true worshipers the knowledge of God. Thus the way of the knowledge of God lies from one Spirit through the one Son to the one Father, and conversely, the natural goodness and the inherent holiness and the royal dignity extend from the Father through the Only-begotten to the Spirit. Thus there is both acknowledgment of the hypostases and the true doctrine of the divine monarchy is preserved. As for those who create a hierarchy of three divine beings, they ought to be told that they are introducing into Christianity the polytheism of heathen error. What they have in effect is a first, second and third god. As for us, we shall stick with the order prescribed by the Lord, and anyone guilty of transgressing that order will be no better than an ungodly heathen. ON THE HOLY SPIRIT 18.47.[145]

SAMENESS AND DIFFERENCE.

GREGORY OF NYSSA: The person of the Father, from whom the Son is begotten and from whom the Holy Spirit proceeds, is one and the same. Therefore, because the cause of the persons caused is properly one, we say that he is the one God and that he exists in eternity with the others. The persons of the Godhead do not differ in time, or in place, or in will, or in occupation, or in activity or in any of the emotions and passions that characterize the human race. The only difference between them is that the Father is the Father and not the Son, the Son is the Son and not the Father, and the Holy Spirit is neither the Father nor the Son. ON COMMON NOTIONS.[146]

THE FATHER HAD NO NEED TO BEGET THE SON.

HILARY OF POITIERS: It used to be taught that the Son did not owe his existence to God's will in the way that other things

---

[142]PG 32:693; cf. NPNF 2 8:231. [143]This word is here understood in the ancient sense of "mask" or "superficial appearance," not as the equivalent of hypostasis. [144]PG 32:884; cf. NPNF 2 8:278. [145]PG 32:153; cf. NPNF 2 8:29-30. [146]PG 45:180.

do, in order to avoid the suggestion that the Son exists merely by the Father's will and not because he is God in his own nature. But heretics seized on this and started saying that the Father was forced to beget the Son because of some necessity in his own nature. But such weakness does not exist in God the Father, and in the ineffable and perfect birth of the Son it was neither mere will that begat him, nor was the Father's essence changed or forced by some natural law working in him. The Father needed no extra substance in order to beget the Son, nor is the nature of the begetter changed in the begotten, nor is the Father's uniqueness affected by time. Before all time, the Father, out of the essence of his nature, with a desire devoid of passion, gave to the Son a birth that conveyed the essence of his nature. ON THE COUNCILS 59.[147]

ONLY THE FATHER IS DESCRIBED AS UN-BEGOTTEN. HILARY OF POITIERS: Since God is one, there cannot be two who are unbegotten. God is one (although both the Father and the Son are God) for the simple reason that unbegottenness is the only quality that can belong to one person only. The Son is God precisely because he derives his birth from that unbegotten essence. Our holy faith therefore rejects the idea that the Son is unbegotten in order to affirm that there is only one God who is unbegotten, and therefore only one God, and in order to accept the only-begotten nature, begotten from the unborn essence, in the one name of the unborn God. For the head of all things is the Son, but the head of the Son is God. All things are referred to this one God through this stepping stone and by this confession, since the whole world takes its origin from him for whom God himself is the origin. ON THE COUNCILS 60.[148]

THE ONE DIVINE SUBSTANCE. HILARY OF POITIERS: Beloved, we must not deny that there is one substance shared by both the Father and the Son, but we must not proclaim this without giving reasons for our conviction. The one substance must be derived from the true character of the begotten nature, not from any division or confusion of persons or from any sharing of a prior substance [which has now split into two]. It may be right to assert that there is one substance, and it may be right to keep quiet about it. You believe in the birth and you also believe in the likeness, so why should the word raise suspicions on either side when we look at the matter in the same way? Let us believe and say that there is one substance, but in virtue of the true character of the nature and not to imply a blasphemous unity of persons. Let the oneness be ascribed to the fact that there are similar persons, and not just one solitary person. ON THE COUNCILS 71.[149]

EACH PERSON HAS HIS OWN POWERS AND GIFTS. HILARY OF POITIERS: Jesus commanded his disciples to baptize in the name of the Father, of the Son and of the Holy Spirit.[150] That is to say, with the confession of the Creator, the Only-begotten and the gift. For God the Father is one from whom are all things; and our Lord Jesus Christ the only-begotten, through whom are all things, is one; and the Spirit, God's gift to us, who pervades all things, is also one. Thus each of them is ordered according to the powers possessed and the benefits conferred—the one power from whom all, the one offspring through whom all, the one gift who gives us perfect hope. Nothing is lacking in that supreme union that, in the Father, the Son and the Holy Spirit, embraces infinity in the eternal, his likeness in his express image and our enjoyment of him in the gift [of the Holy Spirit]. ON THE TRINITY 2.1.[151]

---

[147]PL 10:520-21; cf. NPNF 2 9.1.20. [148]PL 10:521; cf. NPNF 2 9.1.20. [149]PL 10:527; cf. NPNF 2 9.1.23. [150]Mt 28:19. [151]PL 10:50-51; cf. NPNF 2 9.1.52.

THE DIFFERENCE BETWEEN BEGINNING AND BIRTH. HILARY OF POITIERS: Since God is a spirit, it is clear that in one born from him there can be nothing alien or different from that spirit from which he was born. Thus the birth of God constitutes [the Son] perfect God. From this it is also clear that we must not say that he began to exist but only that he was born. There is a sense in which beginning is different from birth. A thing that begins to exist either comes into being out of nothing or else changes from one state into another, . . . but in birth the nature of the one who gives birth is preserved in the offspring. ON THE TRINITY 7.14.[152]

THE TRINITY IS AN ARTICLE OF FAITH. HILARY OF POITIERS: I cannot describe the Holy Spirit, just as I cannot describe his pleas on my behalf. As in the revelation that the only-begotten Son was born of the Father before all time, and when we stop struggling with ambiguities of language and the difficulties of thought, the one certainty—that he was born—remains; so I hold fast in my consciousness the truth that the Holy Spirit is from the Father and through the Son, although my intellect cannot comprehend it. ON THE TRINITY 12.56.[153]

TO CALL GOD "FATHER" IS TO NAME HIS ESSENCE. ATHANASIUS: If anyone thinks that God is a compound, or an accident in some other essence, or as someone encompassed by something greater than he is or as being somehow incomplete, so that when we say "God" or "Father" we are not naming the invisible and incomprehensible essence but describing something about it, then they may well complain about the council's statement that the Son is from the essence of God. But let them reflect that in so doing, they are uttering two blasphemies. First of all, they are making God corporeal, and second, they are claiming that the Lord is not the Son of the Father himself but rather of something that characterizes the Father. If God is simple (which he is), it follows that in saying "God" and "Father" we are not defining something about him but rather naming his essence itself. For although it is impossible to comprehend what the essence of God is, it is sufficient to understand that he exists, and if Scripture uses these titles to indicate who he is, then we are merely imitating it when we call him God, Father and Lord. DEFENSE OF THE NICENE DEFINITION 22.[154]

THE SON IS THE FATHER'S COCREATOR. ATHANASIUS: If the Son does what the Father does, and if what he creates is the creation of the Father, but at the same time the Son is the Father's creation, then either the Son will have created himself, which is absurd and impossible, or else he will not be a creature of the Father. If the Son were simply a means to an end, then he could do no more than transmit this quality to other created things and might well have no power to do even that much. DISCOURSES AGAINST THE ARIANS 2.21.[155]

ONE DIVINITY IN THE TRINITY. ATHANASIUS: Just as the Father can never become the Son, so the Son can never become the Father. And just as the Father can never cease to be the only Father, so the Son can never cease to be the only Son. No one but a maniac would say or think that the Son is a brother or that the Father is a grandfather. Thus nowhere in holy Scripture is the Spirit ever called a son, lest he be thought to be the Son's brother, or his son, which would make the Father his grandfather. The Son of the Father is the Son and the Spirit of the Father is called the Spirit, and thus there is one divinity in the Trinity and one faith. FOUR LETTERS TO SERAPION 1.16.[156]

---

[152]PL 10:210-11; cf. NPNF 2 9.1:23-24. [153]PL 10:469-70; cf. NPNF 2 9.1:23. [154]PG 25:453-56; cf. NPNF 2 2:164-65. [155]PG 26:189-91; cf. NPNF 2 4:359. [156]PG 26:569.

THE PERSONS OF THE TRINITY CANNOT BE SEPARATED. ATHANASIUS: Therefore, given the conjunction and unity in the holy Trinity, who would dare to separate the Son from the Father or the Holy Spirit from either the Son or the Father? Or who would be so bold as to suggest that the Trinity is a combination of different natures, so that the Son would have a different substance from the Father? And who would argue that the Spirit is alien to the Son? If anyone asks how it can be that when the Spirit is in us, the Son is said to be in us too, and when the Son is in us, the Father is said to be in us too, or how a Trinity can signify unity, so that when it is said that there is one God in us, this one God is a Trinity—if anyone, I say, should ask this sort of thing—let him first divide brightness from light and wisdom from the wise person, and then he will be able to explain how this can be. But if these things are impossible, how much more daring and absurd must it be to attempt the same in the case of God? The truth is that divinity is not communicated by arguments but by faith. It is not linked to reason but to godliness. FOUR LETTERS TO SERAPION 1.20.[157]

THE INNER LIFE OF GOD. MARIUS VICTORINUS: "He will receive of mine."[158] In this one act, Christ is the agent and the Holy Spirit also. The first is to live, and then on that basis to understand. To live is Christ, to understand is the Spirit. Therefore, the Spirit receives from Christ as Christ receives from the Father, so that the Spirit too is from the Father. They are all one, and all from the Father. AGAINST ARIUS 1.13-14.[159]

THE EXISTENCE OF EACH PERSON IMPLIES THE EXISTENCE OF THE OTHERS. DIDYMUS THE BLIND: Just as it is impossible for the Father not to have been Father from eternity (not in time, because the name was not added to him later on), so it is impossible for the Son the Word and his Spirit not to have existed from eternity out of his nature and hypostasis. For as long as the Father has existed, the former has been begotten and the latter proceeds from him. The fact that he is the Father of the only-begotten [Son] and that he has his Spirit proceeding from him cannot be taken away, and the thing that makes him the Father does not differ in time or in substance from the Son or from his Spirit. ON THE TRINITY 1.15.[160]

THE INDWELLING PRESENCE OF THE FATHER. DIDYMUS THE BLIND: If the Father dwells in those who are worthy, how can it not be, on the ground of the unity and fullness of the divine nature, that the Son and the Holy Spirit would not be present in us also? . . . But nobody wants to suggest that there is a multiplicity of divine beings dwelling in us! There is only the one God, whose three persons exist in the unity of the Godhead. ON THE TRINITY 2.6.7.[161]

IN CREATION AND REDEMPTION. JEROME: When the plural is used of the person of God, it is to be understood in the same sense as it is in Genesis, where we read, "Let us make humankind in our image and likeness"[162]—as a sign that points to the Trinity. And when we read in the Gospel how our Lord said, "I and the Father are one,"[163] we refer the "one" to the divine nature and the "are" to the different persons. COMMENTARY ON ISAIAH 3.6.8.[164]

ONE LORD, ONE FAITH, ONE BAPTISM. JEROME: There is one Lord, and there is one God, because the dominion of the Father and the Son is one divinity. Moreover, there is also said to be one faith, because we believe in the Father, the Son and the Holy Spirit in the same way. There is also one baptism, because we are baptized in exactly the same way into the Father, the Son and the Holy Spirit. We

---

[157]PG 26:576-57. [158]Jn 16:14. [159]PL 8:1048. [160]PG 39:320. [161]PG 39:529. [162]Gen 1:26. [163]Jn 10:30. [164]PL 24:97.

are even immersed three times in order to show that it is one sacrament of the Trinity. Furthermore, we are not baptized in the names of the Father, Son and Holy Spirit but in one name, which is the name of God. COMMENTARY ON EPHESIANS 2.4.5.[165]

DISTINCT BUT INDISTINCT AT THE SAME TIME. AMBROSE: There is something about the substance of the distinct, incomprehensible and ineffable Trinity that is indistinct. For we accept that the Father, Son and Holy Spirit are different from each other, not confused together. Nevertheless this difference is not a separation, nor does it produce a plurality of beings. Therefore, when adoring the divine mystery, we always believe that there is one Father, one Son and one Holy Spirit, not two of any of them. . . . We recognize the distinction but do not understand its secrets. We do not argue about how this came to be but merely maintain the evidences of the distinctions [as we see them.] ON THE CHRISTIAN FAITH 4.8.91.[166]

WE ARE CALLED TO ENJOY THE TRINITY. AUGUSTINE: The true objects of our enjoyment are the Father, the Son and the Holy Spirit, who are at the same time the Trinity, one being, supreme above all and common to all who enjoy him, if he is an object and not rather the cause of all objects, or indeed even if he is the cause of all. For it is not easy to find a name that will adequately express such great excellence, unless it is better to speak in this way: The Trinity, one God of whom are all things, through whom are all things and in whom are all things. The Father, the Son and the Holy Spirit are each by himself God, and at the same time they are all one God, and each of them by himself is a complete substance, and yet they are all one substance. The Father is not the Son or the Holy Spirit, the Son is not the Father or the Holy Spirit, the Holy Spirit is not the Father or the Son, but

only the Father is Father, only the Son is Son, and only the Holy Spirit is the Holy Spirit. To all three belong the same eternity, the same unchangeableness, the same majesty, the same power. In the Father is unity, in the Son equality, in the Holy Spirit the harmony of unity and equality, and these three attributes are all one because of the Father, all equal because of the Son and all harmonious because of the Holy Spirit. CHRISTIAN INSTRUCTION 1.5.5.[167]

THE TRINITY IS A BIBLICAL DOCTRINE. AUGUSTINE: All the orthodox biblical interpreters whom I have been able to read, who have written before me about the Trinity, who is God, have set out to teach the scriptural doctrine that the Father, Son and Holy Spirit share a divine unity of one and the same substance in indivisible equality, and therefore they are not three gods but one God. However, the Father has begotten the Son, and so he is not the Son, and the Son has been begotten by the Father, so he is not the Father. The Holy Spirit is neither the Father nor the Son but rather the Spirit of both the Father and the Son, co-equal with them and belonging to the unity of the Trinity. ON THE TRINITY 1.4.7.[168]

GOD'S TRINITARIAN SUBSTANCE. AUGUSTINE: The substance, or more correctly, the essence of God, by which we understand as best we can the Father, the Son and the Holy Spirit, must be invisible because it is completely unchangeable. ON THE TRINITY 3.11.21.[169]

EACH PERSON OF THE TRINITY IS EQUAL TO THE OTHERS. AUGUSTINE: If the Son is said to have been sent by the Father because one is the Father and the other is the Son, this does not stop us from believing that the Son is

---

[165]PL 26:496. The text being discussed is Eph 4:5. [166]PL 16:634-35. [167]PL 34:21; cf. NPNF 2 2:524. [168]PL 42:824; cf. NPNF 1 3:20. [169]PL 42:881-82; cf. NPNF 1 3:65.

equal and consubstantial and co-eternal with the Father, and yet to have been sent by the Father. This is not because one is greater than the other, but because each person is who he is. On the Trinity 4.20.27.[170]

How the Persons Differ from Each Other. Augustine: We do not say that the Father was sent, when from time to time he is perceived by someone, for he has no one of whom to be or from whom to proceed. . . . The Father begat, and the Son is begotten; the Father sent, and the Son was sent. He who begat and he who was begotten, just as he who sent and he who was sent, are one, because the Father and the Son are one. So also the Holy Spirit is one with them, since these three are one. For just as to be born, with respect to the Son, means to be born of the Father, so to be sent, again with respect to the Son, means to be sent from the Father. Likewise, to be the gift of God, with respect to the Holy Spirit, means to proceed from the Father, and to be sent means to proceed from the Father. Nor can we say that the Holy Spirit does not also proceed from the Son, for the same Spirit is not without reason said to be the Spirit of both the Father and the Son. On the Trinity 4.20.28-29.[171]

God Has Inner Relationships. Augustine: Nothing in God is an accident, yet not everything in him is substance either. In created and changeable things, whatever is not part of their substance must be an accident, since whatever can be changed is ultimately accidental to their being and not substantial. This is true also of their relationships, which change according to circumstances. But in God there are no accidents, and nothing ever changes in him. Nevertheless, he has inner relationships that are not substances any more than they are accidents. The Father stands in relation to the Son and the Son in relation to the Father, but this is not an accident because

these relationships have always been there in eternity. . . . If the Son had been born in time, then his existence would indeed be accidental, and if the Father had possessed that name before the birth of the Son, it would necessarily have been part of his substance. But the Father is Father only in relation to the Son and vice versa, so that these relationships are neither part of the divine substance nor merely accidental. They both possess exactly the same substance and differ only according to relation, but because those relations are unchangeable they cannot be called accidents either. On the Trinity 5.5.6.[172]

One Creator and One God. Augustine: The Father, the Son and the Holy Spirit are one beginning with respect to the created order, for they are but one Creator and one God. On the Trinity 5.14.15.[173]

The Trinity Is Not a Compound of Three Elements. Augustine: The Trinity is not to be thought of as a compound of three elements. If that were the case, then the Father by himself or the Son by himself would be less than both of them together. Even though it is hard to see how we can talk about the Father by himself or the Son by himself, since the Father and the Son are inseparably together in eternity. This is not because both are the Father and both the Son but because they are always one in relation to each other and do not appear on their own. On the Trinity 6.7.9.[174]

The Term "Person" Is a Convenient Description. Augustine: If we say that there are three persons in God, as a way of expressing what is common to the Father, the Son and the Holy Spirit, why do we not also

---

[170]PL 42:906; cf. NPNF 1 3:83. [171]PL 42:908; cf. NPNF 1 3:84. [172]PL 42:913-14; cf. NPNF 1 3:89. [173]PL 42:921; cf. NPNF 1 3:94-95. [174]PL 42:929; cf. NPNF 1 3:101.

say that there are three gods? The Father is a person, the Son is a person, and the Holy Spirit is a person. The Father is also God, the Son is God, and the Holy Spirit is God. Why then are there not three gods, or conversely, if all three are one God, why is there not just one person? . . . We use the term "person" of the three not because Scripture does so but because otherwise we would have no way of describing them. Scripture does not authorize us to do this, but neither does it forbid us, and herein lies the difference, because Scripture does forbid us to say that there are three gods. ON THE TRINITY 7.4.8.[175]

THE ATTRIBUTES OF GOD DO NOT BELONG TO EACH PERSON OF THE TRINITY INDIVIDUALLY. AUGUSTINE: Those things that are predicated of each of the persons relative to one another are predicated as belonging to each person individually. . . . The Father is not the Trinity, nor is the Son, nor is the gift [Holy Spirit]. But every description of them is found in the singular, as applying to all three persons in the Trinity. The Father is God, the Son is God, and the Holy Spirit is God. The Father is good, the Son is good, and the Holy Spirit is good. The Father is Almighty, the Son Almighty and the Holy Spirit Almighty. But there are not three gods, three goods or three almighties, but one God, one good and one Almighty, the Trinity itself. . . . They are thus spoken of according to their essence, since in them to be is the same as to be great, good, wise and whatever else is said of each person individually. They are called three persons, not in respect of their essence, where there is no difference, but only so that we may be able to give an answer to whoever might ask us what these three things are. ON THE TRINITY 8, PREFACE.[176]

THE IMAGE OF THE TRINITY. AUGUSTINE: God said, "Let us create humankind in our own image."[177] . . . The word *our* would not

mean anything if humanity were made in the image of only one person, whether the Father, the Son or the Holy Spirit, but it is appropriate because humanity was created in the image of the Trinity. ON THE TRINITY 12.6.6.[178]

THE FATHER KNOWS EVERYTHING. AUGUSTINE: God the Father knows everything in himself and also in the Son. In himself he knows everything for that reason only, but in the Son he knows everything through his Word, the Word that is spoken concerning everything that he has in himself. ON THE TRINITY 15.14.23.[179]

THE TRINITY IS STILL ONLY ONE GOD. AUGUSTINE: There is a good that is simple and unchangeable, and this is God. By this Good all other good things have been created, but the other things are not simple and therefore not unchangeable. God created them, I say; he did not beget them, for what is begotten of him is as simple and good as he is in himself. These two we call the Father and the Son, and both together with the Holy Spirit are one God. In Scripture, the epithet "holy" is given to the Spirit, who is different from either the Father or the Son. He is different but not a different thing, because like the Father and the Son, the Spirit is also simple and good, unchangeable and co-eternal. This Trinity is one God and no less simple for being a trinity. We do not say that the Good is simple because the Father alone possesses it (or the Son alone, or the Holy Spirit alone), nor do we say that the Trinity is only a nominal one, without any real distinction of persons (as the Sabellians teach). We say that the Trinity is simple because it is what it has, apart from the relationship of the persons to each other. For although it is true

---

[175]PL 42:940-41; cf. NPNF 1 3:110. [176]PL 42:947; cf. NPNF 1 3:115. [177]Gen 1:26. [178]PL 42:1001; cf. NPNF 1 3:157. [179]PL 42:1077; cf. NPNF 1 3:213.

that the Father has a Son, he is not himself the Son, just as the Son has a Father without being himself the Father. But apart from that, each person of the Trinity is what he has; for example, each is living because each has life in himself. CITY OF GOD 11.10.1.[180]

WE PREACH THE UNITY IN DIVERSITY THAT IS THE TRINITY. AUGUSTINE: We believe, we maintain, we faithfully preach that the Father begat the Word, that is, Wisdom, by which all things were made, the only-begotten Son, one as the Father is one, eternal as the Father is eternal, and equally with the Father, supremely good; and that the Holy Spirit is the spirit alike of Father and Son and is consubstantial and co-eternal with both, and that this whole Trinity, by reason of the individuality of the persons, and one God by reason of the indivisible divine substance, as also one Almighty by reason of the indivisible omnipotence; yet so that when we enquire regarding each singly, it is said that each is God and Almighty, and when we speak of all together, it is said that there are not three gods or three almighties but one God Almighty, so great is the indivisible unity of these three, which requires that it be so stated. CITY OF GOD 11.24.[181]

DISTINCT PERSONS, BUT CONSTITUTING ONLY ONE GOD. LEO THE GREAT: In the divine Trinity nothing is unlike or unequal, and everything that can be thought concerning its substance admits of no diversity either in power or glory or eternity. And while in the property of each person the Father is one, the Son is another and the Holy Spirit is a third, yet the Godhead is not distinct and different, for while the Son is the only-begotten of the Father, the Holy Spirit is the Spirit of the Father and the Son, not in the way that every creature is the creature of the Father and the Son but as living and having power with both and eternally subsisting of that which is the Father and the Son. SERMON 75.3.[182]

THE TRINITY HAS A SINGLE, SIMPLE NATURE. CYRIL OF ALEXANDRIA: The supreme nature is simple and not compound. It is modulated through the properties of the hypostases and differences of persons and names and goes into the holy Trinity, yet by the unity of its nature and its perfect and universal identity, it comes together as one, which is called and is God. This occurs in such a way that in each person the entire nature is understood, along with its hypostatic property. So each hypostasis remains what it is, and each one possesses these things in its own nature through its natural unity with the others. For the Father is in the Son and in the Holy Spirit, just as the Son and the Holy Spirit are in the Father and in each other also. DIALOGUE ON THE TRINITY 7.[183]

THE FATHER AND THE TRINITY. JOHN OF DAMASCUS: We believe in one Father, the beginning and cause of all, begotten of no one, without cause or generation, alone subsisting, creator of all but Father of only one by nature, his only-begotten Son, our Lord Jesus Christ, and producer of the Holy Spirit. ORTHODOX FAITH 1.8.[184]

DISTINGUISHED BY THEIR PECULIAR PROPERTIES. JOHN OF DAMASCUS: In the case of the Godhead, we confess that there is only one nature but maintain that there are three subsistences actually existing in him. Everything relating to the nature and existence of God is simple, the difference of the subsistences being recognized only in the three properties that distinguish them—unbegottenness in the case of the Father, begottennness in the case of the Son and procession [in the case of the Holy Spirit]. We also know that these three are indivisible and inseparable from each other, united

---

[180]PL 41:325; cf. NPNF 1 2:210-11. [181]PL 41:337; cf. NPNF 1 2:218-19. [182]PL 54:402; cf. NPNF 2 12:190. [183]PG 75:1092. [184]PG 94:809; cf. NPNF 2 9.2:6.

in one and interpenetrating each other without confusion. Nevertheless, they remain three distinct subsistences, even though they are united without confusion or separation. Each has an independent existence and individuality of its own—its own mode of existence—but they are one in their essence and in the properties that belong to that. ORTHODOX FAITH 3.5.[185]

INCOMPREHENSIBLE UNITY. JOHN OF DAMASCUS: The Father is Father and unbegotten. The Son is Son and begotten, not unbegotten, because he is from the Father. The Holy Spirit is not begotten but proceeds, for he is also from the Father. None of these is created, none is inferior, and none is subservient. Rather, there is both unity and Trinity, which was and is and shall be forever. The Trinity is understood and worshiped by faith—by faith, not by inquiry or investigation or demonstration. The harder you look, the less you will find; the more you seek, the more it will be hidden. God ought therefore to be worshiped by believers with an incurious mind. Believe that God exists in three hypostases, but how this can be is beyond our understanding, because God is incomprehensible. ON HERESIES, EPILOGUE.[186]

---

[185]PG 94:1000; cf. NPNF 2 9.2:10. [186]PG 94:780.

THE ALMIGHTY

πιστεύομεν εἰς ἕνα Θεὸν	*Credo in unum Deum*	*We believe in one God,*
πατέρα, **παντοκράτορα,**	*Patrem **omnipotentem;***	*the Father, **the Almighty,***
ποιητὴν οὐρανοῦ καὶ γῆς,	*factorem coeli et terrae,*	*maker of heaven and earth,*
ὁρατῶν τε πάντων καὶ ἀοράτων.	*visibilium omnium et invisibilium.*	*of all that is, seen and unseen.*

HISTORICAL CONTEXT: Centuries of creedal repetition have made it seem natural to associate the words *Father* and *Almighty*, and it now takes special effort to realize that this was not so in the early days of the church. The title "Almighty" is used many times in the Old Testament and in the book of Revelation, but it occurs only once elsewhere in the New Testament,[1] and in no instance is it ever coupled with the word *Father*. No doubt the early Christians were happy to make this identification, but although it seems that they did so almost unconsciously, a case can still be made for saying that there should be a comma between the two words in the first article of the creed, in order to emphasize that the terms are of independent origin.

The word *Almighty* is not an adjective describing a divine attribute but a title given to the God of Israel, a fact that is unfortunately obscured in translation. In our English Bibles, "Almighty" is used to translate the Hebrew name El-Shaddai every time it occurs, and its apparent Greek equivalent, Pantocrator.[2] However, the Greek word is used more than 150 times in the Old Testament, where it sometimes translates El-Shaddai but more

---

[1]2 Cor 6:18. [2]El-Shaddai occurs forty-eight times in the Old Testament, of which thirty-one occurrences are in the single book of Job. Pantocrator is found nine times in the New Testament, eight of them in the book of Revelation.

often Yahweh Sabaoth or the Lord of hosts.[3] Unfortunately neither Latin nor English has exact equivalents of these names. Both Western languages have to fall back on adjectives—*Omnipotens* in Latin and "Almighty" in English—that give a misleading impression.[4] It can nevertheless be seen from the surviving texts that, as long as some knowledge of Greek remained current in the Latin-speaking world, the sense that "Almighty" was a title and not a descriptive adjective was preserved in theological writing. There was, however, some discussion as to its precise meaning. Originally, the word emphasized that God was the ruler of all things, a status that belonged to him by virtue of the fact that he had created them. It was extremely important for the early Christians to maintain this essentially Jewish idea, since without it, the door was open to belief in an independent evil deity that could compete with the true God for power and influence.[5] As time went on, the question arose as to whether God's universal rule implied that he had the ability to do anything and everything, and at first Christians like Origen were inclined to say that it did. This view was modified somewhat later on, as other theologians (like Augustine) realized that God could not do things that contradicted his nature. This was not because he was not omnipotent but because it made no sense to say that God could do such things. They were no more than verbal constructs, with no reality behind them. For example, to ask whether God could commit suicide or do evil was to fall into absurdity, since such concepts could not be applied to his being.

The fact that the New Testament presents Jesus Christ as the co-creator of the universe quickly led the early Christians to recognize that the Son must also be almighty God, and as the doctrine of the Holy Spirit was developed in the fourth century, the term was naturally extended to him as well. Nevertheless, it is remarkable that this theological develop-

ment, which was greatly assisted by the need to react against the claims of Arius, did not find its way into the Nicene Creed. It was the *Quicunque vult*, usually known (inaccurately) as the Athanasian Creed,[6] which seems to date from early sixth-century Gaul and which was never adopted by any council of the church, which became the first creedal document to insist on the applicability of the name "Almighty" to all three persons. In that creed, it is given precedence over the more familiar names God and Lord because, while there were many gods and many lords in a pagan environment, there could only ever be one Almighty. It was the ultimate confession of monotheism, and as such it deserves a special place in any examination of creedal history.

OVERVIEW: God is greater than anything else and rules over everything (THEOPHILUS). All his attributes point to his supreme omnipotence (CLEMENT OF ALEXANDRIA), and all things are possible with him (ORIGEN), though there are some things that he cannot do precisely because he is almighty (AUGUSTINE). God is the absolute and perfect creator of everything (NOVATIAN, HIPPOLYTUS, CYRIL OF JERUSALEM, AUGUSTINE). The almighty

---

[3] The exact number of occurrences depends on which manuscript tradition is followed and on whether one includes the deuterocanonical (apocryphal) books or not. Very often the Greek Old Testament does not translate El-Shaddai at all. In the Pentateuch, for example, the Hebrew name is left out in translation! Note too, that in 2 Corinthians 6:18, the Greek Pantocrator translates the Hebrew Yahweh Sabaoth, as found in 2 Samuel 7:8. [4] What is true of English is equally true of all other languages that have absorbed the Latin theological tradition, including those in parts of the world that have been evangelized only in modern times. [5] This danger was real. Dualism, as it is called, was the official creed of Persia and entered the Roman world in the form of Manichaeism, a philosophical heresy to which the young Augustine was particularly attracted for several years, before he was converted to orthodox Christianity. [6] It may have acquired this name because Athanasius was the classical champion of orthodoxy, which the *Quicunque vult* was designed to uphold. Formally speaking, it is not a creed in the usual sense of the word, though it has come to be regarded as such in the Western tradition. It is unknown in the Eastern churches.

God cannot have been born (ARNOBIUS), but he can reproduce himself without sexual relations (LACTANTIUS). Therefore the Son Jesus Christ is almighty in the same sense as his Father is (HIPPOLYTUS, ATHANASIUS). Because he is almighty, God is fully sovereign and can save whomever he pleases, but his omnipotence does not mean that he saves everyone (AUGUSTINE). The word also implies that he must be invisible and impassible (RUFINUS) and that the creation must be subject to him (ATHANASIUS, CYRIL OF JERUSALEM). Only the almighty God can make something out of nothing (AUGUSTINE), and it is precisely because he is the source of all things that the title is given to him (PSEUDO-DIONYSIUS). Furthermore, everything in the created order bears witness to his almighty power (FULGENTIUS).

The Meaning of God's Omnipotence

GOD IS GREATER THAN ANYTHING ELSE.
THEOPHILUS OF ANTIOCH: This is the attribute of God, the highest and Almighty, the living God—not only to be present everywhere but also to see and hear everything. He is not confined to one place, because if he were, then the place concerned would be greater than he is. God is not contained by anything else; on the contrary, he is the one who contains all things. TO AUTOLYCUS 2.3.[7]

GOD RULES EVERYTHING.
THEOPHILUS OF ANTIOCH: God is Almighty because he rules and embraces everything. The heights of heaven and the depths of the abyss, as well as the ends of the earth, are all in his hand. TO AUTOLYCUS 1.4.[8]

GOD'S ATTRIBUTES ARE PROOF THAT HE IS ALMIGHTY.
CLEMENT OF ALEXANDRIA: We call God the One, the Good, the Mind, the absolute Being, the Father, God, the Creator and Lord. We are not giving him names, but because we have no alternative, we use these words as points of reference so as not to go astray. None of these words by itself expresses God fully, but taken together they are all indicative of the power of the Almighty. STROMATEIS 5.12.[9]

ALL THINGS ARE POSSIBLE WITH GOD.
ORIGEN: Nothing is impossible to the Almighty, nor is anything incapable of being restored by its creator. ON FIRST PRINCIPLES 3.6.5.[10]

GOD IS THE ABSOLUTE AND PERFECT CREATOR OF EVERYTHING.
NOVATIAN: The rule of truth demands that first of all, we must believe in God, the Father and Lord Almighty. He is the absolute and perfect founder of everything. . . . There is no room left for any being superior to him, because he contains all things. . . . He knows no bounds, for there is nothing greater than he is. He is eternal, because there is nothing older than he is. He has no beginning, and so can have been preceded by no one. He is immortal, and dwells outside of time. . . . If he could be understood, he would be smaller than the human mind which could grasp him. ON THE TRINITY 1-2.[11]

JESUS CHRIST IS THE ALMIGHTY GOD.
HIPPOLYTUS: Having become man, Christ is still God forever. John put it like this: "Who is, and who was and who is to come, the Almighty."[12] He was right to call Christ "Almighty," because this is merely what Christ said about himself when he declared: "All things have been delivered unto me by my Father."[13] AGAINST NOETUS 6.[14]

EVERYTHING IS MADE BY GOD'S ALMIGHTY WILL.
HIPPOLYTUS: By the almighty will of God all things are made, and

---

[7]PG 6:1049; cf. ANF 2:95. [8]PG 6:1029; cf. ANF 2:90. [9]PG 9:121-24; cf. ANF 2:464. [10]PG 11:338; cf. ANF 4:346. [11]PL 3:886-90; cf. ANF 5:611-13. [12]Rev 1:8. [13]Lk 10:22. [14]PG 10:812; cf. ANF 5:225.

the things that have been made are preserved, being maintained according to their several principles in perfect harmony by the one who is by nature the almighty God and maker of all things. His divine will remains unalterable, and by it he has made and moves all things, sustained as each of them is by its own natural laws. For the infinite cannot in any manner or by any account be susceptible of movement, inasmuch as it has nothing toward which and nothing around which it can be moved. For in the case of something that is by nature infinite and so incapable of being moved, movement would be a loss of identity. AGAINST BERON AND HELIX 1.[15]

THE ALMIGHTY GOD CANNOT HAVE BEEN BORN. ARNOBIUS OF SICCA: By the unanimous judgment of everyone the almighty God is understood as having never been born. He was never brought out into the light, nor did he ever begin to exist at some point in the past. He is the source of all things, the Father of ages and seasons, for they do not exist of themselves. AGAINST THE NATIONS 1.34.[16]

GOD CAN REPRODUCE WITHOUT SEXUAL RELATIONS. LACTANTIUS: The immortal God has no need of sex or succession. . . . Why should he need the female when, as the almighty God, he can produce sons on his own? DIVINE INSTITUTES 1.8.[17]

THE ALMIGHTY SON IS BORN OF THE ALMIGHTY FATHER. RUFINUS OF AQUILEIA: God is called Almighty because he possesses rule and dominion over all things. But the Father possesses all things by his Son. . . . Just as light is born of light, and truth of truth, so too Almighty is born of Almighty. In the book of Revelation,[18] . . . the one who is to come is called the Almighty, and who is that one, if not Christ, the Son of God? COMMENTARY ON THE APOSTLES' CREED 5.[19]

GOD IS INVISIBLE AND IMPASSIBLE. RUFINUS OF AQUILEIA: These words are not in the creed of the Roman church but were added after "Almighty" in our own church [at Aquileia], because of the Sabellian heresy, known among us as Patripassianism, according to which the Father himself was born of the Virgin Mary, became visible and suffered in the flesh. To exclude such impiety concerning the Father, our ancestors seem to have added these words. It is evident that it was the Son, not the Father, who became incarnate and was made "visible and passible." But as far as his invisible substance of Godhead is concerned, we must believe that neither the Father nor the Son nor the Holy Spirit is "visible and passible." COMMENTARY ON THE APOSTLES' CREED 5.[20]

THE CREATION SUBJECT TO AN ALMIGHTY GOD. ATHANASIUS: If God is almighty and nothing has power over him because he has power over everything else, how can those who deify creation fail to see that their view does not measure up to this definition of God? AGAINST THE HEATHEN 29.2.[21]

GOD IS FAR GREATER THAN ANY OF HIS CREATURES. CYRIL OF JERUSALEM: The Father of our Lord Jesus Christ is not limited to any place, nor is he less than heaven itself, for the heavens are the works of his hands[22] and the whole earth is held in his grasp.[23] He is in and around all things. Do not think that the sun is brighter than he is, or even equal to him, for the one who formed the sun must needs be infinitely greater and brighter than it is. He knows everything that will come to pass and is mightier than all of them. He is not subject to any necessary sequence of events, to generation, chance or fate. He is perfect in

[15]PG 10:829-32; cf. ANF 5:231. [16]PL 5:758; cf. ANF 6:421-22. [17]PL 6:154-55; cf. ANF 7:17. [18]Rev 4:8. [19]PL 21:343-44; cf. NPNF 2 3:545. [20]PL 21:344; cf. NPNF 2 3:545. [21]PG 25:57; cf. NPNF 2 4:19. [22]Ps 8:3 (8:4 LXX). [23]Is 40:12.

everything, possessing every absolute form of virtue, neither diminishing nor increasing but remaining always the same. Catechetical Lectures 4.5.[24]

God Must Have Power Over Everything. Cyril of Jerusalem: Heretics do not acknowledge one almighty God. The one who rules all things is almighty, but those who say that God is lord of the soul but that someone else rules the body, ends up making neither God nor his rival perfect, since each has something that is missing in the other. How can God be almighty if he has power over the soul but not over the body? How can a being be almighty if he has power of bodies but not over spirits? . . . Unless the Father of our Lord Jesus Christ has power over both, how does he subject both of them to punishment? How can he take a body that belongs to someone else and cast it into hell? Catechetical Lectures 8.3.[25]

The Son Possesses Divine Authority. Athanasius: When the prophets spoke of God as almighty, they did not mean to say by this that the Word was subject to him (for they knew that the Son was different from created things and indeed that he was sovereign over them himself, according to his likeness to the Father), but because he is ruler over all things that he has made through the Son and has given authority over them to the Son. But having given this authority to the Son, the Father is still Lord of all things through his Word. Defense of the Nicene Definition 30.[26]

The Almighty God Has Made Everything. Augustine: Since we believe that God is the Father Almighty, we ought to agree that every creature has been made by him. On Faith and the Creed 2.3.[27]

Because God Is Almighty. Augustine: We do not subject God to the inevitability of

necessity if we say that he must live forever and know everything in advance, just as his freedom is not compromised when we say that he cannot die or fall into error. These things are impossible for him, but only because if they were possible, he would cease to be all-powerful. Yet he is rightly called almighty, even if he cannot die or fall into error, because the word *almighty* describes his ability to do what he wills, not his need to suffer what he does not will for himself. Thus there are some things God cannot do precisely because he is almighty! City of God 5.10.1.[28]

We Will Be Saved If God Wants Us to Be. Augustine: When we hear and read in Scripture that God "would have all people to be saved,"[29] although we know perfectly well that not all people are saved, we must not for that reason limit the omnipotence of God but rather understand this passage as meaning that no one is saved unless God wills his salvation. It is not that there is nobody whose salvation he does not will, but that no one is saved apart from his will. Therefore we should pray him to will our salvation, because if he wills it, it must necessarily be accomplished. Enchiridion 103.[30]

God Cannot Be Measured. Augustine: God cannot be measured, because that would imply that he is limited. But he is able to give measure to other things, so that they can exist. Again, God cannot be measured as if he received his limits from someone else. If we say that he is the measure of all things, what we mean is that he is the highest good. On the Nature of the Good 22.[31]

Only the Almighty Can Create Something from Nothing. Augustine: Ev-

[24]PG 33:460; cf. NPNF 2 7:20. [25]PG 33:628; cf. NPNF 2 7:48. [26]PG 25:472; cf. NPNF 2 4:170-71. [27]PL 40:183; cf. NPNF 1 3:322. [28]PL 41:152; cf. NPNF 1 2:92. [29]1 Tim 2:4. [30]PL 40:280; cf. NPNF 1 3:270. [31]PL 42:558; cf. NPNF 1 4:355.

erything that exists and what anyone makes exists either by itself, or has been made out of something else or has been created out of nothing. A human being, because he is not omnipotent, makes children out of himself and makes objects out of something else—for example, an artisan makes a box out of wood and a goblet out of silver. . . . A person can make the box but cannot make the wood. In fact, no human being can make anything out of nothing. But God, who is almighty, has begotten a Son from himself and has made the world out of nothing. He also formed humankind out of the dust of the ground, so as to demonstrate by his actions on all three levels that his power is supreme in all things. Against Felix the Manichaean 2.18.[32]

Why God Is Called the Almighty.

Pseudo-Dionysius: God is called Almighty because he is the source of all things. He contains and embraces everything, he stabilizes and restrains everything. He is the absolute being in himself, and from himself, as from an all-embracing root, he produces everything and binds everything to himself, transforming and containing all that exists. Divine Names 10.1.[33]

The Omnipotence of God.

Fulgentius of Ruspe: The goodness and omnipotence of the Creator is just as great in the making of small things as in great things. For the highest and true wisdom has made all things wisely. For him, wisdom is part of his nature and to do things at all is to do them wisely. Therefore, the simplicity of the multiple wisdom of God manifests the greatness of his exaltedness, not only in the greatness of sublime creatures but also in the smallness of the least. All the good things that he has created are very inferior and dissimilar to their Creator, because they are not taken out of him but made out of nothing. But also, they do not exist in the same manner. Each of them exists as it has been given by God to exist—one in one way and another in a different way. Nor has it been given to corporeal things to exist in the same way as spiritual things. . . . As the apostle Paul says, the brightness of heavenly bodies is one thing and that of earthly bodies is another.[34] . . . Therefore the diversity of corporeal natures demonstrates that each one of them is not what it is because of what it could always have been in and of itself, but because of what it has received from the plan and working of the almighty, unchangeable and all-wise Creator. To Peter, on the Faith 3.26.[35]

One Almighty, Not Three.

Athanasian Creed: So likewise the Father is almighty, the Son almighty and the Holy Spirit almighty, and yet there are not three Almighties but one Almighty. Athanasian Creed.[36]

---

[32]PL 42:547-48. [33]PG 3:936-37. [34]See 1 Cor 15:41. [35]PL 65:683-84; FC 95:76. [36]Book of Common Prayer.

MAKER

πιστεύομεν εἰς ἕνα Θεὸν	*Credo in unum Deum*	*We believe in one God,*
πατέρα, παντοκράτορα,	*Patrem omnipotentem;*	*the Father, the Almighty,*
ποιητὴν οὐρανοῦ καὶ γῆς,	**factorem** *coeli et terrae,*	**maker** *of heaven and earth,*
ὁρατῶν τε πάντων καὶ ἀοράτων.	*visibilium omnium et invisibilium.*	*of all that is, seen and unseen.*

HISTORICAL CONTEXT: The doctrine of creation is one that the early church clearly inherited from Judaism, and it is fundamental to any understanding of Old Testament religion. Like Jews, Christians have always believed that the world was created by a good God, who is a personal being who cares for his creatures. He governs the universe by his providential care, and nothing can happen in it without his permission. Because of this belief, Christians have always had to face the problems of what theologians call theodicy. These can be stated as, first, the problem of the existence of evil, and second, the degree to which evil can affect those who believe in God.

The early Christians did not have to defend their doctrine of creation against Jews, except insofar as to say that it was the work of all three persons of the Trinity, and not of the Father only. This issue became particularly important in the fourth century, after Arius tried to maintain that the Son and the Holy Spirit were the highest of the creatures. Until that time, the bigger problem for the church was to explain and defend its doctrine against the many forms of paganism, including the most sophisticated pagan philosophies, which could not reconcile their understanding of evil with that of a world created by a good and omnipotent God.

As the implications of a divine ordering of the universe sank in, it became clear that God had to be understood as being in complete control of his creation, even when the latter appeared to go against his wishes. This led to an elaborate defense of divine foreknowledge, which included the (future) sin of Adam and eventually to a refined doctrine of predestination, which is associated above all with Augustine. The Fathers were determined to avoid saying that God created evil or made it impossible for some people to be saved, on the ground that they were not predestined, but the logical implications of predestination were hard to escape, and the fundamental dilemma remained for future generations to ponder and attempt to resolve in their own fashion.

Another issue that engaged the Fathers was the distinction between a world fashioned by God (out of preexisting matter) and a world created by him out of nothing. The Bible puts the emphasis on the former without denying the latter, but things were not so clear to the Greek mind, which was often dualistic in this respect. The Fathers argued that the word *maker* implied that God had created matter out of nothing, since it had to come from somewhere. The fact that God had ultimately created it meant that matter must be good, not evil, and it was here that Christian teaching confronted the most widespread pagan beliefs of the time. At the same time, the Fathers did not deny that it was the fashioning of matter into what the Greeks called the *cosmos*, which was the true glory of creation, and they often went into this in great detail. Creedal usage oscillated between "maker" and "creator," with the latter word emphasizing the origin of matter ex nihilo, but it is clear from the comments made on it that both words are meant to convey the same belief in a God who has made everything according to the purpose of his mind and the intention of his will.

Overview: God made everything of his own free will through his Word and his Wisdom (Irenaeus, John of Damascus) and made it out of nothing (Justin Martyr, Hippolytus, Athanasius, Chrysostom, Augustine, Theodoret). All three persons of the Trinity took part in this great work (Basil, Augustine, Fulgentius), but no other being can create anything at all (Chrysostom, Cyril of Alexandria), though humans have a certain power of procreation (Athanasius). The intelligent design of the universe presupposes the existence of a creator (Theophilus, Origen, Lactantius, Augustine, John of Damascus), and providence is the care that God lavishes on the creation once it has been made (John of Damascus). Everything has been made in a particular order (Tertullian) and for a particular purpose (Origen), and the world remains God's personal possession (Arnobius). There is nothing in the universe that God did not make (Basil), and therefore even apparently evil things are good in themselves (Fulgentius, Leo).

God foresaw everything that would come to pass, but his foreknowledge is not incompatible with human free will (Tatian, Tertullian, Eusebius, John of Damascus), and God is in no sense responsible for sin (Chrysostom, Prosper). Sometimes he takes human lives prematurely, but this is because he knows what is best for each one of us (Gregory of Nyssa). Nobody is forced to sin or to perish, even though God knew that these things would happen (Chrysostom). The offer of salvation is made to everyone (Ambrose), but God saves only those who want to be saved (Ambrosiaster, Jerome). Those who are born in Adam's sin are destined to eternal punishment, unless they are chosen for salvation, but those whom God chooses to save are given the faith to persevere in their calling and they cannot fall

away from his grace. The number of those who will be saved is already fixed, and those who are destined to perish have fully deserved their punishment. Predestination is ultimately a mystery, but God's judgments are always righteous, even when we cannot understand them (Augustine, Fulgentius).

God the Creator

God Made Everything Out of Nothing. Justin Martyr: We have received by tradition the belief that God does not need the material offerings that human beings can give him, because he is himself the provider of all things. We have also been taught and are convinced that he accepts only those who imitate his virtues—temperance, justice and love, as well as whatever other virtues are proper to a God who has no name of his own. We have also been taught that in the beginning he made everything out of nothing, because of his goodness and for our sake alone. First Apology 10.[1]

We Perceive the Invisible God by His Works. Theophilus of Antioch: Just as the soul in a person is not seen but is perceived through the body, so God cannot be seen by human eyes but is beheld and perceived through his providence and works. Just as someone who sees a fully-rigged out ship sailing into the harbor will suppose that it has a pilot to steer her, so we must perceive that God is the pilot of the whole universe, although he is not visible to the eyes of the flesh because he is incomprehensible. To Autolycus 1.5.[2]

By His Word and Wisdom. Theophilus of Antioch: God made all things by his Word and his Wisdom. "By his Word were the heavens made, and all the host of them by the breath of his mouth."[3] . . . By his wisdom, God

---

[1]PG 6:340; cf. ANF 1:165. [2]PG 6:1029-32; cf. ANF 2:90. [3]Ps 33:6.

founded the earth, and by knowledge he prepared the heavens. . . . If you understand these things and lead a chaste, holy and righteous life, you can see God. To AUTOLYCUS 1.7.[4]

OF HIS OWN FREE WILL. IRENAEUS: I ought to begin with the most important point, which is that God the Creator made heaven and earth and everything in them, . . . and demonstrate that there is nothing above him or behind him, as well as that he made everything of his own free will, uninfluenced by anyone else. He is the only God, the only Lord, the only Creator, the only Father, the only one who contains all things and who commanded everything else to come into existence. How can there be any other fullness, principle, power or god above him, since it is necessary for God, who is the fullness of all these things, to contain them in his immensity without being himself contained by anyone? AGAINST HERESIES 2.1.1-2.[5]

THROUGH HIS WORD AND HIS WISDOM. IRENAEUS: God always had in himself the Word and Wisdom, the Son and the Spirit, by whom and in whom, freely and spontaneously, he made everything that exists. This is the Creator who has granted the world to the human race and whose greatness is unknown to any of those who have been made by him (for no one has discovered his height, either among the ancients who have gone to their rest or of any of those who are still alive). But as regards his love, he is always known through him by whose means he ordained all things. This is his Word, our Lord Jesus Christ. AGAINST HERESIES 4.20.4.[6]

THE DIFFERENT FACETS OF THE CREATOR. IRENAEUS: In respect of his love, the Creator is our Father; but in respect of his power, he is our Lord, and in respect of his wisdom, he is our maker and designer. By transgressing his commandment, we become his enemies. AGAINST HERESIES 5.17.1.[7]

GOD MADE THE WORLD FOR OUR ENJOYMENT. TERTULLIAN: Ours is the God of nature, who fashioned humankind in such a way that he might desire, appreciate and partake of the pleasures afforded by his creatures. He endowed humanity with certain senses, which act through particular parts of the body, which may be called their instruments. The sense of hearing he has planted in the ears, that of sight he lighted up in the eyes, that of taste he shut up in the mouth, that of smell he wafted into the nose and that of touch he fixed in the tips of our fingers. By means of these organs of the outer person, which do duty for the inner person, the enjoyment of the divine gifts is conveyed by the senses to the soul. What is it about flowers that you particularly enjoy? . . . Either the smell, you say, or the color, or perhaps both. . . . What parts of the body have these senses allotted to them? The eyes and the nose, I presume. With sight and smell, then, make use of flowers, for these are the senses by means of which they are supposed to be enjoyed. . . . The desire for enjoyment comes from God, though the means by which you enjoy the flowers comes from the material world. Never mind—the use of material means does not preclude the enjoyment of the thing desired. Let flowers be what they are—things to be looked at and smelled. THE CHAPLET 5.[8]

HOW CAN THE WORLD EXIST WITHOUT A CREATOR? ORIGEN: I cannot understand how so many distinguished people . . . have thought that the world was uncreated, that is, that it was not formed by God the Creator of all things. They prefer to say that it came into being by chance, thinking that so great a work as the universe could exist without an architect or designer. I am astonished that they should find fault with those who deny either God's creative

---

[4]PG 6:1036; cf. ANF 2:91. [5]PG 7:709-10; cf. ANF 1:359. [6]PG 7:1034; cf. ANF 1:488. [7]PG 7:1169; cf. ANF 1:544. [8]PL 2:82-83; cf. ANF 3:95-96.

power or his providential administration of the world and accuse them of ungodliness for thinking that so great a work as the world could exist without an architect or overseer, while they themselves incur a similar charge of ungodliness by saying that matter is uncreated and co-eternal with the uncreated God. If we suppose then for the sake of argument that matter did not exist and agree with these people that God could not have created something out of nothing, no doubt he would have been idle, having no matter on which to operate! They claim that this matter was provided for him not by his own design but by accident, and they think that something discovered by chance in this way was enough for him to be able to undertake a work of so vast extent. This seems to be to be quite absurd and to be the opinion of people who are altogether ignorant of the power and intelligence of uncreated nature. ON FIRST PRINCIPLES 2.1.4.[9]

INTELLIGENT DESIGN PRESUPPOSES A CREATOR. LACTANTIUS: Cicero said that it is unlikely that matter was made by God. How can you prove this? There is no reason given as to why this should be improbable. On the contrary, it seems to me to be exceedingly probable, nor does it appear this way without reason, when I reflect that there is something more in God, whom you are reducing to the level of human weakness when you credit him with nothing more than mere workmanship. . . . If God cannot make anything unless he is given the material by someone else, it is clear that his power is imperfect and that the one who prepared the original material is more powerful than he is. But who is that? . . . If it is impossible that anything should be more powerful than God, who must necessarily be perfect in strength, power and intelligence, it follows that the one who shaped matter created it also. . . . It is easier to believe that the universe was made by God than to deny it, for nothing can be made without intelligence and

design. DIVINE INSTITUTES 2.9.[10]

SO THAT PEOPLE WOULD COME TO KNOW GOD. ATHANASIUS: For God, being good and loving to the human race and caring for the souls made by him, since he is by nature invisible and incomprehensible, having his being beyond all created existence, for which reason the human race was likely to miss the way toward knowing him, since they are made out of nothing while he is unmade. For this reason, God gave the universe the order it has, using his own Word to do so, so that people who cannot see him, because he is invisible, may come to know him by his works. AGAINST THE HEATHEN 35.1.[11]

CREATION OUT OF NOTHING. CHRYSOSTOM: To say that things that exist were made out of some primary matter and to deny that the Creator of all made everything out of nothing would be the height of stupidity. HOMILIES ON GENESIS 2.2.[12]

THE CREATOR TRINITY. BASIL THE GREAT: In the creation, think first of the original cause of everything that has been made—the Father. Then think of the creative cause—the Son; and then of the perfecting cause—the Holy Spirit. The ministering spirits therefore subsist by the will of the Father, they are brought into being by the action of the Son, and they are perfected by the presence of the Holy Spirit. ON THE HOLY SPIRIT 16.38.[13]

THE CREATOR IS INDEPENDENT OF HIS CREATION. GREGORY OF NYSSA: The world's Creator made time and space as a background to receive what was to come into being; it was on that foundation that he built the universe. It is not possible for anything that has come or

---

[9]PG 11:185; cf. ANF 4:269-70. [10]PL 7:298-303; cf. ANF 7:53-55. [11]PG 25:69; cf. NPNF 2 4:22. [12]PG 53:28. [13]PG 32:136; cf. NPNF 2 8:23.

is now coming into being by means of creation to be outside space and time. But the existence that is all-sufficient, everlasting and world-enveloping is not in space or in time. It is before these and above these in an ineffable way. It is self-contained, knowable by faith alone, immeasurable in centuries, unaccompanied by time, with no associations of past or future. There is nothing beyond or beside itself, whose intervention might make something past or future. Such accidents are confined to the creation, the life of which is divided by time into memory and hope. But within that transcendent and blessed Power all things are equally present as in an instant; past and future are within its all-encircling grasp and its comprehensive view. AGAINST EUNOMIUS 1.26.[14]

GOD CAN ACT WHILE RESTING AND REST WHILE ACTING. AUGUSTINE: We must not believe that God is affected in one way when he works and in another way when he rests. To say that he is not affected at all is an abuse of language, since it implies that something comes into being in his nature that was not there before. He who is affected is acted on, and whatever is acted on is changeable. His leisure therefore is not laziness, indolence or inactivity, just as his work is not labor, effort or industry. He can act while he rests and rest while he acts. He can begin a new work with his already existing eternal design, and what he has not made before he does not now begin to make because he repents of his former rest. . . . Indeed, to speak of former rest and subsequent activity makes sense only with respect to the things created, which formerly did not exist and subsequently came into existence. Perhaps his intention was to demonstrate, to those who have an eye for such things, just how independent he is of his creation and how it is of his own gratuitous goodness that he creates, since from eternity he dwelt without creatures in no less perfect a blessedness. CITY OF GOD 12.17.[15]

WHAT WAS GOD DOING BEFORE CREATION?
AUGUSTINE: What was God doing before he made heaven and earth? I would not answer this question in the way that someone was supposed to have done, by making a joke of it so as to avoid having to face the issue. That person is supposed to have replied, "He was making hell for those who inquire into such deep mysteries." It is one thing to laugh but quite another to grasp the point at issue, and I do not like this reply. I would have preferred him to say, "I am ignorant of what I do not know" rather than reply so as to ridicule someone who has asked an important question and to win applause for the wrong answer. You our God are the creator of every creature, and assuming that "heaven and earth" includes everything that is, I boldly declare that before God made heaven and earth, he was not making anything. CONFESSIONS 11.12.14.[16]

GOD THE CREATOR IS THE TRINITY.
AUGUSTINE: I discern the Trinity in the enigmatic image of the Creator. . . . Where the name of God occurs . . . , have come to understand the Father who made these things. Where the "beginning" is mentioned, I see the Son by whom he made them. Believing that my God is a Trinity, I searched the Scriptures and found your Spirit to be hovering above the waters. There is the Trinity, my God—Father, Son and Holy Spirit, Creator of the whole universe. CONFESSIONS 13.5.6.[17]

GOD MADE MATTER FROM NOTHING. AUGUSTINE: It is quite right to believe that God made everything out of nothing, because even if everything was fashioned out of [preexisting] matter, that matter itself was made out of nothing. We must not be like those who believe that the almighty God could not have

---

[14]PG 45:365-68; cf. NPNF 2 5:69-70. [15]PL 41:367; cf. NPNF 1 2:237-38. [16]PL 32:815; cf. NPNF 1 1:167. [17]PL 32:847; cf. NPNF 1 1:191.

made things out of nothing, merely on the ground that they observe that artisans and workers cannot make anything unless they have the raw materials with which to work. ON GENESIS AGAINST THE MANICHAEANS 1.6.10.[18]

THE CREATION CONTAINS HIDDEN POTENTIAL. AUGUSTINE: There are certain seminal factors present in corporeal things, which develop into the appropriate species on their own, whenever the temporal and causal opportunity is given to them. The angels who do these things are not said to be the creators of animals, nor are farmers said to be the creators of vegetables, trees or whatever else grows in the earth, although they know how to take advantage of the visible opportunities and causes to make them grow. Farmers do this with visible things and angels with invisible ones, but in the end God alone is the creator, who has implanted these causes and seminal factors in the things that exist. QUESTIONS ON THE HEPTATEUCH 2.21.[19]

MATTER IS NOT ETERNAL. CYRIL OF ALEXANDRIA: "In the beginning," says Moses, "God created the heavens and the earth."[20] It is therefore wrong to think, as some do, that matter existed with God from the beginning and is both eternal and uncreated. . . . It was in time, and at its beginning, that God called matter into being and established the creation as something that was brought forth out of nothing according to his will and made to be what it now is. AGAINST THE EMPEROR JULIAN 2.[21]

ONLY GOD CAN CREATE. CYRIL OF ALEXANDRIA: It is totally alien to God's glory to suppose that other beings can create and call into existence things that are not. It is impious to say that those things that are proper and unique to the divine and ineffable nature [of God] could ever be present in created things. The ability to create belongs to him alone and

is part of his glory. AGAINST THE EMPEROR JULIAN 2.[22]

GOD DOES NOT NEED TOOLS TO CREATE. THEODORET OF CYR: The God of all things has no need of anything, whereas human arts need tools for their work. The Maker of all things needs neither tools nor matter to work on, because whereas other artisans require matter, tools, time and labor, as well as skill and diligence, all God needs is his will. CURE FOR GREEK LEANINGS 4.[23]

GOD IS NEVER FAR FROM HIS CREATURES. FULGENTIUS OF RUSPE: It is clear that God is everywhere but is not spatially contained. God is a spirit; indeed, he is the Creator, not created, the Maker of all bodies and all spirits, immutable, eternal, infinite, just and good. Through the infinity of his nature he never departs from the things that he has made. Nor can he be absent from anything that has its existence from him. Yet through his mercy and judgment, because of which the church never ceases to praise him, it is rightly said that he is both present to believers and far away from unbelievers. For what concerns nature, the whole, whatever has been created, whether corporal or spiritual, the holy Trinity alone—one God, Father, Son and Holy Spirit—with one will, one operation, one power, one benevolence and one omnipotence, has made it. Just as the Father fills the whole creature with his power, . . . so the Son fills the whole and so the Holy Spirit fills the whole. BOOK TO VICTOR AGAINST FASTIDIOUSUS THE ARIAN 5.2.[24]

ALL THREE PERSONS TOOK PART IN CREATION. FULGENTIUS OF RUSPE: Can it be said that the Holy Spirit has less than what the Father and the Son have, considering that he made the beginning of the creation together

---

[18]PL 34:178. [19]PL 34:602-3. [20]Gen 1:1. [21]PG 76:584. [22]PG 76:596. [23]PG 83:916. [24]PL 65:513; FC 95:399-400.

with the Father and the Son and has perfected the effect of our redemption along with the Father and the Son? God is said to have made the heavens, but the Son was working alongside the Father in this, as was the Holy Spirit. To Trasamundus 3.35.[25]

The Fragility of Creation. Gregory the Great: It is one thing to exist and quite another to exist as a matter of principle. It is one thing to exist in a changeable state and quite another to be unchangeable. Everything around us exists, but not as a matter of principle, because they do not exist in their own right. If they were not preserved by the hand of the Ruler, they might disappear. . . . Since everything has been made out of nothing, everything would also go back to nothing if the Author of all things did not hold them up by his governing hand. Morals on the Book of Job 16.37.45.[26]

God's Foreknowledge, Providence and Predestination

God Foresaw the Works of the Devil. Hermas: The Lord knows the heart and foreknows everything. He knew the weakness of the human race and the many wiles of the devil. He knew that the devil would inflict evil on the servants of God and would act wickedly toward them. Shepherd, Mandate 2.4.3.[27]

God's Foreknowledge and Human Free Will. Tatian: The power of the Word is able to foresee future events, but those events are not fated to take place. They occur because free agents have chosen them. To the Greeks 7.[28]

God's Foreknowledge Made Creation Possible. Tertullian: If God is good and knows the future and is also able to prevent evil, why did he permit Adam, the very image and likeness of himself and (by the origin of his

soul) his own substance too,[29] to be deceived by the devil and fall from the obedience of the law to death? . . . What can I say about God's foreknowledge, which so many of the prophets have borne witness to? What does it mean to say that the Author of the universe has foreknowledge, when it is precisely that attribute that made it possible for him to create an ordered world in the first place? God must have been aware of sin before it happened, since otherwise he could not have warned Adam about it. . . . God made Adam free, in his own image and likeness. Against Marcion 2.5.[30]

God's Foreknowledge. Eusebius of Caesarea: If we have to say that foreknowledge is not the cause of everything that happens (for God does not prevent a future sinner from sinning), what is even stranger yet true is that the future event is the cause of God's foreknowledge of it. For it does not happen because it was known in advance but rather it was known in advance because it was going to happen. We must make a clear distinction here. If someone interprets "what will be will be" as meaning that a foreknown event must necessarily take place, we do not agree. For we do not say that just because it was known in advance that Judas would be the betrayer of Jesus, that Judas had no choice but to become his betrayer for that reason. Preparation for the Gospel 6.11.[31]

Why Some Children Die. Gregory of Nyssa: God sees the future as well as the past, and for that reason he may sometimes prevent a child from growing into adulthood, so as to protect him from future harm, which he would have suffered had he lived to a mature age. This is what I think about the death of infants. God, who does everything for a reason,

---

[25]PL 65:300. [26]PL 75:1143. [27]PG 2:919-20; cf. ANF 2:22. [28]PG 6:820; cf. ANF 2:67-68. [29]This reflects the Stoic belief that the human soul is a spark of the divine fire. [30]PL 2:289-90; cf. ANF 3:300-301. [31]PG 21:492.

out of his goodness removes all possibility of wrongdoing by not allowing time for the free choice [of evil] which, because of his foreknowledge, he can see coming, because of the child's inbuilt tendency in that direction. ON CHILDREN WHO ARE TAKEN AWAY PREMATURELY.[32]

SCANDALS ARE NECESSARY. CHRYSOSTOM: "It is necessary for scandals to come."[33] . . . Although Jesus uses the word *necessity*, he does not thereby take away free will or human responsibility, nor does he subject anyone's life to the principle of necessity. Rather, he merely predicts what will happen. . . . This prediction does not cause the scandals—God forbid! Nor do they occur merely because he predicted them. He predicted what would happen so that if those who were to cause them should change their minds, they would never come, and if they were never to happen, they would not have been predicted. The scandals came because those who did them were incurably diseased, and Jesus foretold what would come to pass. HOMILIES ON THE GOSPEL OF MATTHEW 59.1.[34]

NO ONE IS FORCED TO PERISH. CHRYSOSTOM: God never compels anyone by necessity or by force but rather desires everyone to be saved. He does not impose any necessity on anyone, as the apostle Paul says: "He desires everyone to be saved and to come to a knowledge of the truth."[35] So how is it that not everyone is saved when God wants everyone to be? The answer is that not everyone chooses to follow his will, and God does not force anyone to do so. HOMILIES ON CERTAIN NEW TESTAMENT TEXTS.[36]

EVERYONE IS PROTECTED BY DIVINE PROVIDENCE. CHRYSOSTOM: God did not simply make the creation, but he also protects and nourishes it now that it has been created. Whether you are speaking about angels,

archangels, higher powers or whatever falls under our gaze or not, everything benefits from his providence, and if they are deprived of his effective working in them, they break up, dissolve and disappear. ON THE DIVINITY OF CHRIST, AGAINST THE ANOMOEANS 12.4.[37]

FOREKNOWLEDGE AND PREDESTINATION. AMBROSE: "Whom he foreknew, he also predestined."[38] God's predestination did not come before his foreknowledge. Rather, he knew in advance what people would deserve and predestined the rewards that they would then receive. ON THE CHRISTIAN FAITH 5.6.83.[39]

HEALING IS AVAILABLE TO ALL. AMBROSE: God saw that those who were struggling could not be saved without help, and so he offered medicine to the sick. Therefore, he provided the means of recovery to everyone, so that if anyone should perish, he would have no one to blame for this but himself for refusing the cure. For the means of healing is available, the mercy of Christ is preached and manifested to everyone, so that those who perish, perish because of their own negligence, whereas those who are saved are delivered according to the statement of Christ, "who desires all people to be saved and to come to a knowledge of the truth."[40] CAIN AND ABEL 2.3.11.[41]

GOD SAVES THOSE WHO WANT TO BE SAVED. AMBROSIASTER: God wants everyone to be saved, but only if they come to him. He does not want those who are unwilling to be saved, though he wants to save them if they so desire. For the one who gave the Law to everyone has not excluded anyone from salvation. Does not a doctor declare publicly that he is willing to heal everyone, as long as he is asked to do so by those who are sick? For salvation

---

[32]PG 46:184-85. [33]Mt 18:7. [34]PG 58:573-74; cf. NPNF 1 10:364. [35]1 Tim 2:4. [36]PG 51:144. [37]PG 48:810-11. [38]Rom 8:29. [39]PL 16:665. [40]1 Tim 2:4. [41]PL 14:346.

means nothing if it is granted to those who do not want it. On 1 Timothy 2:4.[42]

The Preservation of Human Free Will. Jerome: "Lest perhaps they may hear and be converted."[43] The ambiguous word *perhaps* is not appropriate to the majesty of the Lord, but it expresses the human standpoint, so that the free will of humanity is preserved and people are not forced to do or not do something as of necessity, because of divine foreknowledge. Commentary on Jeremiah 5.26.3.[44]

God's Providential Workings. Augustine: It is possible to say that God rested from his creating activity once he had made the world and that he has never made anything new since that time, but at the same time we must say that God continues to govern the things that he made at the beginning and not suppose that on the seventh day he simply gave up controlling all the things in heaven and on earth that he had made by his power. On the Literal Interpretation of Genesis 4.12.22.[45]

Why Did God Create People Who Would Be Condemned to Hell? Augustine: Why did God create people whom he knew would be condemned to hell and not saved by his grace? The blessed apostle explains this as succinctly and as authoritatively as he can when he says . . . that it would indeed be unjust if God had made vessels of wrath for perdition,[46] if they had not belonged to the universal race of the condemned that descends from Adam. What is made a vessel of wrath by birth receives its deserved punishment, but what is made a vessel of mercy by rebirth receives undeserved grace. Epistle 190.3.9.[47]

Those Who Are Saved Are Saved Only in Christ. Augustine: Scripture says, "Even so in Christ shall all be made alive."[48] This means that even though there are a great many

people who will be punished with eternal death, all those who receive eternal life receive it in and through Christ, and in no other way. Likewise the verse that says "God wants everyone to be saved"[49] means that although there are a great many people whom he does not want to be saved, those who are saved are saved only because he wants them to be. Letter 217.6.19.[50]

We Can Be Saved Only If God Wants Us to Be. Augustine: "No one can come to me unless it is given to him by my Father."[51] Therefore all those who are saved and come to a knowledge of the truth are saved because God wills it. They come because God wills it. There are those who, like small children, are born again by the will of their Creator, even before they come to the age of discretion. By contrast, those who have reached the age of discretion cannot will their own salvation unless God wills it and comes to help them achieve it by preparing their will for it. Against Julian 4.8.44.[52]

Divine Foreknowledge and Human Memory. Augustine: Just as your memory does not make you force past events to take place, so God's foreknowledge does not force him to bring about events in the future. And just as you remember some of the things that you have done in the past but have not actually done all the things you remember, so God knows in advance everything that he will do but is not thereby the doer of everything that he knows beforehand. For he is not the wicked doer of evil things but the just avenger of them. On Free Will 3.4.11.[53]

God Knows What He Will Do Before He Does it. Augustine: In God's wisdom

[42]PL 17:466. [43]Jer 26:3. [44]PL 24:844. [45]PL 34:304. [46]See Rom 9:20. [47]PL 33:359-60. [48]1 Cor 15:22. [49]1 Tim 2:4. [50]PL 33:985-86. [51]Jn 6:65. [52]PL 44:760. [53]PL 32:1276.

all the plans he has for making things can be found, even before they are actually made. For all things are made by his wisdom, but it is not itself made, because it is the Word of which it is said, "All things were made through him."[54] For God knew everything that he has made even before he made it. For we cannot say that he has made things of which he was totally ignorant and then taught us about them as if they had not yet been made. To Orosius 8.9.[55]

God Foreknew the Sin of Adam. Augustine: God knew in advance that the will of Adam and Eve would become bad. He knew this, and because his foreknowledge cannot be mistaken, it was not his will but theirs that was evil. Why then did he create them, when he knew that they would turn out like that? Because, just as he knew that they would do something wicked, so he also knew that he would do something good with the wickedness that they had committed. He made them in such a way as to leave it up to them what to do, and at the same time whatever they might choose to do sinfully, they would find that he was using their misdeeds to bring glory to himself. So they had their own evil will, but they received both a good nature and a just punishment from God. On the Literal Interpretation of Genesis 11.9.12.[56]

God Planned to Use Adam's Sin for His Own Good Purposes. Augustine: If God had wanted to preserve the first man in the good estate in which he had created him and to lead him on to better things at the right time, after he had had children and before the coming of death, so that not only would he not have committed sin but he would not even have wanted to sin, Adam would have desired to remain without sin, just as he had been created, and God would have known in advance that he would have the will to do so. But because God knew that Adam would misuse his free will and that he would sin, he prepared his

own will for that eventuality, so that he might do something good even when Adam had done the opposite. Thus the good desire of the Almighty was not destroyed by the evil will of humanity, but fulfilled. Enchiridion 104.[57]

Those Who Are Not Saved by Grace. Augustine: Those who have never heard the gospel, those who have heard it and who have been changed for the better by it but who have not received the grace of perseverance, those who have heard the gospel and who have failed to respond, . . . those who were too young to believe and who died without baptism—all these are exactly the same as the great mass of those who are condemned. . . . Some are made different, however, not by their own merits but by the grace of the Mediator; that is to say, they are justified freely in the blood of the second Adam. . . . No one can earn this status; it is a gift of God, and those who have it have received it by divine grace. On Rebuke and Grace 7(12).[58]

All Who Are Predestined Will Be Saved. Augustine: The apostle Paul says, "To those who love God all things work together for good, to them who are called according to his purpose. Those whom he foreknew he predestined to be conformed to the image of his Son, that he might be the firstborn of many brothers. Those whom he predestined he also called, and those whom he called he justified, and those whom he justified he glorified."[59] None of these can perish because they are all elect. They are elect because they were called according to God's purpose, of which Paul says, "That the purpose of God according to election might stand not of works but of him who calls, it was said to her that the elder should serve the younger."[60] . . . The elect are obviously also called, but not everyone who

---

[54]Jn 1:3. [55]PL 42:674. [56]PL 34:434. [57]PL 40:281. [58]PL 44:923; cf. NPNF 1 5:476. [59]Rom 8:28-30. [60]Rom 9:11-12.

is called is elect. Those who are elect are called according to God's purpose, and they are also predestined and foreknown. If any of them perishes, God is mistaken, but of course none of them perishes, because God is not mistaken. If any of them perishes, God is overcome by human sin, but none of them perishes, because God is overcome by nothing. ON REBUKE AND GRACE 7(14).[61]

GOD'S GRACE IS BEYOND OUR UNDERSTANDING.

AUGUSTINE: It is amazing that God regenerates some people in Christ and gives them the gifts of faith, hope and love, yet does not add to these the gift of perseverance, when at the same time there are others whose wickedness he forgives and by bestowing his grace on them, makes them his children. Is this not amazing? . . . It is also true that some children of believers die without baptism, though God can certainly make up for this later if he so desires, since he can do anything. Yet it seems that he alienates children from the kingdom into which he has brought their parents, whereas others who are children of his enemies, he brings into the kingdom. He does this in spite of the fact that in the former case, the children have deserved nothing bad, whereas in the latter case they have deserved nothing good. The judgments of God are righteous and deep and can neither be blamed nor penetrated. So too is the mystery of perseverance, which can only lead us to exclaim, "O the depth of the riches of the wisdom and knowledge of God. How unsearchable are his judgments."[62] ON REBUKE AND GRACE 8(18).[63]

THE ORIGIN OF EVIL IS PART OF GOD'S FOREKNOWLEDGE.

AUGUSTINE: The God and Lord of all things, who in his strength created all things good, and foreknew that evil things would arise out of good and knew that it pertained to his almighty goodness to do good out of evil things rather than not to allow evil things to exist at all, so ordained the life of angels and people that he might first of all show what their free will was capable of and then what the kindness of his grace and the judgment of his righteousness could do to put things right. ON REBUKE AND GRACE 10(27).[64]

THE NUMBER OF THE SAVED IS FIXED.

AUGUSTINE: The number of those who are predestined to the kingdom of God is so certain that there is not one who can be added to or subtracted from it—not even one of those who, after he had preached and spoken, were multiplied beyond number. They may be said to be called but not chosen, because they are not called according to the purpose. That their number is fixed . . . is proved also by the following verse in the book of Revelation: "Hold fast to what you have, lest someone else should take your crown."[65] If it is impossible for another person to receive a crown unless someone should first lose it, the overall number of those with crowns is clearly fixed. ON REBUKE AND GRACE 13(39).[66]

THE REPROBATE ARE JUSTLY PUNISHED FOR THEIR SINS.

AUGUSTINE: Those who do not belong to the number of the predestined are . . . most justly judged according to their deservings. Either they lie under the sin that they have inherited from Adam and die without having had that debt put away by regeneration, or they have added further sins to the original one by their own free will. This will is free but not freed—it is free from righteousness but enslaved to sin. . . . Because they have not received the gift of perseverance, they are sent away by the righteous and hidden judgment of God. ON REBUKE AND GRACE 13(42).[67]

---

[61]PL 44:924; cf. NPNF 1 5:477. [62]Rom 11:33. [63]PL 44:926-27; cf. NPNF 1 5:478-79. [64]PL 44:932; cf. NPNF 1 5:482. [65]Rev 3:11. [66]PL 44:940; cf. NPNF 1 5:487-88. [67]PL 44:942; cf. NPNF 1 5:489.

In What Way God Wills Everyone to Be Saved. Augustine: It is written, "He wills all people to be saved,"[68] but all people are not saved. This may be understood in a number of different ways, . . . but here I will say one thing above all else. . . . It refers to all those who are predestined, since they come from every kind of human being. It was said to the Pharisees, "You tithe every herb,"[69] which clearly means that they tithed every herb that they had, not every herb that exists. Similarly, it also says, "I please all people in all things,"[70] which does not mean that Paul went out of his way to please his persecutors but rather that he pleased every type of person who gathered in Christ's church, whether they were established believers or newcomers. On Rebuke and Grace 14(44).[71]

God Wants Us to Desire the Salvation of Everyone. Augustine: In our ignorance of who exactly will be saved, God commands us to desire this for everyone to whom we preach the gospel and works this in us by diffusing that love in our hearts by the Holy Spirit, who is given to us. On Rebuke and Grace 15(47).[72]

Why God Does Not Teach Everyone the Way of Salvation. Augustine: Why does God not teach everyone the way of salvation in Christ? It must surely be because those whom he teaches, he teaches in mercy, whereas those whom he does not teach, he judges. "He has mercy on those whom he chooses, and he hardens those whom he chooses."[73] When he gives good things he has mercy, but when he repays people what they deserve he hardens them. Predestination of the Saints 8.14.[74]

Christ Foreknew Who Would Be Saved. Augustine: What can be more true than that Christ knew beforehand who would be saved, and where and when they should be converted? I do not think there is any need to discuss whether this would come about by their own preaching of Christ to themselves or only through a direct gift from God—in other words, did God merely know in advance that they would be saved, or did he actually predestine them? . . . Christ willed to appear to the human race at the time that he did, and that his gospel should be preached among those whom he knew, who had in fact been elected in him before the foundation of the world. Predestination of the Saints 9.18.[75]

The Difference Between Predestination and Grace. Augustine: The only way anyone can merit salvation is by God's grace and predestination. The difference between these two things is that predestination is the preparation for grace, whereas grace is the gift itself. When the apostle Paul says, "Not of works, lest anyone should boast. For we are his workmanship, created in Christ Jesus for good works,"[76] it is grace, but what follows ("which God has prepared, that we should walk in them") is predestination, which cannot exist without foreknowledge, although foreknowledge may exist without predestination, because God foreknew by predestination those things that he was about to do. . . . Moreover, he is able to foreknow even things that he does not do—like sins. Predestination of the Saints 10.19.[77]

The Twofold Calling. Augustine: God calls many predestined children of his in order to make them members of his only predestined Son. He does not do this with the calling with which those who would not come to the marriage were called,[78] since that was the calling with which he called the Jews, to whom Christ

---

[68]1 Tim 2:4. [69]Lk 11:42. [70]1 Cor 10:33. [71]PL 44:943; cf. NPNF 1 5:489. [72]PL 44:945; cf. NPNF 1 5:491. [73]Rom 9:18. [74]PL 44:971; cf. NPNF 1 5:505. [75]PL 44:974; cf. NPNF 1 5:507. [76]Eph 2:9-10. [77]PL 44:974-75; cf. NPNF 1 5:507. [78]See Mt 22:3.

crucified is an offense, and also the Gentiles, to whom Christ crucified is foolishness. Rather, he called them with that calling that the apostle distinguished when he said that he preached Christ, the wisdom of God and the power of God, to all who were called, both Jews and Greeks.[79] He says "unto those who were called"[80] in order to show that there were some who were not called, knowing that there is a certain sure calling of those who are called according to God's purpose, whom he has foreknown and predestined to be conformed to the image of his Son. PREDESTINATION OF THE SAINTS 16.32.[81]

THE ELECT ARE CALLED. AUGUSTINE: The Lord says, "You have not chosen me, but I have chosen you."[82] If they had been chosen because they already believed, then they would have chosen him first by believing in him, in order to deserve their election. But by saying this, Jesus takes this supposition away. At the same time it is quite clear that in fact they did choose him when they believed, but this was because he had first chosen them for belief. . . . His mercy stepped in beforehand according to his grace, and not because of some debt which he owed to their choice of him. He chose them out of the world while he was in the flesh, but they had already been chosen by him from before the foundation of the world. This is the changeless truth concerning predestination and grace. PREDESTINATION OF THE SAINTS 17.34.[83]

THOSE WHOM GOD WANTED TO MAKE RIGHTEOUS. AUGUSTINE: "He has chosen us in himself before the foundation of the world, that we might by holy and unblemished."[84] It was not because we were going to be holy, but so that we might become holy, . . . that he predestined us by his grace. . . . In this mystery of his will he placed the riches of his grace, according to his good pleasure, not according to ours, which could not possibly be good unless

he himself, according to his own good pleasure, should help it become so. PREDESTINATION OF THE SAINTS 18.36.[85]

THE BEGINNING OF FAITH IS GOD'S GIFT. AUGUSTINE: The faith of the Ephesians was new and followed on the preaching of the gospel to them, and when the apostle Paul heard of it, he gave thanks to God on their behalf.[86] Now if he were to give thanks to a person for something that he thinks or knows that that person has not given, it would be flattery or mockery, not a true giving of thanks. But God is not mocked.[87] His gift is also the beginning of faith, unless Paul's giving of thanks is mistaken or fallacious. . . . It would be pointless for him to give thanks to someone who had not done the work concerned, and because this thanksgiving is not a waste of time, it must mean that God had done what he is being thanked for. When the Ephesians heard the word, they heard it not as the word of people but as the word of God. God therefore works in the hearts of people by calling them according to his purpose, that they should not hear the gospel in vain but should be converted and believe, receiving it not as the words of people but as the word of God, which in truth it is. PREDESTINATION OF THE SAINTS 19.39.[88]

WHY GOD WANTS US TO PRAY. AUGUSTINE: God wanted to be asked that we should not be led into temptation, because if we are not led, we do not depart from him. He might have done this for us without our praying for it, but by our prayer he wanted us to be reminded from whom we receive this benefit. . . . The church should not look for quarrels about this kind of thing but consider its own daily prayers. We pray that the unbelieving may

---

[79]1 Cor 1:22-25. [80]1 Cor 1:24. [81]PL 44:983; cf. NPNF 1 5:513. [82]Jn 15:16. [83]PL 44:985; cf. NPNF 1 5:515. [84]Eph 1:4. [85]PL 44:987; cf. NPNF 1 5:516. [86]Eph 1:13. [87]See Gal 6:7. [88]PL 44:989; cf. NPNF 1 5:517.

believe, and because of that, God wins people to the faith. We pray that believers may persevere, and so God gives perseverance to the end. God knew in advance that he would do this. This is the very predestination of the saints, whom he has chosen in Christ from before the foundation of the world.[89] ON THE GIFT OF PERSEVERANCE 7.15.[90]

WHY IS ONE TAKEN AND ANOTHER LEFT?

AUGUSTINE: Why is it that of two infants, each of whom is bound by original sin, one is taken and the other left? Why is it that of two wicked people of maturer years, one should be called to follow Christ and not the other? The judgments of God are unsearchable. Even more, why is it that of two godly people, one is granted perseverance to the end while the other falls by the wayside? Here the judgments of God are even more unsearchable! Yet to believers it ought to be crystal clear that in each case, the former is predestined to eternal life and the latter is not. One of the predestined, who had learned this secret from the Lord's breast, put it like this: "If they had been of us, certainly they would have remained with us."[91] . . . Both were created by God and born of Adam. Both had been called and had followed the one who called them. Both had been converted from wickedness to righteousness, and both had been born again. . . . All this is true, and to that extent, both belonged to us. Yet with respect to another distinction they were not both of us, for if they had been, then they would both have remained with us. What then is that distinction? God's books lie open; let us not turn away our view. The divine Scripture cries aloud, let us give it a hearing. They were not of us because they were not called according to the purpose, they had not been chosen in Christ from before the foundation of the world, they had not gained an inheritance in him, they had not been predestined according to the purpose of him who works all things. If they had been, then they would have been of

us and they would have remained with us. ON THE GIFT OF PERSEVERANCE 9.21.[92]

GOD'S WAYS ARE PAST FINDING OUT.

AUGUSTINE: "His judgments are unsearchable, and his ways are past finding out; all the ways of the Lord are mercy and truth."[93] God's mercy is past finding out. He has mercy on those whom he wants to have mercy, without any merit of the recipient. Likewise, the truth by which he hardens whom he wills, even when the person concerned may have done meritorious works, is beyond our understanding. . . . There is no unrighteousness with God, but his ways are past finding out. Therefore, let us believe in his mercy in the case of those who are delivered and in his truth in the case of those who are punished, without any hesitation, and let us not try to look into what is inscrutable or to trace what cannot be discovered. ON THE GIFT OF PERSEVERANCE 11.25.[94]

GOD GIVES GRACE TO BELIEVE AND TO PERSEVERE.

AUGUSTINE: The grace of God, which is given both to believe and to persevere to the end, is not given according to our merits but according to his most secret and at the same time most righteous, wise and beneficent will. . . . No one can be said with certainty to belong to this calling until he has departed this life, because as long as we are here on earth we must take heed lest we fall.[95] Since those who will not persevere . . . are mingled together with those who will, we must learn not to be proud but to be humble and to "work out our own salvation in fear and trembling, for it is God who works in us both to will and to do his good pleasure."[96] We therefore will, but God also works in us to will. We work, but God also works in us to work for his good pleasure. We must believe and say this because

---

[89]Eph 1:4. [90]PL 45:1001-2; cf. NPNF 1 5:531. [91]1 Jn 2:19. [92]PL 45:1004-5; cf. NPNF 1 5:532-33. [93]Ps 25:10; Rom 11:33. [94]PL 45:1007-8; cf. NPNF 1 5:534-35. [95]1 Cor 10:12. [96]Phil 2:12-13.

it is godly and true. Our confession must be humble and submissive, and all the glory should be given to God. On the Gift of Perseverance 13.33.[97]

What Predestination Is. Augustine: Would anyone dare say that God did not foreknow those to whom he would give the power to believe or whom he would give to his Son, that he should lose none?[98] If he foreknew these things, he must also have foreknown his own kindness, which he continues to bestow on us. This is the predestination of the saints—nothing else; to wit, the knowledge and the preparation of those kindnesses of God by which those who are to be delivered are saved. And where are the rest left by the righteous divine judgment, if not in the mass of ruin where the people of Tyre and Sidon were left? They might have believed if they had seen Christ's miracles, but since they were not predestined to believe, the means of believing were also denied to them.[99] From this it appears that some have in their understanding itself a naturally divine gift of intelligence by which they may be moved to faith, if they hear the words or see the signs that correspond to what is already in their minds. But if, in the higher judgment of God, they are not separated from the mass of perdition by the predestination of grace, neither those divine words nor those deeds reach them in order that they might believe. Even the Jews were left in this mass of ruin because they could not believe the great and mighty works that were done among them. . . . The Gospel itself[100] explains the reason for this by quoting the prophet Isaiah, who said, "Lord, who has believed our report, and to whom has the arm of the Lord been revealed?"[101] They could not believe because, as Isaiah said again: "God has blinded their eyes and hardened their heart, that they should not see with their eyes or understand with their hearts and be converted and I should heal them."[102] . . . No one comes to Christ unless it

is given to him to do so, and it is given to those who have been chosen from before the foundation of the world. On the Gift of Perseverance 14.35.[103]

Why Prayer Is Necessary. Augustine: There are some people who either do not pray at all or else pray half-heartedly, because they have learned from the Lord's own words that God knows what we need before we ask him, and so why should they bother?[104] Should we drop this belief and take it out of the gospel merely because of these people? Of course not! It is clear that God has prepared some things, like conversion, to be given to those who have not prayed for them, but it is equally clear that other things will not be given to us unless we pray for them, notably the gift of perseverance to the end. Obviously someone who thinks he already has this gift in himself will see no need to pray for it. Therefore we must be careful not to stifle prayer and encourage arrogance because we are afraid that our exhortation to the former may grow lukewarm [if we feel that it is not needed.] On the Gift of Perseverance 16.39.[105]

We Must Preach the Doctrine of Predestination. Augustine: Either predestination must be preached in the way and degree in which the holy Scripture plainly declares it, so that the gifts and calling of God might be without repentance in those who are predestined, or it must be said that God's gifts are given according to our merits, which is the opinion of the Pelagians. . . . Grace precedes faith, because if it were the other way around, then the will would certainly precede faith, because there cannot be faith without will. But if grace precedes faith because it precedes will, it must certainly precede all obedience

[97]PL 45:1012-13; cf. NPNF 1 5:538. [98]Jn 18:9. [99]See Mt 11:21. [100]See Jn 12:37-38. [101]Is 53:1. [102]Is 6:10. [103]PL 45:1014; cf. NPNF 1 5:539. [104]Mt 6:8. [105]PL 45:1017; cf. NPNF 1 5:541.

and love, by which alone God is truly obeyed. Grace brings about all these things in those to whom it is given, and therefore it must precede all these things. On the Gift of Perseverance 16.41.[106]

THE CONDEMNATION OF THE APPARENTLY INNOCENT. AUGUSTINE: God is good, God is just. He can save people without good works because he is good, but he cannot condemn anyone without evil works, because he is just. A child who is only eight days old cannot have done any evil works himself, so why is he condemned if he is not circumcised? The reason is that he was condemned from the beginning [regardless of any works.] AGAINST JULIAN 3.18.35.[107]

THE SIN OF ADAM EXTENDS TO EVERYONE. AUGUSTINE: "We were all in Adam, and when he perished, we all perished."[108] But you say that no one should have perished because of someone else's sin. It is true that Adam's sin was the sin of another person, but he is our ancestor, and for this reason his sins are ours, by the law of insemination and reproduction. Who can deliver us from this perdition, except the one who came to seek and to save that which was lost? Therefore we find mercy in those whom he sets free but recognize the most secret judgment of God on those whom he does not set free, and we also know that this judgment is very just. AGAINST JULIAN (FRAGMENT) 1.48.[109]

GOD'S CONDEMNATION IS ALWAYS JUST. AUGUSTINE: What I see the apostle most clearly teaching is what I hold to be true, which is that all human beings are headed toward condemnation because they are born of Adam, unless they are reborn in Christ. Furthermore, God has provided that they should be born again before they die, and he is the most generous donor of grace to those whom he has predestined to eternal life, just as he

is the most righteous avenger on those whom he has predestined to eternal death, and not merely against those who have done something wrong but also against infants who have not done anything at all, because of their original sin. This is how I understand the matter; the hidden works of God have their secret that I believe by faith. On the Soul 4.11.16.[110]

GOD IS NOT RESPONSIBLE FOR SIN. PROSPER OF AQUITAINE: Just as good works can be attributed to God who inspires them, so bad works must be attributed to those who sin. No one is abandoned by God in order that the person might then abandon him, but people have abandoned him and are abandoned and have been changed from good into evil by their own will. Even if some of them have subsequently been born again and justified, they may not be predestined because God did not know them from the beginning. REPLIES TO OBJECTIONS 3.[111]

GOD KNEW THAT PEOPLE WOULD SIN. CYRIL OF ALEXANDRIA: God knows the future, not just when it happens, but even before the foundation of the world, he knew what was coming in the last days. Therefore, when he made things as they ought to be, it was not after we were made, but long before, that he planned out everything to do with us. Even before he made the heavens and the earth, he knew all about us. Indeed, he grounded his Son in his foreknowledge so that we, who would fall into corruption through our sins, might rise again and be built on him in incorruption. For God knew that we would perish because of sin. THESAURUS ON THE TRINITY 15.[112]

JUDAS WAS CHOSEN, YET HE FELL. CYRIL OF ALEXANDRIA: Christ chose Judas and

---

[106]PL 45:1018; cf. NPNF 1 5:542. [107]PL 44:721. [108]See Rom 5:12. [109]PL 45:1071. [110]PL 44:533-34. [111]PL 51:159. [112]PG 75:292.

made him one of his holy disciples, because he at first seemed to be an ideal follower. But a little while later Satan tempted him with filthy lucre, . . . and then Jesus dismissed him because he had turned traitor as a result. But the one who chose him in the first place bore no responsibility for this. Commentary on John 9.[113]

God's Foreknowledge Does Not Imply Direct Causation. Theodoret of Cyr: Those whose intention God foreknew he predestined from the beginning. Those who are predestined he called and justified by baptism. Those who were justified he glorified, calling them children. . . . Let no one say that God's foreknowledge was the unilateral cause of these things. It was not his foreknowledge that justified people, but God knew what would happen, because he is God. Commentary on Romans 8.30.[114]

Those Who Are Predestined to Condemnation. Fulgentius of Ruspe: God could, if he wished, predestine some to glory and others to punishment. But those whom he predestined to glory, he predestined to righteousness. Those whom he predestined to punishment, however, he did not predestine to guilt. A sin might be attributed to the predestination of God if it were possible to sin justly. But no one sins justly, even if God rightly allows him to sin. Therefore God justly abandons those who have abandoned him. To Monimus 1.13.[115]

The Promise of Future Rewards and Punishments. Fulgentius of Ruspe: God predicted and promised that the righteous would enjoy their reward; he did not promise but predicted that the unrighteous would be punished. Nor did he predestine the unrighteous to turn away from the righteousness that he predestined the saints to receive, because the merciful and righteous God could free

whomever he chose from the bondage of sin. He himself has never been the cause of sin, because no one has even been a sinner except in so far as he has turned away from God. God did not predestine this turning away, although his divine understanding knew in advance that it would happen. To Monimus 1.25.[116]

God Gives His Grace to Those Who Are Predestined. Fulgentius of Ruspe: Grace and the beginning of good will are given to us so that we may believe, and help is provided to our will so that it may accomplish the good that it wants to do. For God, who created humankind, has by his own predestination prepared the gift of enlightenment for the purpose of believing, the gift of perseverance for the purpose of growing in grace and remaining in it and the gift of glorification so that those whom he wills may reign with him forever. No one can achieve these things other than as they have been determined by his eternal and unchangeable will. Letter 17.67.[117]

Providence Is the Care God Takes Over Existing Things. John of Damascus: Providence is the care that God takes over existing things. It is the will of God through which all existing things receive their due consummation. If providence is God's will, then it follows that everything that comes into being through it must be so fair and so excellent that it cannot be surpassed. The creator and sustainer of all creation must be the same person, since it is not fitting for one to create and another to sustain what has been created. If there were two separate persons, both would be imperfect, since the creator would not be able to sustain his creation, and the sustainer would not be able to create. Orthodox Faith 2.29.[118]

[113]PG 74:129. [114]PG 82:141-44. [115]PL 65:162. [116]PL 65:172. [117]PL 65:492-93. [118]PG 94:964; cf. NPNF 2 9.2:41.

GOD DOES NOT PREDETERMINE EVERYTHING. JOHN OF DAMASCUS: We ought to understand that while God knows everything beforehand, he does not predetermine everything. He knows beforehand what things are in our power, but he does not predetermine them. It is not his will that there should be wickedness, nor does he choose to compel virtue in such a way as to make predetermination the work of a divine command based on foreknowledge. However, God determines those things that are not in our power, in accordance with his foreknowledge. God has already judged everything in accordance with his goodness and justice. ORTHODOX FAITH 2.30.[119]

GOD'S FOREKNOWLEDGE AND OURS. JOHN OF DAMASCUS: The foreknowledge of the powerful God does not depend on us, but knowing in advance what we plan to do does, for if we did not intend to do it, he would not have prescribed it in advance and it would not happen. And yet the foreknowledge of God is true and inviolable, though it is not the cause of everything that happens; rather, he knows in advance that we must do this or that. DIALOGUE AGAINST THE MANICHAEANS 79.[120]

[119]PG 94:969-72; cf. NPNF 2 9.2:42.   [120]PG 94:1577.

OF HEAVEN AND EARTH

πιστεύομεν εἰς ἕνα Θεὸν	Credo in unum Deum	We believe in one God,
πατέρα, παντοκράτορα,	Patrem omnipotentem;	the Father, the Almighty,
ποιητὴν **οὐρανοῦ καὶ γῆς**,	factorem **coeli et terrae,**	maker **of heaven and earth,**
ὁρατῶν τε πάντων καὶ ἀοράτων.	visibilium omnium et invisibilium.	of all that is, seen and unseen.

HISTORICAL CONTEXT: To counter pagan objections, Christians argued that the intelligent design of the universe presupposes the existence of a supremely intelligent Creator. The complexity of the created order is such that it can hardly have emerged out of chaos by itself. Apparent anomalies, like the superiority of the human race to animals that are bigger and stronger than we are, cannot be explained by chance evolution. Furthermore, Christians maintained that everything in the world was good in and of itself and became evil only through misuse. They also claimed that the creation was not eternal and generally believed that time and space had been made together at the beginning of God's great work. This flew in the face of a commonly held pagan view that matter was eternal and, by its nature, opposed to the spiritual world from the beginning.

OVERVIEW: The order of creation did not evolve naturally out of a primordial chaos but was inherent in it from the beginning (ORIGEN, DIONYSIUS), although the created order contains undeveloped potential that comes to fruition in the course of time (AUGUSTINE). God does not need the world but made it for his own pleasure (LACTANTIUS). The creation was planned by God beforehand and is fundamentally good (AUGUSTINE, JOHN OF DAMASCUS), having been made out of a spirit of love (PSEUDO-DIONYSIUS). It was made for our enjoyment (Tertullian), but it is not eternal (Athanasius, Cyril of Alexandria, Gregory the Great). Time was made on the first day of creation (Augustine) and through the agency of Christ the mediator (Hilary). God exists independently of his creation (Gregory of Nyssa), though he sustains it by the power of his will (Fulgentius, John of Damascus), and the universe is not governed by an impersonal fate (Eusebius). Even though he is said to have rested on the seventh day, he is still at work in maintaining what he has made (Ambrose, Augustine).

The Creation

The Glory of the Six Days' Work. Theophilus of Antioch: No one can give a worthy explanation and description of every aspect of the six days' work; even if he had ten thousand tongues and mouths or lives ten thousand years, he would still not be able to say anything worthy of these things, because of the exceeding greatness and riches of the wisdom of God that can be found in the six days' work narrated in Genesis 1. To Autolycus 2.12.[1]

God Made Everything in a Particular Order. Tertullian: God made all his works in a particular order. First he laid out the raw material, so to speak. Then he fashioned them into their finished beauty. He did not suffuse the light all at once with the splendor of the sun, nor did he immediately modify the darkness with the soothing beam of the moon. He did not at first adorn the heavens with the constellations and stars, nor did he at once fill the seas with teeming monsters. He did not first endow the earth with its different kinds of vegetation but first brought it into existence and then filled it. Against Hermogenes 29.[2]

The Creation Has Definite Limits. Origen: Let us . . . examine the beginning of creation, at least to the extent that it is possible to understand how God's creation began. We must understand that at the beginning, God created the exact number of rational, intellectual creatures . . . that he thought would be sufficient. It is certain that he made a definite number of them, and that number was predetermined by him. We cannot imagine, as some have supposed, that creatures have no limit, because where there is no limit there can be no comprehension. If that were the case, created things could neither be restrained nor administered by God, for whatever is infinite is also incomprehensible. Scripture says, "God has arranged everything in number and measure,"[3] which means that there is a definite number of rational creatures, which can then be arranged, governed and controlled by God. On First Principles 2.9.1.[4]

The Creation Story Is Symbolic. Origen: Who would think that the first, second and third days of creation, which include an evening and a morning, could have existed without sun, moon and stars? Who would think that the first day was without a sky? . . . No one doubts that these things are figures that speak of certain mysteries, the history having occurred symbolically and not literally. On First Principles 4.1.16.[5]

Wild Beasts. Origen: Lions, bears, leopards, wild boars and similar beasts have been given to us in order to bring out our latent manly character. Against Celsus 4.78.[6]

We Have Much to Learn from Irrational Animals. Origen: We should admire the divine power that gave even irrational animals the ability to imitate rational beings, perhaps in order to put us to shame. For

---

[1]PG 6:1069; cf. ANF 2:99. [2]PL 2:222-23; cf. ANF 3:493. [3]Wis 11:20. [4]PG 11:225-26; cf. ANF 4:289. [5]PG 11:377; cf. ANF 4:365. [6]PG 11:1152; cf. ANF 4:532.

example, by looking at ants, human beings might become more industrious and more thrifty in the management of their possessions. By considering the bees, they might subject themselves to their ruler and play their proper part in the government that ensures the safety of cities. AGAINST CELSUS 4.81.[7]

GOD MADE EVERYTHING OUT OF NOTHING.
HIPPOLYTUS: The one and only God . . . had nothing equally eternal with himself. There was no infinite chaos, no measureless water, no solid earth, no dense air, no warm fire, no refined spirit, no azure canopy covering the firmament. He was one, alone in himself. By an exercise of his will he created things that are, which previously had no existence, except that he willed to make them. For he is fully acquainted with whatever is about to take place, since foreknowledge is also present to him. First of all he made the different elements out of which everything else would then come into being—fire, spirit, water and earth. He formed some objects from a single element, but others he made compounds of two, three and four of them. Those formed from a single element were immortal, since they can never be dissolved into their component parts. Those that are compounds however can be dissolved, which is why they are termed mortal. The dissolution of the elements has been called death. I think that I have now given an explanation of creation that will satisfy any rational person. REFUTATION OF ALL HERESIES 10.32(28).[8]

WHO OWNS THE WORLD? ARNOBIUS OF SICCA: Does it not occur to you to reflect and to examine whose property it is that you live on? Who owns the earth that you cultivate? Who owns the air that you breathe? Who owns the fountains that you enjoy in such abundance? Whose water is it? . . . O great and supreme Creator of all things, you alone are truly worthy, if only mortal tongue could speak of you! All breathing, intelligent crea-

tures should constantly be thankful to you and say so. AGAINST THE NATIONS 1.30-31.[9]

ORDER DID NOT EVOLVE NATURALLY.
DIONYSIUS OF ALEXANDRIA: Who can stand to hear it said that this mighty universe, which is composed of heaven and earth, . . . was established in all its order and beauty by those atoms that keep their course, a course that in itself is devoid of order and beauty? Who can bear the thought that a state of disorder has naturally evolved into an orderly universe? FRAGMENT 3 FROM THE BOOKS OF NATURE.[10]

CREATED BY A HIGHER INTELLIGENCE. LACTANTIUS: There is no one so uncivilized and ignorant who, when he looks up to the heavens, . . . does not understand from the very size of the objects, from their motion, arrangement, consistency, usefulness, beauty and disposition, that there is some providence and that the things that exist in such wonderful order must have been created by some higher intelligence. . . . Why do we need many to govern the universe, unless we should happen to think that if there were more than one, each of them would possess varying degrees of might and strength? This is what polytheists imagine, but God, who is the eternal mind, is undoubtedly excellent, complete and perfect in every part. If that is true, then he must of necessity be one, since absolute power or excellence has its own particular integrity. DIVINE INSTITUTES 1.2-1.3.[11]

GOD DOES NOT NEED THE WORLD. LACTANTIUS: It cannot be said that God made the world for his own sake, since he can exist without the world. . . . It is obvious, therefore, that the world was made for the benefit of living beings, since it is those beings who enjoy what it contains. DIVINE INSTITUTES 7.4.[12]

---

[7]PG 11:1153-56; cf. ANF 4:533. [8]PG 16/3:3446-47; cf. ANF 5:150. [9]PL 5:754-75; cf. ANF 6:420-21. [10]PG 10:1253; cf. ANF 6:86. [11]PL 6:121-22; cf. ANF 7:11. [12]PL 6:747; cf. ANF 7:198.

THE UNIVERSE IS NOT SUBJECT TO FATE AS A LAW OF NATURE. EUSEBIUS OF CAESAREA: In their folly, the great majority of people ascribe the regulation of the universe to "nature," though some think that fate or accident is the cause. As far as those who attribute everything to fate are concerned, do they not know that in saying this they are just uttering a word that does not stand for any active power or anything that has real or active existence? What can this "fate" be, if nature is the first cause of all things? What is nature, indeed, if we think that the law of fate is inviolable? The very assertion that there is a law of fate implies that the law is the work of a lawgiver, and so if fate is a law, it must have been devised by God. All things therefore are subject to God, and nothing is beyond the sphere of his power. If it is said that fate is the will of God, we admit the fact but must ask how justice, self-control or the other virtues can depend on it. . . . Vice has its origin in nature, and virtue is the proper regulation of natural character and disposition. . . . What happens to us depends on the way we live our lives, [and not on some impersonal fate]. God delights in goodness but turns away from all ungodliness. He accepts the humble spirit but abhors presumption and rejects that pride that exalts itself above what is seemly for a creature. THE ORATION OF CONSTANTINE 6.[13]

GOD AND HUMANITY BOTH CREATE. ATHANASIUS: God creates, and human beings are also said to create. God has being, and so do we, having received this gift from God as well. But does God create the way we do? Is his being like ours? Certainly not! We understand these terms in one way when we are talking about God and in another way when we are talking about ourselves. When God creates, he does so out of nothing, but when we create, . . . we can do so only out of some preexisting material. Similarly, we are incapable of self-

existence and are limited in time and space, whereas God is self-existent and unlimited in that way. . . . Because of these basic differences and in line with them, generation in God means something different from what is implied in human birth. DEFENSE OF THE NICENE DEFINITION 11.[14]

GOD CREATED EVERYTHING OUT OF NOTHING. ATHANASIUS: If God did not make matter but was able only to fashion things out of preexisting substances, he would be weak, because he would be unable to produce anything without the material at hand. . . . If that material had not existed, then God would never have made anything! In that case, how could he be called the creator and designer? On such a theory, God would be a mere mechanic and not a creator out of nothing. It really makes no sense to call him a creator, unless he also created the matter out of which everything is actually made. ON THE INCARNATION 2.4.[15]

"HEAVEN AND EARTH" INCLUDES THE WHOLE WORLD. BASIL THE GREAT: By naming the two extremes of heaven and earth, God indicates the substance of the whole world, granting heaven the privilege of seniority and putting earth in the second rank. All the intermediate beings were created at the same time as the two extremes. Thus, although there is no mention of the elements, fire, water and air, imagine that they were all compounded together, and you will find water, air and fire in the earth. Fire leaps out from stones as we see from iron, which is dug out of the earth and produces fire in plentiful measure when it is struck. Fire lurks hidden in bodies without harming them, but as soon as it is released it consumes what has previously preserved it. The earth contains water,

---

[13]PG 20:1245-48; cf. NPNF 2 1:564. [14]PG 25:433; cf. NPNF 2 4:157. [15]PG 25:100; cf. NPNF 2 4:37.

as diggers of wells teach us. It contains air too, as we see from the vapors that it exhales under the sun's warmth when it is damp. According to their nature, heaven occupies the higher and earth the lower position in space. Everything that is light ascends up toward heaven, and everything that is heavy falls to the ground. Since therefore height and depth are the points most opposed to each other, it is enough to mention the most distant parts in order to include everything that fills the intervening space. Do not ask for a complete list of all the elements—just guess from what holy Scripture indicates, all that is passed over in silence. HOMILIES ON THE HEXAMERON 1.7.[16]

THE LIMITATIONS OF CREATED THINGS.

DIDYMUS THE BLIND: No created thing fills the entire world, or contains everything in itself or exists in everything else. Even intelligent powers have limits and a definite size. Only God fits the description I have just given. ON THE TRINITY 2.6.2.[17]

THE EARTH RESTS ON THE POWER OF

GOD. AMBROSE: The earth is not suspended in the middle of the universe like a balance hung in equilibrium, but God's majesty holds it together by the law of his own will, so that what is fixed might prevail over the void and unstable. The prophet David bears witness to this when he says, "He set the earth on its foundations; it can never be moved."[18] God is revealed not only as an artist but also as one who is almighty, who suspended the earth not from some central point but from the firmament, according to his command, and did not allow it to sway. The measurement did not come from the center but from a divine decree, because it is not a measurement of art but one of power, justice and knowledge. All things do not escape his knowledge as if they were immeasurable but underlie his knowledge as if they were already measured. When we read,

"I have established the pillars thereof,"[19] we cannot believe that the world is actually supported by columns but rather by that power that props up the substance of the earth and sustains it. SIX DAYS OF CREATION 1.6.22.[20]

GOD CREATED IN A UNIQUE WAY. CHRYSOSTOM: Notice how the divine nature shines out of the very way in which the creation was made. Look how God executes it in a way contrary to human procedures, first stretching out the heavens and then laying out the earth beneath, first the roof and then the foundation. Who has ever seen anything like this? Who has ever heard of it? No matter what human beings produce, things could never have happened with us. But when God decides to do something, everything yields to his will and becomes possible. So do not pry too closely into the works of God with your human reasoning. Instead, let the works lead you to marvel at their maker. HOMILIES ON GENESIS 2.3.(11).[21]

GOD CREATED WHAT HE ALREADY KNEW.

AUGUSTINE: God does not know his creatures because they exist; on the contrary, they exist because he knows them. He was not ignorant of what he was about to create and so created what he already knew. Nor did he know them after their creation in any different way than before, because his divine wisdom remained unchanged, and what came into being conformed to that wisdom in every particular. ON THE TRINITY 15.13.22.[22]

CHANGE AND DEVELOPMENT. AUGUSTINE: The heaven and the earth exist and by the fact that they change and are variable, they proclaim that they were made. Whatever has not been made but yet has being has nothing in it that was not there before, but things that are

---

[16]PG 29:20; cf. NPNF 2 8:56. [17]PG 39:509. [18]Ps 104:5. [19]Ps 75:3. [20]PL 14:133; FC 42:21-22. [21]PG 53:30; FC 74:35. [22]PL 42:1076; cf. NPNF 1 3:212.

changeable and varied can and do develop new things. Confessions 11.4.6.[23]

Five Different Interpretations of Genesis 1:1. Augustine: Some people say . . . that when Moses used the word *heaven* he did not mean the spiritual or intellectual creation, which eternally looks on God's face, nor did he intend formless matter when he used the word *earth*. . . . They say that Moses meant to signify in general and concise terms the entire visible world, so that under the successive days he could arrange each category of created being in the way which the Holy Spirit chose to list them. Because the character of the people was rough and carnal, Moses decided to present only the visible works of God to them. However, they also agree that if the words "without form and void" and "dark abyss" refer to formless matter, there is no incongruity. For it was from that that all visible things were created and ordered on the subsequent days, as the following verses show.

Another interpretation suggests that the phrase "heaven and earth" is used by anticipation to mean formless and chaotic matter, since it was out of that that the visible world was created and perfected.

A fourth interpretation might be that "heaven and earth" is a good way of describing invisible and visible nature and that these two words cover the entire created order that God made in his wisdom, that is to say, in the beginning. Nevertheless, everything that exists was made, not out of the substance of God but out of nothing, because they are not being itself (as God is) and they all have a certain mutability, whether they are permanent, like the eternal house of God, or changing, like the human soul and body. So the common material of all things, visible and invisible, is the matter from which heaven and earth originate. On this view, the formless creation is what is intended by the words "without form and void" and "darkness above the abyss," but with the difference that the former phrase means matter before it was given form and shape, whereas the latter phrase means the spiritual realm before its uncontrolled fluidity was checked and before it was enlightened by wisdom.

There is a further interpretation that can be held, which is that in this text the words "heaven and earth" do not mean already perfect and formed natures, whether they are visible or invisible, . . . but a still unformed beginning of things. What these words refer to is a matter capable of being formed and open to creativity. In this primeval state things were confused, but now they have been separated and formed into their own orders. They are called "heaven and earth," the former referring to the spiritual creation and the latter to the physical one. Confessions 12.17.24-26.[24]

The Created Order Is Good. Augustine: By the words "God saw that it was good"[25] it is sufficiently intimated that God made what was made not from any necessity nor for the sake of supplying any want but solely from his own goodness, that is to say, because it was good. This is stated after the creation had taken place, that there might be no doubt that the thing made satisfied the goodness on account of which it was made. And if we are right in understanding that this goodness is the Holy Spirit, then the whole Trinity is revealed to us in the creation. City of God 11.24.[26]

The Goodness of Creation Tells Us of a Good Creator. Augustine: How far can we speak of God's goodness? Who can conceive of this in his heart or apprehend how good the Lord is? Let us therefore look at ourselves and recognize him in us. Let us praise our Maker in his works, because we are unworthy to contemplate him in himself. We

---

[23]PL 32:811; cf. NPNF 1 1:165. [24]PL 32:834-35; cf. NPNF 1 1:182. [25]Gen 1:10. [26]PL 41:338; cf. NPNF 1 2:219.

may hope that one day, when our hearts are purified by faith, we may be able to contemplate him as he is and rejoice in the truth, but for the time being let us look at his works, so that we may not live without praising him. EXPOSITIONS OF THE PSALMS 135(134).4.[27]

EVERYTHING IS CREATED IN ITS OWN WAY. AUGUSTINE: Individual things are all created according to their own principles. And where are these principles decided, if not in the mind of God? For God did not discover something outside himself and then decide to make his creation along those lines; it would be blasphemous to imagine that! Now if the principles of everything that has been or will be created are present in the mind of God, and nothing can exist in God's mind that is not eternal and immutable, and Plato calls these rational principles ideas, then not only are they ideas, but they are true because they are eternal and for that reason are also unchangeable, determining what exists in reality and how it exists. ON EIGHTY-THREE VARIED QUESTIONS 46.2.[28]

GOD KNEW WHAT HE WOULD CREATE. AUGUSTINE: In God's wisdom all the principles of things to be created existed even before they were made. Everything was made by the wisdom of God, but that wisdom was not itself created, since it is the Word of which it is said, "Everything was made through him."[29] For God knew everything he would make even before he made it. For we cannot say that he made things that he knew nothing about or that he knew nothing about anything that he had not already made. TO OROSIUS 8.9.[30]

GOD CREATED EVERYTHING AT THE SAME TIME. AUGUSTINE: Just as the seed contains everything that will later sprout and grow into the tree, so we ought to think of the creation of the world. God created everything at the same time, because everything that he created contained in it whatever it would eventually

produce. ON THE LITERAL INTERPRETATION OF GENESIS 5.23.45.[31]

CREATED WITH PROPER QUALITIES AND LIMITATIONS. AUGUSTINE: The elements of this material world have their own definite quality and power, which determines what they are and what they are not, what can be made out of them and what cannot. From the beginning of time, everything has come into being in its proper order and has decayed and vanished in a similar way. So it is that beans are not produced from grains of wheat, nor is wheat produced from beans. Human beings do not come from cattle, nor cattle from human beings. The power of the Creator is able to alter the movement and course of natural things, . . . but he has not given them the power to do this by themselves. ON THE LITERAL INTERPRETATION OF GENESIS 9.17.32.[32]

THERE ARE NO LIMITS TO GOD. CYRIL OF ALEXANDRIA: There is no place that holds divinity, yet it is absent from nothing at all, for it fills all things, goes through all things, is beyond all things and yet within all things too. COMMENTARY ON JOHN 11.9.[33]

GOD MADE NOTHING EVIL. LEO THE GREAT: The true and universal faith confesses that the substance of all creatures, whether spiritual or material, is good, and that there is no evil nature, because God, who is the creator of the universe, made nothing that was not good. LETTER 15.6.[34]

GOD MADE SCORPIONS. FULGENTIUS OF RUSPE: What is so displeasing about scorpions that anyone should think that they have not been made by God? There is nothing in the body of a scorpion that does not suggest the

---

[27]PL 37:1741; cf. NPNF 1 8:624-25. [28]PL 40:30. [29]Jn 1:3. [30]PL 42:674. [31]PL 34:338. [32]PL 34:406. [33]PG 74:525. [34]PL 54:683.

praise of the Creator. First of all, that bodily structure of members, put together and arranged harmoniously, the symmetry and equality of the parts, then the soul giving life and feeling to the body—who would dispute that these are all good things? Without question, that power of poison that is found to be harmful to human beings is regarded as something to be dreaded in the body of the scorpion. Would that human beings might learn from it to pay attention to the punishment for their transgressions and stop attributing the good works of God to the devil! LETTER TO SCARILA 28.[35]

GOD CREATED THE WORLD OUT OF LOVE.

PSEUDO-DIONYSIUS: True reason will dare to say that the one who is the cause of all things loves everything, makes everything, perfects everything, contains everything and draws everything to himself on account of the excellence of his goodness. The divine love is good because the good is good in itself. DIVINE NAMES 4.10.[36]

THE CREATION HAS BEEN DESIGNED BY GOD.

JOHN OF DAMASCUS: What is it that gave order to things of heaven and things of earth and everything that moves in the air and in the water, or rather, to what was in existence before these were created, namely, heaven and earth and air, and the elements of fire and water? What was it that mingled and distributed these? What set them in motion, and what is it that keeps them in their endless and unchanging course? Was it not the designer of these things, and the one who implanted in everything the law by which the universe is governed and directed? Who then is this Designer? Is it not he who created them and who brought them into existence? Something so complicated could never have come into being spontaneously. Even if we accepted that their existence was spontaneous, who or what put them in order? What is it that keeps them going? This cannot be mere spontaneity, and who

else is there who could have done this, apart from God? ORTHODOX FAITH 1.3.[37] (FOLLOWING GREGORY OF NAZIANZUS THEOLOGICAL ORATIONS 28.16.)[38]

THE CAUSE AND BEGINNING OF EVERYTHING.

JOHN OF DAMASCUS: God is the cause and beginning of all, the essence of all that have essence, the life of the living, the reason of all rational beings, the intellect of all intelligent beings, the recalling and restoring of those who fall away from him, the renovation and transformation of those who are thrown into unholiness, the steadfastness of those who have stood firm, the way of those whose course is directed to him and the hand stretched out to guide them upwards. He is the Father of all his creatures, for the God who brought us into being out of nothing is strictly speaking more our Father than our human parents are, since they too have derived their being from him. ORTHODOX FAITH 1.12.[39]

AN EXPRESSION OF GOD'S GOODNESS.

JOHN OF DAMASCUS: God who is good and more than good did not find satisfaction in self-contemplation, but in his exceeding goodness he wished certain things to come into existence, which would enjoy his benefits and share in his goodness. He therefore brought all things out of nothing into being and created them, both what is visible and what is invisible. ORTHODOX FAITH 2.2.[40]

CERTAIN BASIC ELEMENTS.

JOHN OF DAMASCUS: Our God, whom we glorify as three in one, created the heaven and the earth and all that they contain, and he brought all things into being out of nothing. He made some things out of no preexisting matter, like heaven, earth, air, fire and water, and the rest

---

[35]PL 65:589; FC 95:450. [36]PG 3:708. [37]PG 94:796-97; cf. NPNF 2 9.2:3. [38]PG 36:48; cf. NPNF 2 7:294. [39]PG 94:844; cf. NPNF 2 9.2:13. [40]PG 94:864-65; cf. NPNF 2 9.2:18.

out of these elements that he had created, such as the living creatures, plants and seeds. These are all made up out of earth, air, fire and water, at the command of the Creator. ORTHODOX FAITH 2.5.[41]

Space and Time

GOD'S WORKS ARE NOT ETERNAL. ATHANASIUS: If God was always a maker, and if the power to create things is not accidental to him, does it follow that his works are as eternal as he is? This is a nonsensical argument, and the parallel that the Arians draw between God as Father and God as Creator must be rejected. . . . A work is external to the creator's nature, but a child is an offspring of his parent's being. It follows from this that a work need not always have existed, since the artisan creates it whenever he wants to, but an offspring is not created at will—it belongs to the Father's essence. A person may be called a maker, even before he does his work, but a parent cannot be so called unless and until he produced offspring—the two things go together. If someone wants to know why God always had the power to make things but did not do so in eternity, the answer is given in Scripture as follows: "Who has known the mind of the Lord, or who has been his counselor?"[42] and "Shall the thing formed say to the potter, why did you make me like this?"[43] AGAINST THE ARIANS 1.29.[44]

TIMES AND WORLDS MADE THROUGH CHRIST THE MEDIATOR. HILARY OF POITIERS: There is one mediator between God and humankind, who is himself both God and man—mediator, both in the giving of the Law and in taking on our body.[45] Therefore, no one else can be compared with him, for he is one, born from God into God, and it was through him that all things in heaven and on earth were created, through him also that times and worlds were made. Everything that exists owes its existence to his action. ON THE TRINITY 4.42.[46]

TIME WAS CREATED AT THE BEGINNING OF THE WORLD. AUGUSTINE: If the sacred and infallible Scriptures say that it was in the beginning that God created the heavens and the earth,[47] in order that it might be understood that he had not made anything else before them, . . . then it is clear that the world was not made in the course of time but simultaneously with time itself. Things that are made in time are made in the context of "before" and "after," but when the world was created there was no "before," because there was no creature by which time could have been measured. But the world was made simultaneously with time, if change and motion were created at the same time as the world, which seems clear from the order of the first six or seven days. For on those days the morning and the evening were counted, until all things were finished on the sixth day, and the rest of God was mysteriously and sublimely signified. Of course, what kind of days these were is extremely difficult, even impossible, for us to conceive. CITY OF GOD 11.6.[48]

WHAT IS TIME? AUGUSTINE: Who can explain easily and concisely what time is? Who can comprehend it even in his or her own mind, so as to be able to formulate that conception in words? But what do we speak of in ordinary conversation more often than we speak of time? We surely know what we mean when we speak of it! We also know what is meant when we hear someone else talking about it. But what exactly is time? As long as nobody asks me, I know. If I want to explain it to an inquirer, I do not know. But I can say with complete certainty that I know that if nothing passes away, there is no past time; if nothing arrives, there is no future time; and if nothing existed, there would be no present

---

[41]PG 94:880; cf. NPNF 2, 9.2:21. [42]Rom 11:34. [43]Rom 9:20. [44]PG 26:72; cf. NPNF 2 4:323. [45]1 Tim 2:5. [46]PL 10:128; cf. NPNF 2 9:84. [47]Gen 1:1. [48]PL 41:321-22; cf. NPNF 1 2:208.

time. Look at the past and the future. How can they exist when the past is gone and the future has not yet come? But if the present were always present, it would never vanish into the past. In fact, it would not be time at all, but eternity. But if the present is made in such a way that it must become past, how can we say that it exists? The essence of its being is that it will cease to be! Therefore we cannot really say that time exists, except in the sense that it tends towards nonexistence. CONFESSIONS 11.14.17.[49]

---

[49]PL 32:816; cf. NPNF 1 1:168.

OF ALL THAT IS, SEEN

πιστεύομεν εἰς ἕνα Θεὸν	*Credo in unum Deum*	*We believe in one God,*
πατέρα, παντοκράτορα,	*Patrem omnipotentem;*	*the Father, the Almighty,*
ποιητὴν οὐρανοῦ καὶ γῆς,	*factorem coeli et terrae,*	*maker of heaven and earth,*
ὁρατῶν τε πάντων καὶ ἀοράτων.	**visibilium omnium** *et invisibilium.*	**of all that is, seen** *and unseen.*

HISTORICAL CONTEXT: The human race was the supreme act of God's creation, as is stated in the book of Genesis. This supremacy is not because human beings are the highest of the creatures (a distinction that belongs to angels) but because we combine both the spiritual and the material in one being and for that reason have been given dominion over the creation in obedience to God. To the fathers of the church, it was highly significant that although God revealed himself to us by the agency of angels, when he wished to appear on earth himself, it was as a man that he came. The incarnation of the Son of God validated the goodness of the material world and ensured that it would be redeemed along with the spiritual order. Once this point was established, the way was open for Christians to explore the natural world as a gift from God, and many early Christian writers took great delight in its wonders, which they often described at great length. The six days of creation were a favorite theme for commentators, and virtually every major patristic writer has left us at least one treatise on the subject.[1] It would be untrue to say that the triumph of Christianity in the fourth century led to a new era of scientific exploration, and it would take many more centuries before the implications of the Christian doctrine of creation began to do its work at that level, but it can still be said that the church fathers prepared the way for a more positive approach to the natural world, and when the scientific revolution finally came, their writings could be appealed to as confirmation that Christians had indeed inherited dominion over the earth.

OVERVIEW: God created Adam out of love (IRENAEUS, TERTULLIAN) and wanted him to be happy (THEOPHILUS). Human beings are special in God's eyes (CLEMENT OF ALEXANDRIA), although they are not the biggest or the strongest of the creatures (LACTANTIUS), and they were made perfect at the beginning

---

[1]Often called the Hexaemeron, from the Greek words for "six days."

(CYRIL OF ALEXANDRIA). A human being consists of body, soul and spirit (AUGUSTINE) and is both spiritual and material in nature (JOHN OF DAMASCUS). Women were created out of Adam's body, but they have souls of their own (EPHREM). Both male and female reflect the nature of the rational soul, which holds the primary place in God's creation (AUGUSTINE). In Christ, human beings are now being restored to the image of God in which they were created (EPHREM, LEO).

Evil was the result of Adam's rebellion against God (IRENAEUS) and disobedience to his will (METHODIUS, AUGUSTINE). It was a free choice on Adam's part (TATIAN, IRENAEUS, CLEMENT OF ALEXANDRIA, AUGUSTINE, JOHN OF DAMASCUS), but God knew that it would happen (AUGUSTINE, CYRIL OF ALEXANDRIA). God gave us free will, which makes evil possible (TERTULLIAN), but this is right, because otherwise virtue would have no meaning (ORIGEN). The existence of evil helps us to appreciate the good all the more (LACTANTIUS), and suffering is an agent of good (CLEMENT OF ALEXANDRIA). Human sin was caused by disobedience (METHODIUS), and it brought suffering and death into the world (ATHANASIUS), but God can and does use suffering to bring about good (CLEMENT OF ALEXANDRIA, AUGUSTINE). Human beings lost the likeness of God when they fell (BASIL, AMBROSE). The root of all evil is pride (AUGUSTINE), but in the end, even evil will be turned to good by the power of God (GREGORY OF NAZIANZUS). Adam and Eve were mortal beings protected from the power of death (AUGUSTINE), but when they sinned this protection was taken away, and they died (JOHN OF DAMASCUS).

The Creation of Man and Woman

THE TRUTH OF THE ACCOUNT IN GENESIS.
THEOPHILUS OF ANTIOCH: God made humankind on the sixth day and revealed this creation after the seventh day, when he also made para-

dise, so that humans might be in a better and obviously superior place. The fact itself proves that this is true. For how can one miss seeing that the pains that women suffer in childbirth and the oblivion of their labors that they afterwards enjoy are sent in order that the Word of God may be fulfilled and that the human race may increase and multiply? Do we not also see the judgment of the serpent—how despicably he crawls on his belly and eats the dust—so that this too is a proof of the things that were said in ancient times? To AUTOLYCUS 2.23.[2]

THE NATURE OF HUMANKIND.
THEOPHILUS OF ANTIOCH: Was humankind made mortal or immortal? . . . Neither. If God had made humanity immortal, he would have made them God. If he had made them mortal, God would appear to be the cause of their death. Humanity was therefore neither mortal nor immortal but capable of becoming either. If they inclined toward immortal things, keeping God's commandments, they would have been rewarded with immortality and become God. If they turned to the things of death, disobeying God, they would bring death on themselves. God made humanity free, with the power to decide their own destiny. People brought death on themselves through carelessness and disobedience, but God grants the gift of life to everyone who obeys him. For as disobedient people brought death on themselves, the one who obeys God's will is able to obtain life everlasting. God has given us a law and holy commandments, and everyone who keeps these can be saved. To AUTOLYCUS 2.27.[3]

GOD CREATED ADAM BECAUSE HE WANTED TO.
IRENAEUS: God formed Adam not because he needed him, but in order to have someone on whom he could confer all his blessings. AGAINST HERESIES 4.14.1.[4]

---

[2]PG 6:1088-89; cf. ANF 2:103. [3]PG 6:1093-96; cf. ANF 2:105.
[4]PG 7:1010; cf. ANF 1:478.

God Was Wholly Absorbed in Creation of Humankind. Tertullian: Imagine God wholly absorbed in the creation of human beings—in his hand, his eye, his labor, his purpose, his wisdom, his providence and most of all, his love. All these things were shaping the outline of humankind, for whatever form and expression he gave to the clay of the earth, it was always in his mind that one day Christ would become a man. . . . For the Father had already said to the Son, "Let us make humankind in our image, after our likeness."[5] And God made humankind after his image, which is the image of Christ. . . . Therefore that clay that was even then putting on the image of Christ, who was to come in the flesh, was not only the work but also the pledge and surety of God. On the Resurrection of the Flesh 6.[6]

God Made the Human Race by His Own Hand. Clement of Alexandria: Humanity is dear to God because they are his workmanship. The other works of creation, God made by his word of command alone. But he framed the human race by his own hand and breathed into them what was peculiar to himself. What God made after his own likeness was either held by him to be desirable in itself or else desirable for some other purpose. If a person is an object that is desirable for itself, then he who is good loved what is good. . . . But if humankind was a desirable object for some other purpose, God had no reason for creating them other than to prove that he is a good creator or for humanity to come to the knowledge of God. . . . It therefore seems logical that God made humankind because he found them desirable in themselves and not for some ulterior motive. Furthermore, what is desirable is loveable, and so humanity is loved by God. Christ the Educator 1.3.[7]

Wisdom Can Supply What Is Missing. Lactantius: Our creator and parent, God, has given us perception and reason, so that it might be clear that we are descended from him who is himself intelligence, perception and reason. He did not give these things to the other animals, and so he provided them with what they needed to survive—their own natural hair . . . and their own defense mechanisms for fending off predators. . . . But God did not make humankind with the things that are given to the other animals, because wisdom is able to supply those things that the condition of nature has denied them. On the Workmanship of God 2.[8]

People Have Dominion Over Other Creatures. Lactantius: When we see that even elephants . . . are subject to people, can anyone complain about God merely because people have received only moderate strength and a small body? On the Workmanship of God 3.[9]

The World Was Made for Humankind. Lactantius: God designed the world for the sake of humankind, but he made humankind for his own sake. People were called to be priests of the divine temple, observers of God's works and of heavenly things. They are the only earthly beings who can understand God, . . . being intelligent and rational. . . . Of all living creatures, people alone were created to walk upright, a sign that they were made in order to be able to contemplate their parent. For this reason they received the gift of language, so that they can declare the majesty of their Lord. It was for this reason that everything was put under their control, so that they might be under the control of God, their maker and creator. On the Wrath of God 14.[10]

The Threefold Nature of Adam's Creation. Ephrem the Syrian: We under-

---

[5]Gen 1:26. [6]PL 2:802; cf. ANF 3:549. [7]PG 8:257; cf. ANF 2:210-11. [8]PL 7:14-15; cf. ANF 7:282. [9]PL 7:19; cf. ANF 7:284. [10]PL 7:122; cf. ANF 7:271.

stand the creation of Adam in the image and likeness of God in three different ways. As a creature, he would not be called the likeness of God, except in relation to his freedom and to his dominion over the creatures. Similarly, we understand the image of God in three ways. First, because just as the power of God is present in all things, so Adam was given dominion over all things. Second, because Adam received a pure soul in which he acquired every kind of divine virtue and grace. Third, because by means of the rational part of the mind and by controlling himself, he can go anywhere and conjure up in himself images of whatever he chooses. COMMENTARY ON GENESIS 1.[11]

EVE TOOK ADAM'S BODY BUT NOT HIS SOUL.

EPHREM THE SYRIAN: "God took a rib from Adam and made woman."[12] He did this so that there would be only one source of the human race, on which he drew in order to fulfill what was written: "Male and female made he them."[13] He did this in order to avoid the suspicion that Eve had some other maker, but he did not breathe Adam's spirit into her. Her soul was not generated from his. The text of Scripture says, "Bone of my bone," not "soul of my soul," and "The two shall be one flesh," not "one soul."[14] COMMENTARY ON GENESIS 2.[15]

GOD HAD NO NEED OF HUMANKIND.

HILARY OF POITIERS: God did not create humankind because he had any need of them but because he is good. He made people to be participants in his own blessedness and fashioned them as rational animals with life and sense, so that he could extend the scope of his own eternity. We know this from what he says himself. HOMILIES ON THE PSALMS 2.15.[16]

THE TRIPARTITE VIEW OF HUMANKIND.

AUGUSTINE: A human being consists of three things—body, soul and spirit, which are often spoken of as two, because soul and spirit are taken together, the rational part of the soul (which animals do not possess) being termed "spirit." In us the principal part is the spirit; then comes the soul, which is the life of the body; and finally the visible body itself. This "whole creation groans and labors up till now,"[17] but God has given it the firstfruits of the Spirit in that it has believed him and is now of a good disposition. This spirit is also called the mind, of which the apostle Paul says, "With my mind I serve the will of God."[18] The same apostle likewise says, "For God is my witness, whom I serve in my spirit."[19] Moreover, the soul, when it lusts after carnal things, is called the flesh. For there is a certain part of it that resists the Spirit, not by virtue of its nature but because of the habit of sin, which is why Paul says, "With my mind I serve the law of God but with my flesh the law of sin."[20] This habit has become our nature according to mortal generation, thanks to the sin of the first man. This is why Paul wrote, "We were once the children of wrath by nature,"[21] that is, we were children of vengeance, through which it has happened that we now serve the law of sin. The nature of the soul, however, is perfect when it is made subject to its own spirit and when it follows that spirit as the same follows God. This is why "the soulish person does not receive the things that belong to the Spirit of God."[22] The soul is not as readily subdued to the spirit for the purpose of good works as the spirit is to God for the flourishing of true faith and good will. Sometimes its tendency to head downwards towards things that are temporal and carnal takes time to put in reverse. ON FAITH AND THE CREED 10.23.[23]

---

[11]ESOO 1:128. [12]Gen 2:22. [13]Gen 1:27. Ephrem interprets the creation of Eve as a fulfillment of this verse, which precedes it in the text of Genesis. [14]Gen 2:23. [15]ESOO 1:129. [16]PL 9:269. [17]Rom 8:22. [18]Rom 7:25. [19]Rom 1:9. [20]Rom 7:25. [21]Eph 2:3. [22]1 Cor 2:14. [23]PL 40:193-94; cf. NPNF 1 3:331-32.

HUMANITY IS CREATED IN THE IMAGE OF THE TRINITY. AUGUSTINE: There is something in humanity that can be compared only with the excellence of the Trinity, which is God. . . . It is said that he created us "according to his image."[24] This ought to be understood as referring to the Trinity. Therefore we recognize these three things in the soul of a person—memory, intelligence and will—and everything we do is done by these three. AGAINST THE ARGUMENT OF THE ARIANS 16.[25]

MALE AND FEMALE REFLECT THE NATURE OF THE RATIONAL SOUL. AUGUSTINE: We see the face of the earth covered with earthly creatures and with human beings, made in your image and likeness, who are put in authority over all irrational animals by your image and likeness, that is to say, by the power of reason and intelligence. Just as in his soul there is one element that deliberates and aspires to domination and another element that is submissive and obedient, so in the bodily realm, woman is made for man. In mental power she has an equal capacity for rational intelligence, but by the sex of her body she is submissive to the male. This is analogous to the way in which the impulse for action is subordinate to the rational mind's prudent concern that the act is right in itself. Thus we see that each particular aspect, as well as the whole taken together, is very good. CONFESSIONS 13.32.47.[26]

THE CREATION AND NATURE OF THE HUMAN SOUL. AUGUSTINE: I can affirm nothing about the human soul, which God breathed into Adam by blowing on his face, except that it comes from God in such a way as not to be part of God's substance but yet still incorporeal, that is to say, it is not a body but a spirit. It was not begotten from the divine substance, nor does it proceed from it, but it was made by God. It was not made out of any corporeal or irrational nature, but out of nothing. In one sense, it may be said to be immortal, because

it cannot now cease to exist, but because it is changeable and can become better or worse, it probably ought to be regarded as mortal, because the only one who has true immortality is the one of whom it is said, "Who alone has immortality."[27] ON THE LITERAL INTERPRETATION OF GENESIS 7.28.43.[28]

PRIMARY PLACE IN GOD'S CREATION. AUGUSTINE: I say that the soul was made by God, just as everything else was also made by him, and that among the things that the almighty God has made, the place of honor is given to the soul. AGAINST FORTUNATUS THE MANICHAEAN 13.[29]

ADAM WAS CREATED PERFECT. CYRIL OF ALEXANDRIA: Our first ancestor Adam does not seem to have acquired wisdom in the course of time, the way we do, but to have possessed perfect intelligence from the moment of his creation, having in himself a pure and undefiled natural understanding given by God and the full dignity of his nature. COMMENTARY ON JOHN 1.9.[30]

THE SOUL DID NOT FALL INTO THE BODY. CYRIL OF ALEXANDRIA: It is crazy to suppose that the soul existed before the body and that it was sent down into earthly bodies because of sins it had previously committed. COMMENTARY ON JOHN 1.9.[31]

WE WERE CREATED IN GOD'S IMAGE. LEO THE GREAT: If we comprehend faithfully and wisely the beginning of our creation, we shall find that human beings were made in God's image,[32] to the end that they might imitate their creator and that our race attains its highest natural dignity by the form of the divine goodness being reflected in us as in a mirror.

---

[24]Gen 1:26. [25]PL 42:695. [26]PL 32:866; cf. NPNF 1 1:206, CConf 302. [27]1 Tim 6:16. [28]PL 34:372. [29]PL 42:117. [30]PG 73:128. [31]PG 73:133. [32]Gen 1:27.

And assuredly it is to this form that the Savior's grace is daily restoring us so long as that which fell in the first Adam is raised up again in the second. SERMON 12.1.[33]

THE SOULS OF PEOPLE WERE NOT PREEXISTENT. GENNADIUS OF CONSTANTINOPLE: We do not believe that the souls of people existed from eternity among the intellectual creatures or that they were all created at the same time, as Origen imagined, or that they are inseminated with the body by means of sexual intercourse, as the Luciferians, Cyril and some of the Latin fathers presume to say, as if they were an inevitable part of human nature. Rather, we say that only the body is inseminated through sexual intercourse and that only the Creator of all things knows how the soul is created. BOOK OF ECCLESIASTICAL DOGMAS 14.[34]

GOD CREATED US AS MIXED BEINGS. JOHN OF DAMASCUS: God created beings that can be perceived by the senses, that is heaven and earth and the intermediate region between them, and so he created both the kind of being that is similar to him in nature . . . and the kind that, precisely because it can be known by the senses, is separated from him by an abyss. God also determined that there should be a mixture of both kinds of being, . . . a connecting link between the visible and the invisible . . . this is the human race, created after God's own image and likeness. Our bodies belong to the earth, but he breathed into us our mind and soul, by which we are said to be created in his image. ORTHODOX FAITH 2.12.[35]

Evil and the Fall

HUMAN BEINGS FELL BY THEIR OWN FREE WILL. TATIAN: Why are you fated to grasp at things, only to die? Die to the world, and repudiate the madness in it. Live to God, and in apprehending him, lay aside your old nature.

We were not created to die, but we die by our own fault. Our free will has destroyed us. We who were free have become slaves; we have been sold through sin. Nothing evil has been created by God; we ourselves have manifested wickedness, but we who have manifested it are able again to reject it. TO THE GREEKS 11.[36]

THE REBELLIOUS BRING DARKNESS ON THEMSELVES. IRENAEUS: God foreknew everything and prepared dwellings for both the good and the wicked. He conferred the light that they desire on those who seek the light of incorruption, but for those who despise and mock the light and blind themselves to it, he has prepared darkness and inflicted the appropriate punishment on those who try to avoid his rule. AGAINST HERESIES 4.39.4.[37]

EVIL WAS THE RESULT OF A FREE CHOICE. CLEMENT OF ALEXANDRIA: Evil originated from voluntary apostasy. It is the greatest achievement of divine providence that this evil is not allowed to remain without any purpose. It is the work of divine wisdom to . . . ensure that whatever happens through the evil hatched by someone, a good and useful result will come of it. STROMATEIS 1.17.[38]

SUFFERING ENCOURAGES SELF-DISCIPLINE. CLEMENT OF ALEXANDRIA: Disease, accident and death come to the spiritual, but by the power of God they are used to become the medicine of salvation. They encourage discipline, which helps those who find it hard to reform. These plagues are distributed according to providence, which is fundamentally good. STROMATEIS 7.11.[39]

GOD GAVE PEOPLE FREE WILL. TERTULLIAN: If God is good and knows the future,

---

[33]PL 54:168-69; cf. NPNF 2 12:121-22. [34]PL 58:984. [35]PG 94:920; cf. NPNF 2 9.2:30-31. [36]PG 6:829; cf. ANF 2:69-70. [37]PG 7:1111; cf. ANF 1:523. [38]PG 8:801; cf. ANF 2:320. [39]PG 9:485; cf. ANF 2:540.

why did he permit human beings, made in his own image and likeness, to be deceived by the devil and fall from obedience to death? . . . The answer is that God made us to be free, masters of our own will and power. AGAINST MARCION 2.5.[40]

IF VIRTUE IS NOT FREE, IT IS NOT GOOD.
ORIGEN: Why was it not possible for God to create people who had no need of improvement? Why is it not possible for evil to be eradicated? These questions may perplex foolish and ignorant minds, but not someone who understands the nature of things. For if you take away the freedom of virtue, you destroy its essence. AGAINST CELSUS 4.3.[41]

THE ROOT CAUSE OF EVIL.
METHODIUS: After their creation, the first human beings received a commandment from God. It was from this that evil sprang, because they did not obey the command. Disobedience is the root cause of all evil. ON FREE WILL.[42]

THE EXISTENCE OF EVIL HELPS US TO APPRECIATE WHAT IS GOOD.
LACTANTIUS: God arranged for there to be a distinction between good and evil things so that we might learn to appreciate the value of what is good. Observing the good also helps us to understand the meaning of evil. Neither good nor evil can really be understood without the presence of the other. DIVINE INSTITUTES 5.7.[43]

HUMAN BEINGS WERE CORRUPTED BY THEIR SIN.
ATHANASIUS: God has made humankind and willed that they should abide in incorruption, but people, having despised and rejected the contemplation of God and devised instead evil for themselves, received the condemnation of death that they had been threatened with. Once that happened, they no longer remained in the state in which they were made but were corrupted, and death had the mastery over them. Transgression of

the commandment of God meant that just as they were created out of nothing to begin with, so they could only look forward to being dissolved back into nothing at the end. For if human beings were called into existence out of their natural state of nothingness by the presence and loving kindness of the Word, it follows naturally that once we were deprived of our knowledge of God and turned back to what does not exist (for evil does not exist, but only good), we should disintegrate and dwell in death and corruption since we derive our being entirely from the God who is in himself. ON THE INCARNATION 4.4-5.[44]

HUMAN BEINGS LOST THE LIKENESS OF GOD WHEN THEY FELL.
BASIL THE GREAT: People were made in the image and likeness of God, but sin corrupted the beauty of the image when the soul was driven to give in to harmful desires. For God, who made humankind, is true life. Therefore, if someone has lost the likeness of God, he has lost the inheritance of life, because whoever is outside of God cannot enjoy the life of blessedness. Let us therefore return to the grace that was given to us at the beginning, from which we turned away through sin, and let us once again adorn ourselves according to the image of God and become like our Creator by putting off all sinful desires. ASCETIC SERMON 1.[45]

EVIL IS NOT GOD'S WORK.
GREGORY OF NAZIANZUS: Believe that everything in the world, all that is seen as well as all that is unseen, was made by God out of nothing, and is governed by the creator's providence and will one day be changed into a better state. Believe also that evil has no substance or dominion, either uncreated or self-existent or created by God. Evil is our work and the devil's; it came on us because of

[40]PL 2:289-90; cf. ANF 3:300-301. [41]PG 11:1032-33; cf. ANF 4:498. [42]PG 18:265; cf. ANF 6:362-63. [43]PL 6:570; cf. ANF 7:142. [44]PG 25:104; cf. NPNF 2 4:38. [45]PG 31:869-72.

our disobedience and was not sent by our Creator. ON HOLY BAPTISM, ORATION 40.45.[46]

THE DIFFERENCE BETWEEN CREATED AND FALLEN SOULS. AMBROSE: The soul as created by God has the grace of all virtues and shines with the splendor of godliness. That soul is well made from which the image of divine activity radiates. That soul is well made in which we find the splendor of glory and the image of the Father's substance. Because of that image that shines in it, the created soul is very precious. This was what Adam was like before the fall, but when he sinned, he lost the image of the heavenly and instead took on the image of earthly things. SIX DAYS OF CREATION 6.7.42.[47]

PRIDE IS THE ROOT OF ALL EVIL. AUGUSTINE: The true cause of the blessedness of the good angels is that they cling to the One who supremely is. If we ask what the cause of the misery of the bad angels is, it occurs to us, not unreasonably, that they are miserable because they have turned away from him who supremely is and have turned in on themselves, who have no such essential good in them. What is this vice other than pride, which is the beginning of sin?[48] They were unwilling to preserve their strength for God, and given that adherence to God was the condition of their enjoying an ampler being, they diminished it by preferring themselves to him. This was the first defect and the first impoverishment and the first flaw in their nature, which was created not as supremely existent in itself but finding its blessedness in the enjoyment of the supreme Being. By abandoning him, they became not nothing at all but rather natures with a less full existence and therefore miserable. If we go on to ask what the efficient cause of their evil will was, there was none. For what is it that makes the will bad, when it is the will that makes the action bad? The bad will is the cause of the bad action, but there is nothing that forces the will to be bad. CITY OF GOD 12.6.[49]

EVIL WAS THE FRUIT OF DISOBEDIENCE. AUGUSTINE: If the good angels made their own will good, did they use their will to do this? If not, then they did not do so willingly. If so, was that will good or bad? If it was bad, how could a bad will give rise to a good one? If it was good, then they already had a good will. So who made this will that they already had, other than the God who created them with a good will? . . . Thus we are driven to believe that the holy angels never existed without a good will. . . . But the angels who were created good and have now become evil have become so by their own will. This will was not made evil by their good nature but was brought about rather by a departure from what was good. Good is not the cause of evil, but a departure from good is. The angels who fell thus either received less of the divine love than those who persevered in doing good, or if both types of angel were created equally good, then while the one type fell by their evil will, the others were more fully supported and attained to that level of blessedness where they became certain that they should never fall from it. CITY OF GOD 12.9.[50]

ADAM COULD HAVE RESISTED SIN. AUGUSTINE: God made Adam with free will, and although he was ignorant of his future fall, he was happy because he thought he had the power not to die or be miserable. If he had willed by his own free will to continue in this state of uprightness and freedom from sin, he would surely . . . have received the blessing that belongs to the holy angels, that is, the impossibility of falling any more and the certainty of this knowledge. . . . But because he forsook God of his own free will, he experienced God's just judgment, which was that he and all his race should be condemned. Those of this race

---

[46]PG 36:424; cf. NPNF 2 7:376-77. [47]PL 14:258. [48]Eccles 10:13. [49]PL 41:353; cf. NPNF 1 2:229. [50]PL 41:357; cf. NPNF 1 2:231.

who have been delivered by divine grace have certainly been delivered from this fate, but those who have not have no reason to blame God for their punishment. On Rebuke and Grace 10(28).[51]

Adam Chose to Sin. Augustine: At creation God gave Adam a good will, because it was in his own good will that God had made him. He also provided help without which humanity could not continue therein, but he left it up to human free will to decide whether to make use of this help or not. Adam was therefore perfectly able to continue in goodness if he wanted to, because the help that he needed for this was not lacking. But he did not do so, and the blame for this rests on the man himself, just as the merit for obeying would have accrued to him if he had chosen that instead. This is what the holy angels did, when they stood firm of their own free will when other angels fell—again of their own free will. On Rebuke and Grace 11(32).[52]

Adam Could Have Avoided Sin. Augustine: What is the difference between being able not to sin and not being able to sin? Between being able not to die and not being able to die? Between being able not to forsake good and not being able to forsake good? The first man was able not to sin, not to die and not to forsake good, but can we say that he was incapable of sin? Or that he could not die, when God said to him, "If you sin you shall surely die"?[53] Or that he could not forsake good, when he did so by sinning and died? The first freedom of the will was that of Adam, but the second freedom, [the freedom of the resurrection in Christ], will be much greater, because it will be a freedom not to be able to sin. Likewise, the second immortality will be the inability to die, and the second perseverance in goodness will be the inability not to do good. However, the mere fact that the second blessings will be better does not mean that the

first ones were not blessings also or were mere trifles. On Rebuke and Grace 12(33).[54]

How We Became Sinners. Cyril of Alexandria: This is how we became sinners through the disobedience of Adam. He had been created in immortality and life, and his holy food was located in a paradise of delights. His mind was wholly and always on the vision of God, and his body dwelled in peacefulness and quiet, without any wicked desire, for there was no disturbance in him caused by any irrational impulses. But when he fell into sin and succumbed to corruption, impure desires broke into the nature of the flesh, and a cruel law was born inside us. Our nature contracted the disease of sin "by the disobedience of the one man," that is, Adam, and so "many became sinners,"[55] not because they sinned together with Adam (for they did not yet exist) but because they have his nature, which had fallen under the law of sin. Commentary on Romans 5.18.[56]

People Sinned by Choice. John of Damascus: God made people by nature sinless and endowed them with free will. By sinless, I mean not that sin could find no place in them, for that is the case with the Godhead alone, but that sin is the result of the free will that they enjoy and not an integral part of their nature. People have the power to continue and advance in the path of goodness by cooperating with the divine grace, and likewise to turn from good and take to wickedness, for God has permitted this by conferring freedom of the will on them. Orthodox Faith 2.12.[57]

The Loss of Original Innocence. John of Damascus: Adam and Eve were originally naked, because they were covered by divine

[51]PL 44:933; cf. NPNF 1 5:483. [52]PL 44:935; cf. NPNF 1 5:484. [53]Gen 2:17. [54]PL 44:936; cf. NPNF 1 5:485. [55]Rom 5:19. [56]PG 74:789. [57]PG 94:924; cf. NPNF 2 9.2.31.

grace. They had no bodily clothing, but were covered with an incorruptible vestment whose size was measured by the degree of their obedience, and thus of their closeness to God. After they became disobedient, they lost this protecting grace. They were denuded of their access to God and enjoyment of him. They

saw the nakedness of their bodies and began to look for clothing. They had been cast out into a mean and fruitless existence. HOMILY ON THE WITHERED FIG TREE 3.[58]

---

[58]PG 96:580-81.

AND UNSEEN

πιστεύομεν εἰς ἕνα Θεὸν	Credo in unum Deum	We believe in one God,
πατέρα, παντοκράτορα,	Patrem omnipotentem;	the Father, the Almighty,
ποιητὴν οὐρανοῦ καὶ γῆς,	factorem coeli et terrae,	maker of heaven and earth,
ὁρατῶν τε πάντων **καὶ ἀοράτων.**	visibilium omnium **et invisibilium.**	of all that is, seen **and unseen.**

HISTORICAL CONTEXT: The question of the spiritual creation is not often raised nowadays, but the church fathers gave it detailed and special treatment in its own right. To modern readers, this doctrine often appears quite strange, and the way in which the Fathers dealt with it often seems to us to be less satisfactory than other aspects of their creation doctrine. It is all the more important, therefore, that we understand the historical context in which they were writing and the specific problems that they were forced to address.

Everyone in the ancient world believed in the presence and power of spiritual forces, for good and for evil. The Jews thought of them either as messengers from God (the word *angel* means "messenger") or as rebellious spirits who had been cast out of his presence but were still allowed to operate within certain limits on earth. Pagans knew no such distinction, and for them particular spirits could often be either good or bad, depending on the circumstances. From the Jewish point of view, it was easy to identify the pagan gods as evil spirits

who had deceived the people, though this opinion had to compete with the more widely-held assumption that the gods were nothing but figments of the imagination.

The Old Testament is remarkably reticent on the question of spiritual forces, and in particular, it says virtually nothing about the fall of Satan and his angels from heaven. The church fathers recognized this, but felt that they had a duty to supply what was missing by speculating as to the significance of certain mysterious passages like Genesis 6:1, where it says that the "sons of God married the daughters of men." This was taken by many to be a reference to the fall of the angels, who, through their lust for human women, created a race of demons even more rebellious than they were. They also relied on Ezekiel 28:12-19, which was addressed to the king of Tyre but uses such extravagant language that it is difficult to interpret it in any way other than as an explanation of the fall of the devil from heaven.

The main concern that the church fathers had was to reassure Christians that they had nothing to fear from these spiritual powers. They promoted the idea that all believers had a guardian angel who looked after them personally, and they did what they could to insist that demonic forces had no power over Christians. This was not an easy claim to maintain, however, since various diseases and disabilities were attributed to demonic action, and Christians clearly were not exempt from them. At the popular level, the church waged a constant and not very successful battle against superstition, which was much easier to dismiss intellectually than it was to eradicate at the popular level. After Christianity became the official state religion, the various oracles and soothsayers who had flourished under the pagan dispensation were forbidden, but their trade merely went underground, to become what we now think of as the occult. It would be many centuries more before magic and astrology were finally banished from respectable society, and they are still popular though publicly unacceptable today.

On a more sophisticated theological level, the Fathers of the fourth and fifth centuries began to explore the structure of the spiritual world as part of their attempts to systematize Christian teaching generally. They began to examine the qualities of angels, their ranking in the celestial hierarchy and their different functions. The greatest expression of this was the *Celestial Hierarchy*, an anonymous treatise written by someone who claimed to be Dionysius the Areopagite, a man who had professed faith following Paul's preaching at Athens.[1] His claim was accepted throughout the Middle Ages, which gave his writings extraordinary authority, though they are now universally recognized to date from the early sixth century and probably came from Syria.

The Fathers paid less attention to the demonic world and said remarkably little about hell, though what they did say was very much in accordance with the teaching of the New Testament, and in particular, with the hard

sayings of Jesus. However, it must be said that they found it difficult to accept the eternal nature of divine punishment and tended toward the view that in the end, God would redeem everything and turn it to good. Most of them recognized that what they were saying was largely speculative, because Scripture did not give enough information for them to be certain one way or another. Modern readers, who are generally disinclined to follow their speculations, must bear this in mind when they read what the Fathers had to say. Like us, they were doing their best to make sense of something that intrigued them but lay beyond the bounds of human understanding. At their best, they were prepared to admit their limitations and to put their trust in the God whom they knew would protect them on earth and save them from destruction at the end of time.

OVERVIEW: Angels are numerous (CLEMENT OF ROME, ATHENAGORAS), and their role is essentially beyond our comprehension (IGNATIUS). They are agents of God's judgment (BARDESANES, JOHN OF DAMASCUS) and of his salvation (ORIGEN). They helped to preach the gospel (AUGUSTINE) and may take on human form (TERTULLIAN). They pray and watch for God, and spiritual people pray with them (CLEMENT OF ALEXANDRIA). The angels are spirits of fire (GREGORY OF NAZIANZUS) who share in God's goodness (EUSEBIUS), and they see God to the extent that they are able to do so (CYRIL OF JERUSALEM), though they are not gods and must not be worshiped (ORIGEN, LACTANTIUS). They were created at the beginning of time (EPIPHANIUS, GENNADIUS) but they are not holy by nature and must earn their sanctification by their obedience to God (BASIL, FULGENTIUS). They do not have bodies in the human sense, nor can they have sexual relations (CHRYSOSTOM, JOHN CASSIAN). They fully understand creation (AUGUSTINE), though they

---

[1]Acts 17:34.

did not take part in it (IRENAEUS), and they have specific tasks assigned to them by God (CLEMENT OF ALEXANDRIA, ORIGEN). They intercede for us in prayer (TERTULLIAN, HILARY) and reveal the glory of creation to us (CHRYSOSTOM). At the last judgment, the angels will separate the good from the wicked (ORIGEN).

Angels dwell in believers (HERMAS) and protect us from evil spirits (ORIGEN). Every Christian has a guardian angel, as do churches and nations (CLEMENT OF ALEXANDRIA, ORIGEN, THEODORET). Even illegitimate children have them (METHODIUS). Guardian angels bear witness to the dignity of human beings (JEROME). As imperfect people we need them to help us in our spiritual life (ORIGEN). There is a hierarchy of angelic beings, called by different names in holy Scripture (JEROME, AUGUSTINE, GREGORY THE GREAT).

Angels have free will (ATHENAGORAS, BARDESANES, AUGUSTINE, FULGENTIUS, JOHN). Some of them fell from God by rebelling against him (TATIAN, JUSTIN MARTYR, ORIGEN), which they did of their own free will (AUGUSTINE). Because they are higher than human beings, their fall was greater, but no more will fall away (AUGUSTINE, GREGORY THE GREAT). The fallen angels will be judged by God and punished (IRENAEUS), and they have no hope of salvation (TERTULLIAN).

The disobedient angels were attracted away from God by a desire for human women and through them brought an even more wicked race of demons into being (JUSTIN MARTYR, TERTULLIAN, CLEMENT OF ALEXANDRIA, COMMODIAN). These demons mislead us and provoke heresies (JUSTIN MARTYR). They can possess us (ORIGEN) and often are the cause of diseases and disabilities (MINUCIUS FELIX), but they can also be exorcized (THEOPHILUS). They have no secret knowledge of our thoughts but must discern them by observing the way we act (JOHN CASSIAN). Demons dwell in the lower parts of the earth and have become what they are because they disobeyed God (ORIGEN). The demons harm only those who fear them (LACTANTIUS), and Christians have no reason to be afraid of their power (ORIGEN). At the end of time, they will be judged and will perish everlastingly (IRENAEUS, TERTULLIAN, AUGUSTINE, FULGENTIUS).

Demons were well-known to the pagan philosophers (TERTULLIAN), and they were the ones who invented astrology and magic (LACTANTIUS). Their leader is called Satan, who sinned of his own free will (TERTULLIAN) and was given the form of a serpent by God (IRENAEUS). The church's teaching about Satan is not very clear (ORIGEN), but he cannot rule over God's servants (HERMAS). He can do his best to deceive us but cannot step outside the bounds laid down for him by God (TERTULLIAN, CYPRIAN). Most probably, human beings would have sinned even if the devil had never existed (ORIGEN). Satan fell because of his pride (ATHANASIUS, AUGUSTINE), and he is the ultimate source of all evil in the world (FULGENTIUS).

Hell is where unbelievers are punished after death (JUSTIN MARTYR), and it is a place of unrelieved torment (PSEUDO-CYPRIAN), though its fire is a spiritual concept that is not to be taken literally. (AUGUSTINE). Punishment there does not have to wait for the final judgment but can be meted out to the soul even as it waits for the general resurrection on the last day (TERTULLIAN). Hell has different parts, some of which contain the righteous dead who are waiting for the resurrection on the last day (HIPPOLYTUS). Hellfire cannot be material, because it affects spiritual beings, but it is not evil either (AUGUSTINE). Punishment in hell is eternal and never comes to an end (FULGENTIUS).

Angels

THE GREAT NUMBER OF THE ANGELS.

CLEMENT OF ROME: Let us consider the great number of his angels—how they stand always ready to minister to his will. For Scripture says, "Ten thousand times ten thousand stood around him, and thousands of thousands ministered to him."[2] 1 CLEMENT 1.34.[3]

THEIR ROLE IS INCOMPREHENSIBLE.

IGNATIUS: Even though I am in chains [as a martyr] and can therefore understand heavenly things, including the ranks of the angels, the hierarchy of [spiritual] princes and of everything visible and invisible, . . . I am still only a learner [in these matters]. TO THE TRALLIANS 5.[4]

THE ANGEL OF PUNISHMENT. HERMAS: The

angel of punishment belongs to the righteous angels and is appointed to punish, so he takes those who have wandered away from God and walked in the desires and deceits of this world and punishes them. SHEPHERD, SIMILITUDE 6.2-3.[5]

A LARGE NUMBER OF ANGELS. ATHENA-

GORAS: We accept that there is a large number of angels and spiritual ministers, whom God, as the maker and designer of the universe, has distributed and appointed to different functions by his Logos. A PLEA REGARDING CHRISTIANS 10.[6]

ANGELS CAN CHOOSE GOOD OR EVIL.

ATHENAGORAS: Other angels were created by God and given control over matter and its forms. Like human beings, they can choose either good or evil. Some have chosen the good and continue to do the things God had ordained for them. But others went against their own nature and the trust placed in them. They fell into sexual lust and were overcome by the flesh. . . . The people we now call giants were born from the union of these angels with human virgins.[7] A PLEA REGARDING CHRISTIANS 24.[8]

ANGELS HAVE PERSONAL FREEDOM. BARDE-

SANES: The angels have personal freedom,

because if they did not, they would never have consorted with the daughters of humans,[9] thereby sinning and falling from their position. In the same way, those angels who did the Lord's will were raised to a higher rank because of their self-control. BOOK OF THE LAWS OF COUNTRIES.[10]

THE WORLD WAS NOT CREATED BY AN-

GELS. IRENAEUS: Those who say that the world was created by angels . . . are wrong in thinking that the angels could make such a great creation contrary to the will of the most high God. That would imply that the angels were more powerful than God or perhaps that he failed to pay attention to what they were doing! AGAINST HERESIES 2.2.1.[11]

ANGELS SOMETIMES TOOK ON HUMAN

FORM. TERTULLIAN: The Creator's angels were sometimes changed into human form and had so real a body that Abraham even washed their feet[12] and Lot was rescued from the Sodomites by their hands.[13] Furthermore, an embodied angel wrestled so hard with a man (Jacob) that the latter begged him to let go.[14] Is it then the case that angels, who are inferior to God, have been allowed to go on being angels, even after they have been changed into the form of a human body? Will you then claim that this ability has been denied to God, after he became human flesh in Christ? ON THE FLESH OF CHRIST 3.[15]

ANGELS PRAY. TERTULLIAN: The angels all

pray; every creature prays. ON PRAYER 29.[16]

ANGELS ARE THOSE WHO WATCH FOR

GOD. CLEMENT OF ALEXANDRIA: Those

---

[2]Dan 7:10. [3]PG 1:276; cf. ANF 1:14. [4]PG 5:680; cf. ANF 1:68. [5]PG 2:968; cf. ANF 2:37. [6]PG 6:909; cf. ANF 2:133-34. [7]See Gen 6:1-4. [8]PG 6:945-48; cf. ANF 2:142. [9]See Gen 6:1-4. [10]*BLC* 14; ANF 8:725. [11]PG 7:713; cf. ANF 1:361. [12]Gen 18:1-4. [13]Gen 19:15. [14]Gen 32:24-26. [15]PL 2:757-58; cf. ANF 3:523. [16]PL 1:1196; cf. ANF 3:691.

who watch for God are blessed because they make themselves like the angels, whom we call watchers. CHRIST THE EDUCATOR 2.9.[17]

ANGELS DWELL IN THE HIGHEST PART OF THE WORLD. CLEMENT OF ALEXANDRIA: The best thing in heaven . . . is an angel, who partakes of the eternal and blessed life. . . . Christ gave philosophy to the Greeks by means of the lower angels. The angels are distributed among the nations by an ancient, divine order. STROMATEIS 7.2.[18]

SPIRITUAL PEOPLE PRAY WITH THE ANGELS. CLEMENT OF ALEXANDRIA: The spiritual person prays along with the angels. . . . He is never out of their keeping, because even when he prays alone, the holy ones are standing there beside him. STROMATEIS 7.12.[19]

GOD WORKS THROUGH ANGELS. CLEMENT OF ALEXANDRIA: God works through angels and archangels, who are known as spirits of Christ. FRAGMENT OF A COMMENTARY ON 1 PETER 1:3.[20]

ANGELS HELP GOD IN HIS WORK OF SALVATION. ORIGEN: There are some good forces, angels of God, that help him in the work of saving the human race. But it is not clearly stated when they were created, what their nature is or how they exist. ON FIRST PRINCIPLES, PREFACE 10.[21]

ANGELS HAVE BEEN GIVEN PARTICULAR TASKS. ORIGEN: Responsibilities have not been assigned to particular angels in an arbitrary manner. Raphael has been given the task of curing and healing. Gabriel has been given the conduct of wards. Michael has the duty of attending to the prayers and supplications of human beings. Each of them obtained his position by his merits and by the great qualities that he displayed before the creation of the world. ON FIRST PRINCIPLES 1.8.1.[22]

ANGELS ARE QUITE DIFFERENT FROM DEMONS. ORIGEN: The divine and holy angels are different, both in their nature and in their composition, from any earthly demon. AGAINST CELSUS 3.37.[23]

ANGELS ARE NOT TO BE WORSHIPED. ORIGEN: In the Bible, angels are sometimes called "God" because of their divine character. But this does not mean that we are supposed to worship and honor them instead of God, to whom alone all prayers and supplications should be directed. AGAINST CELSUS 5.4.[24]

WE SHOULD IMITATE THE ANGELS. ORIGEN: God's holy angels work on our behalf, so we should imitate them in our relationship with God, as far as human nature can. AGAINST CELSUS 5.5.[25]

ANGELS WILL SEPARATE THE GOOD FROM THE WICKED. ORIGEN: The parable of the tares[26] tells us that the angels will be entrusted with the task of separating the good from the wicked, for it is said, "The Son of Man shall send out his angels, and they shall gather out of his kingdom everything that causes stumbling and those who do iniquity, and they shall cast them into the furnace of fire; there shall be weeping and gnashing of teeth."[27] COMMENTARY ON THE GOSPEL OF MATTHEW 10.12.[28]

NOT NECESSARILY SUPERIOR TO THE ANGELS. ORIGEN: It does not follow that human beings who are saved in Christ are superior to the angels. . . . Some people may indeed be superior to some angels but not to all of them. . . . We know that we shall judge angels,[29] but the Bible does not say that we shall judge all of

---

[17]PG 8:493; cf. ANF 2:258. [18]PG 9:408-9; cf. ANF 2:524. [19]PG 9:509; cf. ANF 2:545. [20]PG 9:729-30; cf. ANF 2:571. [21]PG 11:120-21; cf. ANF 4:241. [22]PG 11:176; cf. ANF 4:264-65. [23]PG 11:968; cf. ANF 4:479. [24]PG 11:1185; cf. ANF 4:544. [25]PG 11:1185; cf. ANF 4:544-45. [26]Mt 13:36-43. [27]Mt 13:41-42. [28]PG 13:864; cf. ANF 9:420. [29]1 Cor 6:3.

them. Commentary on the Gospel of Matthew 10.13.[30]

Proclamation of the Gospel. Origen: The angels cannot have been excluded from the work of proclaiming the gospel. This is why an angel stood over the shepherds and created a bright light around them. Commentary on John 1.13.[31]

The Angels Do Not Want to Be Called Gods. Lactantius: The angels . . . do not want to be called gods and do not allow us to do this, because their one and only aim is to submit to God's will and to do only what he commands. Divine Institutes 2.17.[32]

God Created the Angels to Share in His Goodness. Eusebius of Caesarea: God, being as he is the only good and the source and origin of every good thing, wanted there to be many others who could share the riches of his treasures and so decided to create an entire rational creation, including incorporeal, intelligent and divine powers, angels and archangels, nonmaterial and completely pure spirits. Proof of the Gospel 4.1.[33]

The Angels Behold God as They Are Able to Do So. Cyril of Jerusalem: Is it not written that the angels of the little ones always behold the face of the Father in heaven?[34] Yes, but the angels see God not as he is, but as far as they are able to see him. Jesus said, "No one has seen the Father, but the one who is of God, he has seen the Father."[35] The angels therefore behold as much as they can bear, and archangels as much as they are able, and thrones and dominions more than the former, but yet less than his worthiness, for only the Son and the Holy Spirit can really behold him. Catechetical Lectures 6.6.[36]

When the Angels Were Created. Epiphanius of Salamis: The Word of God makes it quite clear that the angels were not created after the stars or before the heavens and the earth. For this statement is firm and certain, that before the foundation of the heavens and the earth there was nothing at all in existence, since it was "in the beginning" that "God created heaven and earth"[37] and before that happened, there was nothing at all anywhere. Panarion 65.5.[38]

Angels Are Not Holy by Nature. Basil the Great: The principalities and powers and other creatures of that type are not holy by nature but acquire their holiness by diligence and effort. They seek the good so that they may receive a measure of holiness by reason of their love for God. . . . In this they differ from the Holy Spirit, who is holy by nature. Against Eunomius 3.2.[39]

The Angels Intercede for Us. Hilary of Poitiers: We recall that there are many spiritual powers who are called angels, or rulers of churches. . . . The nature of God does not demand their intercession, but rather our human weakness. For they are sent on behalf of those who will inherit salvation, not because God is unaware of what we are doing but in our weakness, to request and obtain what we need by their ministry of spiritual intercession. Homilies on the Psalms 129(130).7.[40]

Angels Reveal the Glory of Creation. Chrysostom: Although visible things are enough to teach us all about the greatness of the Creator's power, if you look at the invisible powers and stretch your mind to consider the armies of angels, archangels, supernatural powers, thrones, dominions, principalities,

---

[30]PG 13:864-65; cf. ANF 9:420-41. [31]PG 14:45; cf. ANF 9:304. [32]PL 6:337-38; cf. ANF 7:65. [33]PG 22:252. [34]Mt 18:10. [35]Jn 6:46. [36]PG 33:545-48; cf. NPNF 2 7:34. [37]Gen 1:1. [38]PG 42:20. [39]PG 29:660. [40]PL 9:722.

powers, cherubim, seraphim—what mind, what tongue could tell of his ineffable majesty? HOMILIES ON GENESIS 4.5.[41]

ANGELS CANNOT HAVE SEXUAL RELATIONS. CHRYSOSTOM: How great was the madness of those who said that the angels were thrown down in such a way as to have sexual relations with women and join their bodiless nature to human bodies! Were they unaware of what the Lord said about the substance of the angels: "In the resurrection they shall neither marry nor be given in marriage, but they will be like the angels of God"?[42] It is quite impossible for an incorporeal being to have such relations! HOMILIES ON GENESIS 22.2.[43]

ANGELS DO NOT HAVE BODIES AS WE HAVE. CHRYSOSTOM: In 1 Corinthians 13:1 the apostle Paul speaks about the tongues of angels, but he does not mean by this that angels have a body. What he is saying is this: "Even if I could speak in the way that angels speak to one another, without love I am nothing." . . . Similarly, when he says elsewhere, "Every knee shall bow in heaven and on earth and under the earth,"[44] he is not saying that angels have knees and legs—far from it! Rather, he wants to indicate their intense and great adoration by using the imagery to which we are accustomed. Here too, he talks about the tongue but is not referring to the physical organ. Instead, he is talking about their conversation among themselves, using language that is familiar to us in order to do so. HOMILIES ON 1 CORINTHIANS 32.3.[45]

ANGELS ARE SPIRITS OF FIRE. GREGORY OF NAZIANZUS: God is said to make his angels spirits and his ministers a flame of fire,[46] though perhaps the making really means preserving them by that Word that brought them into existence. The angel is therefore called spirit and fire, spirit as being a creature of the intellectual sphere and fire as being of a purifying nature, for I know that the same names

belong to the first nature. But in relation to us at least, we must consider the angelic nature to be incorporeal, or as nearly so as possible. Do you see how we get confused at this point and cannot go any further than acknowledging that there are angels, archangels, thrones, dominions, principalities, powers, splendors, ascents, intelligences, pure natures and unalloyed, immovable to evil or scarcely so, ever circling in chorus round the first cause, illuminated by it with the purest illumination . . . so conformed to beauty that they become secondary lights, enlightening others by the overflowing of the first light? Ministers of God's will, they are strong with both native and imparted strength, traversing all space, readily present to all at any place through their zeal for ministry and the agility of their nature. ON THEOLOGY, THEOLOGICAL ORATIONS 2(28).31.[47]

ANGELS SERVE THE PRIMARY SPLENDOR. GREGORY OF NAZIANZUS: Self-contemplation alone could not satisfy Goodness, which had to reach out beyond itself to multiply the objects of its beneficence, for this was essential to the highest goodness. He first conceived the heavenly and angelic powers, a conception that was a work carried out by his Word and perfected by his Spirit. Thus the secondary splendors came into being as the ministers of the primary splendor, whether we are to conceive of them as intelligent spirits, or as fire of an immaterial and incorruptible kind or as something else of this kind. I would like to say that they were unable to move toward evil and that they were inclined entirely toward the good, . . . but I am obliged to stop short of saying that because of Lucifer, whose pride caused him to become and to be called darkness, along with the apostate hosts who are subject to him. ON THE THEOPHANY, ORATION 38.9.[48]

---

[41]PG 53:44. [42]Mt 22:30; Mk 12:25; Lk 20:35. [43]PG 53:188. [44]Phil 2:10. [45]PG 61:268. [46]Ps. 104:4. [47]PG 36:72; cf. NPNF 2 7:300. [48]PG 36:320-21; cf. NPNF 2 7:347.

A Hierarchy of Angelic Beings. Jerome: No one would be called an archangel unless he were greater than the ordinary angels, and in the same way, principalities, powers and dominions would not be so called unless they had subjects and others of inferior rank to themselves. Against Rufinus 1.23.[49]

The Angels Know the Creation in the Wisdom of God. Augustine: The holy angels come to the knowledge of God not by audible words but by the presence in their souls of immutable truth, that is to say, of the only-begotten Word of God, and they know this Word himself, and the Father and their Holy Spirit, and that this Trinity is indivisible, and that the three persons in it are one substance, and that there are not three gods but one God. Furthermore, they know this in such a way that they understand it better than we understand ourselves. They also know the creation not in and of itself but in a better way—in the wisdom of God. As a result, they know themselves better in God than in themselves, though they have self-knowledge as well. They were created and are different from their creator. In him they have what you might call a noonday knowledge, whereas in themselves they have, as it were, a twilight knowledge. City of God 11.29.[50]

Preaching the Gospel. Augustine: Those who are already spirits, who are spiritual, not carnal, God makes his angels (messengers) by sending them to preach his gospel. Expositions of the Psalms 104(103.)3.[51]

The Differences Among the Angels. Augustine: The apostle Paul speaks of "thrones, dominions, principalities and powers."[52] I am convinced that there are indeed thrones, dominions, principalities and powers in the heavenly places and that there is some difference among them. But I do not know what they are or how exactly they differ from one another. To Orosius 11.14.[53]

The Bodies of Angels. John Cassian: Let us declare that there are some spiritual natures, like angels, archangels and other powers, as well as our own souls and even the air itself, which are in no sense incorporeal. For they each have a body in which they subsist, even if it is a good deal more refined than our human bodies are. The apostle Paul expressed this as follows: "There are heavenly bodies and there are earthly bodies,"[54] and again, "It is sown a physical body; it will be raised a spiritual body."[55] There is nothing that does not have a body, except God himself. Conferences 7.13.[56]

When the Angels Were Created. Gennadius of Constantinople: "In the beginning God created heaven and earth,"[57] and also the water, out of nothing. And while the darkness was still covering the water and the water was still hiding the land, the angels and all the heavenly powers were created, so that God's goodness would not be left with nothing to do but would have many opportunities for manifesting its goodness, and thus it was that this invisible world was made and fashioned out of the things that had already been created. Book of Ecclesiastical Dogmas 10.[58]

Angels Have Free Will. Fulgentius of Ruspe: Angels and people both, by virtue of the fact that they were created as rational beings, have by divine inspiration received the gift of eternity and blessedness in the creation of their spiritual nature. Thus, if they had remained bound to the love of their creator, they would also have remained eternal and blessed, but if they dared to exercise their free will against the rule of their creator, the blessing would immediately depart from the

---

[49]PL 23:416. [50]PL 41:343; cf. NPNF 1 2:222. [51]PL 37:1353; cf. NPNF 1 8:510. [52]Col 1:16. [53]PL 42:678. [54]1 Cor 15:40. [55]1 Cor 15:44. [56]PL 49:684-85. [57]Gen 1:1. [58]PL 58:983.

guilty ones and an eternity of misery, marked with errors and griefs, would be left to them as punishment. And as far as angels are concerned, God so ordered and determined matters that if any of them lost the goodness of their will, they would never regain it by any divine grace. TO PETER, ON THE FAITH 3.30.[59]

ANGELS ARE NOT DIVINE BY NATURE. FULGENTIUS OF RUSPE: Neither the angels nor any other creature is of the same nature as the most high Trinity according to its natural divinity, which is one by nature. . . . Nor were they—he who made them and those whom he made—able to be of one nature. . . . Every creature made by the unchangeable God is changeable by nature, though none of the holy angels can now be changed for the worse. They have all received eternal bliss, in which they enjoy God forever, so that they cannot lose him. But this state . . . was not implanted into them by nature but was conferred on them after their creation by the generosity of the divine grace. For if the angels had been made unchangeable by nature, the devil and his angels would never have fallen away from their company. TO PETER, ON THE FAITH 22.65–23.66.[60]

THE FAITHFUL ANGELS. GREGORY THE GREAT: The angelic nature, when it was created, received free will, either to choose to remain in humility and in the presence of almighty God or to give way to pride and fall from blessedness. But those angels who remained faithful in their blessedness when the others fell received this additional grace, which was that they can no longer fall at all. HOMILIES ON EZEKIEL 1.7.18.[61]

NINE DIFFERENT ORDERS OF ANGELS. GREGORY THE GREAT: We have said that there are nine orders of angels that, according to the witness of holy Scripture, are as follows: angels, archangels, rulers, powers, principalities,

dominions, thrones, cherubim and seraphim. That there are angels and archangels is attested on virtually every page of holy Scripture. The prophetic books, as is well known, often refer to cherubim and seraphim. Then there are the four that the apostle Paul mentions in his letter to the Ephesians, that is to say, principalities, powers, rulers and dominions, to which may be added thrones.[62] . . . When these five that are specifically named are added to the other four, you arrive at a total of nine orders of angels. FORTY GOSPEL HOMILIES 2.34.7.[63]

ANGELS ARE SPIRITUAL BEINGS WITH FREE WILL. JOHN OF DAMASCUS: An angel is an intelligent being, a perpetual motion, with free will. Angels are incorporeal; they minister to God and have obtained by grace an immortal nature, whose limits are known to the Creator alone. . . . All the angels were created through the Word and were brought to perfection by the sanctifying power of the Holy Spirit. They are circumscribed, because when they are in heaven they are not on earth, and when they are sent down to earth by God they are no longer in heaven. They are not hemmed in by walls and doors, and in this sense they are quite unlimited. . . . They behold God according to their ability, and this is their food. They are above us because they are incorporeal and are free of all bodily passion, but they are not passionless because only God is passionless.

They take different forms at their Master's bidding and thus reveal themselves to people and unveil the divine mysteries to them. They have heaven for their dwelling-place and have only one duty—to sing God's praise and carry out his divine will. ORTHODOX FAITH 2.3.[64]

[59]PL 65:686-87. [60]PL 65:700; FC 95:98-99. [61]PL 76:849. [62]Eph 1:21; Col 1:16. [63]PL 76:1249-50. [64]PG 94:865-72; cf. NPNF 1 9.2:19-20.

Guardian Angels

THE TWO ANGELS WHO ARE WITH YOU.
HERMAS: There are two angels who dwell with
a person, one of righteousness and the other
of iniquity. . . . The angel of righteousness is
gentle, modest, humble and peaceful. When he
comes into your heart, he speaks about these
things and about every other righteous deed
and glorious virtue. When you are thinking
about such things, then you know that the
angel of righteousness is with you. . . . Look
now at the works of the angel of iniquity. He
is wrathful and bitter; he is foolish, and his
works are evil, ruining the servants of God.
When he enters your heart, realize who he is
by his works. When anger comes on you, or
harshness, know that he is in you. You will
discern his presence when you are attacked by
a longing after wealth, drunkenness, . . . sex
and pride. When these things enter your heart,
you know that the angel of iniquity is in you.
SHEPHERD, MANDATE 2.6.2.[65]

GUARDIAN ANGELS EXIST. CLEMENT OF
ALEXANDRIA: The Bible says that the angels of
the little ones see God,[66] so there is evidence
for the existence of guardian angels. STRO-
MATEIS 5.14.[67]

**ANGELS ARE DISTRIBUTED EVEN TO INDI-
VIDUALS.** CLEMENT OF ALEXANDRIA: Hosts
of angels are distributed among nations and
cities, and some may be assigned to particular
individuals. STROMATEIS 6.17.[68]

**CHURCHES, APOSTLES AND INDIVIDUAL
BELIEVERS.** ORIGEN: The Ephesian church
had its own angel,[69] and so did the church at
Smyrna.[70] Peter had an angel, and so did Paul,
and so on through every one of the little ones
that are in the church, for those angels who
daily behold the face of God must be assigned
to each one of them.[71] So there must also be
some angels who camp around everyone who

fears God.[72] ON FIRST PRINCIPLES 1.8.1.[73]

EVERY BELIEVER HAS A GUARDIAN ANGEL.
ORIGEN: Every believer, even the humblest in
the church, has a guardian angel, who, according to the Savior, always beholds the face of
God the Father.[74] . . . But if that person dis-
obeys God, the angel is taken away from him
because he has become unworthy. ON FIRST
PRINCIPLES 2.10.7.[75]

NATIONS HAVE THEIR ANGELS. ORIGEN:
Individual nations have their own spiritual
prince. In Daniel, we read that there was a
prince of the kingdom of Persia and a prince
of the kingdom of Greece,[76] neither of whom
can have been a human being, as the context
clearly demonstrates. They were both spiritual
powers, and in Ezekiel, the prince of Tyre is
also shown to be a kind of spiritual power.[77]
ON FIRST PRINCIPLES 3.3.2.[78]

GOOD ANGELS AS OUR GUARDIANS. ORI-
GEN: God has set his good angels over those
who believe in him, so that no hostile angel,
not even the "prince of this world,"[79] can do
them any harm. AGAINST CELSUS 8.36.[80]

PROTECTION FROM EVIL SPIRITS. ORIGEN:
We ask God to help us by entrusting us to the
guardianship of holy and good angels, who can
defend us from the spirits of this world who
are intent on fulfilling their lusts. AGAINST
CELSUS 8.60.[81]

IMPERFECT PEOPLE NEED HELP. ORIGEN:
As long as we are imperfect and need someone to help us escape from evil, we are in need
of an angel. It was of just such an angel that

[65]PG 2:928; cf. ANF 2:24. [66]Mt 18:10. [67]PG 9:133-36; cf.
ANF 2:466. [68]PG 9:389; cf. ANF 2:517. [69]Rev 2:1. [70]Rev 2:8.
[71]Mt 18:10. [72]Ps 34:7. [73]PG 11:176; cf. ANF 4:265. [74]Mt
18:10. [75]PG 11:240; cf. ANF 4:296. [76]Dan 10:20. [77]Ezek
28:2. [78]PG 11:315; cf. ANF 4:335. [79]Jn 12:31. [80]PG 11:1572;
cf. ANF 4:653. [81]PG 11:1608; cf. ANF 4:662.

Jacob said, "The angel who delivered me from all evils."[82] COMMENTARY ON THE GOSPEL OF MATTHEW 13.26.[83]

AFTER WE ARE BORN AGAIN. ORIGEN: There is no holy angel present with those who are still dead in their trespasses and sins. At that time, they are still under the power of Satan. But after we have been born again, the One who has redeemed us by his own blood assigns a holy angel to us, who also, because of his purity, beholds the face of God. . . . Another possibility is that perhaps an angel has been given to a person at his birth and starts off wicked, but later he comes to faith in the same degree as the person does. The angel may then improve so much that he may become one of those who continually beholds the Father's face. COMMENTARY ON THE GOSPEL OF MATTHEW 13.28.[84]

ILLEGITIMATE CHILDREN HAVE GUARDIAN ANGELS. METHODIUS: We have received from the inspired writings that even children born out of wedlock are committed to guardian angels. But if they came into being in opposition to the will and decree of the blessed nature of God, how should they be committed to angels, to be nourished with much gentleness and indulgence? If they had to accuse their own parents, how could they stand confidently before the judgment seat of Christ and say, "You did not begrudge us the common light, O Lord, but these people appointed us to death because they despised your command?" For he says, "Children begotten of unlawful beds are witnesses of wickedness against their parents at their trial."[85] BANQUET OF THE TEN VIRGINS 2.6.[86]

BEARING WITNESS TO THE DIGNITY OF HUMAN BEINGS. JEROME: So great is the dignity of human souls that each one has a guardian angel assigned to it from the moment of its birth. COMMENTARY ON THE GOSPEL OF MATTHEW 3.18.10.[87]

ANGELS GIVEN TO INDIVIDUALS, ARCHANGELS TO NATIONS. THEODORET OF CYR: Each of us has received a guardian angel to look after us individually and to protect us from the tricks of demons. Archangels, however, are entrusted with the care of nations, as the blessed Moses taught,[88] and as the blessed Daniel agreed when he wrote of the "prince of the kingdom of the Persians" and somewhat later of "the prince of the Greeks." He also called Michael the prince of Israel.[89] COMMENTARY ON DANIEL 10:13.[90]

Demons

DEMONS ARE SPIRITUAL IN NATURE. TATIAN: None of the demons possesses flesh. They are spiritual in nature, like fire or air. The bodies of demons can therefore be seen only by those whom the Spirit of God indwells and strengthens, not by others. . . . The nature of the demons has no place for repentance, for they are the reflection of matter and of wickedness. TO THE GREEKS 15.[91]

ANGELS SINNED AGAINST GOD. JUSTIN MARTYR: Angels sinned and rebelled against God. DIALOGUE WITH TRYPHO 79.[92]

THE DEMONS DECEIVE US. JUSTIN MARTYR: We warn you to be on your guard against those demons who are out to deceive you and distract you from reading and understanding what we have to say. They strive to hold you in slavery and servanthood. Sometimes by appearing in dreams and sometimes by magical impositions, they subdue those who fail to resist. FIRST APOLOGY 14.[93]

THE DEVILS MISLEAD PEOPLE. JUSTIN

---

[82]Gen 48:16. [83]PG 13:1165; cf. ANF 9:490. [84]PG 13:1168-69; cf. ANF 9:491. [85]Wis 4:6. [86]PG 18:57; cf. ANF 6:316. [87]PL 26:130. [88]See Deut 32:8. [89]Dan 10:13-20. [90]PG 81:1197. [91]PG 6:840; cf. ANF 2:71. [92]PG 6:661; cf. ANF 1:238. [93]PG 6:348; cf. ANF 1:167.

MARTYR: After the coming of Christ, . . . the demons put forth tricksters like the Samaritans Simon and Menander, who did great works of magic and deceived many. . . . They also ensure that people who live irrationally, who were brought up licentiously in wicked customs and who are prejudiced in their own opinions, kill and hate us. . . . They also put forward Marcion of Pontus, who even now is teaching people to deny that God is the maker of all things in heaven and on earth. . . . The devils are interested in nothing else than to seduce people away from the God who made them. FIRST APOLOGY 56-58.[94]

ANGELS TRANSGRESSED. JUSTIN MARTYR: The angels transgressed their appointed limits and were captured by the love of women. Thus they gave birth to children and to those whom we call demons.[95] Afterwards they subdued the human race to themselves, partly by magical writings and partly by fears and the punishments they occasioned, and partly by teaching them to offer sacrifices. SECOND APOLOGY 5.[96]

EXORCISMS STILL TAKE PLACE. THEOPHILUS OF ANTIOCH: Even today, the demon-possessed are sometimes exorcised in the name of the living and true God. The spirits of error themselves confess that they are the demons who once inspired the poets. TO AUTOLYCUS 2.8.[97]

FALLEN ANGELS WILL BE JUDGED. IRENAEUS: After the angels sinned, they fell to earth to be judged. AGAINST HERESIES 4.16.2.[98]

ETERNAL FIRE FOR THE FALLEN ANGELS. IRENAEUS: The Lord has said that the devil has angels for whom an eternal fire is prepared.[99] . . . However, the devil did not create his angels, since all things were created by God. AGAINST HERESIES 4.41.1.[100]

DEMONS STIMULATE DISEASES AND DIS-

ABILITIES. MINUCIUS FELIX: The demons . . . lurk behind statues and images, and by their aura they attain the authority of a deity. They are breathed into prophets who dwell in these shrines, and sometimes they animate the fibers of entrails, control the flight of birds, decide which way the lot will be cast and give out oracles of falsehood. They are both deceived and deceiving. They are ignorant of the simple truth and do not confess what they know, to their own destruction. They weigh people down and take them away from heaven, calling them from the true God to the worship of material things. They disturb life and make people unruly all the time. Secretly creeping into human bodies with subtlety (because they are spirits), the demons simulate diseases, alarm people's minds and distort their limbs. They do this in order to force people to worship them. Then they leave the body, and by putting an end to these convulsions, they give the impression that they have cured it. OCTAVIUS 27.[101]

NO RESTORATION IS PROMISED TO THE FALLEN ANGELS. TERTULLIAN: Christ took on human flesh in order to save us. . . . But there was no such reason for him to take on the nature of angels. No restoration is ever promised to those angels who will be destroyed in "the fire prepared for the devil and all his angels."[102] Christ never received any instructions of this kind from the Father. ON THE FLESH OF CHRIST 14.[103]

PAGANS ARE WELL AWARE OF THE EXISTENCE OF DEMONS. TERTULLIAN: We agree that there are certain spiritual essences, and their name is quite familiar to us. The philosophers acknowledge that there are demons; Socrates himself waited on a demon's will.

[94]PG 6:413-16; cf. ANF 1:182. [95]See Gen 6:1-4. [96]PG 6:452; cf. ANF 1:190. [97]PG 6:1061-64; cf. ANF 2:97. [98]PG 7:1016; cf. ANF 1:481. [99]Mt 25:41. [100]PG 7:1115; cf. ANF 1:524. [101]PL 3:323-24; cf. ANF 4:189-90. [102]Mt 25:41. [103]PL 2:777; cf. ANF 3:533.

Why not, since it is said that an evil spirit attached itself especially to him even from his childhood, turning his mind away from what was good? The poets are all acquainted with demons too; even the ignorant common people often curse by them. In fact, they call on Satan, the demon chief, in their execrations, as though from some instinctive soul knowledge of him. Plato also admits the existence of angels. The magicians, no less, come forward as witnesses to the existence of both kinds of spirits. We are instructed moreover by our sacred books how from certain angels, who fell of their own free will, there sprang a more wicked demon brood, condemned of God along with the authors of their race, and that chief we have referred to.

It will be enough for the present to give some account of their work. Their great business is the ruin of humankind. From the very first, spiritual wickedness sought our destruction. They inflict on our bodies diseases and other grievous calamities, while by violent assaults they hurry the soul into sudden and extraordinary excesses. Their marvelous subtleness and tenuity give them access to both parts of our nature. As spiritual beings they can do no harm, because . . . we are not aware of their actions except by their effects, as for example when some inexplicable, unseen poison in the breeze blights the apples and the grain at blossom time, or kills them in the bud or destroys them when they have reached maturity. . . . Similarly, . . . demons and angels breathe into the soul and rouse up its corruptions with furious passions and vile excesses, or with cruel lusts accompanied by various errors, of which the worst is the one by which these deities are commended to the favor of deceived and deluded human beings, that they may get the proper food of flesh fumes and blood when that is offered up to idol images. What is daintier food to the spirit of evil than turning people's minds away from the true God by the illusions of a false divination?

Let me explain how these delusions are managed. Every spirit, angelic or demonic, is possessed of wings. Thus there can be everywhere in a single moment—the whole world is as one place to them, and they can know whatever is going on in the world without needing to have it reported to them. Their swiftness of motion is mistaken for divinity, because their true nature is unknown. Sometimes they want people to think that they are the cause of what they proclaim, and no doubt it is true that the bad things sometimes are their doing, but never the good ones. They have learned the purposes of God from the lips of the prophets, and they pick them up every time they hear their works being read aloud. In this way they can set themselves up as rivals to the true God, by stealing his words. . . . Because they live in the air and the clouds, . . . they can know when it is going to rain and tell people that it is on the way. They are also very kind to us in the way they heal diseases. Having caused them in the first place, they fake miracles by proposing some new and untried remedy that seems to work because in fact they withdraw their malign influence, and can thus claim to have brought about a cure! What further need do I have to speak of their deceptive power as spirits? APOLOGY 22.[104]

FALLEN ANGELS LUSTED AFTER HUMAN BODIES. TERTULLIAN: If a woman is told to cover her head because of the angels,[105] this must apply equally to virgins. For if they are told to do this on account of the angels, that is to say, those angels who had already fallen away from God and heaven because of their lust for women, who can assume that these angels lusted only after human bodies that had already been defiled, and not after virgins as well? ON THE VEILING OF VIRGINS 7.[106]

---

[104]PL 1:404-9; cf. ANF 3:36-37. [105]1 Cor 11:10. [106]PL 2:899; cf. ANF 4:32.

FALLEN ANGELS INVENTED JEWELRY.

TERTULLIAN: The angels who fell from heaven invented jewelry, and for this they were condemned to death. They are the very same angels who rushed down from heaven and seized the daughters of humans.[107] THE APPAREL OF WOMEN 1.2.[108]

FALLEN ANGELS INVENTED ASTROLOGY.

TERTULLIAN: The angels who deserted God and chose the love of women also invented astrology, for which they were condemned by God. . . . The astrologers are expelled just like the fallen angels. . . . Before the coming of Christ they were tolerated up to a point, and the magi were even led to him. But since Christ's birth astrology has been forbidden, so that now no one can interpret anybody's birth by reference to the skies. . . . Exactly the same thing is true of the magical arts. . . . Simon Magus, shortly after becoming a believer, . . . tried to buy the gift of the Holy Spirit from the apostles, and he was thrown out of the church for that.[109] Similarly, the other magician who associated with Sergius Paulus was punished with the loss of his sight because he set himself up against the apostles.[110] Astrologers would have suffered the same fate if they had crossed the apostles' path, for it is but a species of magic. ON IDOLATRY 9.[111]

FALLEN ANGELS PREFERRED A FADING BEAUTY.

CLEMENT OF ALEXANDRIA: The angels fell from heaven to earth because they rejected the beauty of God and preferred a fading beauty instead. CHRIST THE EDUCATOR 3.2.[112]

FALLEN ANGELS REVEALED SECRETS GIVEN TO THEM.

CLEMENT OF ALEXANDRIA: The angels who had reached the greater heights fell into lust and told their women the secrets that they had learned. But the other angels kept their secrets, or rather held them back until the coming of Christ. STROMATEIS 5.1.[113]

LACKING COMPLETE UNITY WITH GOD.

CLEMENT OF ALEXANDRIA: Some of the angels were thrown down to earth because of their lack of diligence. They had not yet obtained complete oneness with God. STROMATEIS 7.7.[114]

THE BEAUTY OF WOMEN.

COMMODIAN: The beauty of women was so great that it turned the angels away from God. Once they were contaminated, they could not go back to heaven, and since they were rebels against God, they started to speak badly of him. It was then that God pronounced his judgment on them. From their seed the giants are supposed to have been born,[115] and it was they who taught people the arts and how to dye wool. After their deaths, people erected idols to them. THE INSTRUCTIONS OF COMMODIANUS 3.[116]

THE NATURE OF DEMON POSSESSION.

ORIGEN: Evil spirits operate in one of two ways. Sometimes they take complete and entire possession of the mind and do not allow their captives the power of understanding or feeling. This is the case with those who are commonly called possessed. . . . At other times, these forces use wicked suggestions to corrupt a conscious and intelligent soul with thoughts of various kinds—persuading it to do evil. Judas is an example of this kind of thing. ON FIRST PRINCIPLES 3.3.4.[117]

INHABITING THE LOWER PARTS OF THE EARTH.

ORIGEN: It is certain wicked demons of the race of titans or giants who have been guilty of impiety toward the true God and the angels in heaven. They have fallen away from it and haunt the darker parts of the body. They also frequent unclean places on earth. Because

---

[107]Gen 6:1-4. [108]PL 1:1305; cf. ANF 4:14. [109]Acts 8:9-24. [110]Acts 13:6-11. [111]PL 1:671-73; cf. ANF 3:65-66. [112]PG 8:576; cf. ANF 2:274. [113]PG 9:24; cf. ANF 2:446. [114]PG 9:465; cf. ANF 2:536. [115]See Gen 6:1-4. [116]PL 5:203-4; cf. ANF 4:203. [117]PG 11:317; cf. ANF 4:336.

they have no earthly bodies, they have a certain power to foretell future events. They do just that, in order to lead the human race away from the true God. They also secretly enter the bodies of the more predatory, savage and wicked animals and stir them up to do whatever they want to. Against Celsus 4.92.[118]

Because They Fell Away from God.

Origen: Demons were not originally so but became what they are when they turned away from God. This is why the name "demon" is given to those spiritual beings who have fallen away from God. Therefore, those who worship God must not serve demons. We can also learn the true nature of demons if we consider the practice of those who call on them by incantations to prevent certain things or for many other purposes. This is the method they adopt . . . in order to induce the demons to do as they ask. For this reason, the worship of demons is inconsistent with the worship of the true God. Against Celsus 7.69.[119]

Christians Have Nothing to Fear from Demons.

Origen: A Christian who has submitted to God and his Word will suffer nothing from the power of demons, for he is mightier than they are. The Christian will suffer nothing, for "the angel of the Lord will encamp around those who fear him and will deliver them."[120] Against Celsus 8.36.[121]

Demons Harm Only Those Who Fear Them.

Lactantius: The demons do injure some people, but only those who fear them. The powerful and lofty hand of God does not protect them because they have not been initiated into the sacrament of truth. On the other hand, the demons fear the righteous who worship God. Divine Institutes 2.16.[122]

Evil Spirits Invented Astrology and Magic.

Lactantius: Evil spirits invented astrology, soothsaying and divination, as well as oracles, necromancy, magic and anything else like that which people practice either openly or in secret. Divine Institute 2.17.[123]

Demons Try to Lead People into Error.

Lactantius: When they are abjured, the most wicked spirits confess that they are demons, but when they are worshiped, they falsely claim to be gods, in order to lead people into error. Divine Institutes 4.27.[124]

Light and Darkness.

Augustine: We know that some angels sinned and were cast into the lowest parts of this world, which is a kind of prison for them, where they are confined until the condemnation that will come at the day of judgment. We know this on the authority of the apostle Peter, who says, "God did not spare the angels who sinned. He thrust them into the prison of the darkness below and handed them over, to be kept for punishment at the judgment."[125] Can anyone doubt that God separated these angels from the others in his foreknowledge and by his creative act? Who can deny that the good angels are rightly called light, seeing that even human beings, who are still living in faith and hoping for equality with angels, are already called light by the apostle. As he says, "Once you were darkness, but now you are light in the Lord."[126] That darkness is a most apt name for those apostate angels will be readily appreciated by all those who believe that the rebellious angels are worse than unbelieving humans. City of God 11.33.[127]

God Allowed the Angels to Fall.

Augustine: It is God who in the beginning created the world full of all visible and intelligible beings, among which he created nothing

---

[118]PG 11:1169; cf. ANF 4:538. [119]PG 11:1517; cf. ANF 4:638. [120]Ps 34:7. [121]PG 11:1572; cf. ANF 4:653. [122]PL 6:334; cf. ANF 7:64-65. [123]PL 6:336; cf. ANF 7:65. [124]PL 6:534; cf. ANF 7:130. [125]2 Pet 2:4. [126]Eph 5:8. [127]PL 41:346; cf. NPNF 1 2:224.

better than those spirits that he endowed with intelligence and made capable of contemplating and enjoying him, and united in our society that we call the holy and heavenly city, and in which the material and blessedness of their sustenance and blessedness is God himself, as it were their common food and nourishment. It is he who gave to this intellectual nature free will of such a kind that if he wished to forsake God, who was his blessedness, misery should be the immediate consequence. It is he who, when he foreknew that certain angels would in their pride desire to suffice for their own blessedness and would forsake their great good, did not deprive them of this power, deeming it to be more fitting to bring good out of evil than to prevent evil from coming into existence. And indeed evil would never have come into being if the mutable nature, which was created by the most high God, who is the immutable good, had not brought evil on itself by sin. Indeed, the sin itself proved that the nature had originally been good. For if it had not been good, though of course not equal to its creator, the desertion of God as its light cannot have been evil as far as it was concerned. . . . It is God who, by a very just punishment, doomed the angels who voluntarily fell, to everlasting misery, and rewarded those who continued in their attachment to the supreme good with the assurance of endless stability as the gift for their fidelity. City of God 22.1.[128]

When Angels Fell, They Fell Further Than Did Humans. AUGUSTINE: Some people think that human beings are higher than the angels, because (they say) Christ died for us and not for the angels. But what sort of argument is this? Is it not just a desire to glory over our own wickedness? Paul said, "Christ in due time died for the ungodly."[129] . . . What sort of person wants to be praised because he has become so abominably diseased through his own wickedness that only the death of his physician can heal him? . . . Do we prefer

ourselves because, while there are also angels who have sinned, no labor of healing has been expended on their account? As if their need was small compared with ours! But even if that had been the case, we might still wonder whether it was because we once stood higher than they do or because we are now in a more desperate position than they are. Knowing, as we do, that the Creator of all good has imparted no grace for the healing of angelic evils, why do we not come to the conclusion that their fault was all the more damnable because their nature was of a loftier sublimity to begin with? For being superior to us in nature, they had less excuse than we had for falling into sin. But in offending against the Creator they became all the more detestably ungrateful for his blessing in that they were created capable of enjoying much greater blessing. Nor was it enough for them to desert God; they had to become our deceivers as well. This therefore is the great goodness of God shown toward us, that for Christ's sake we may be equal to the holy angels. We were created inferior to them in nature, and by our sin we have fallen into such greater depths of unworthiness as to make it fitting that we should in some respect be made equal to them. TRACTATES ON THE GOSPEL OF JOHN 110.7.[130]

No More Angels Will Fall Away from God. AUGUSTINE: We most properly confess what we most correctly believe, which is that the God and Lord of all things, who in his strength created all things good and foreknew that evil things would arise out of good, and knew that it pertained to his most omnipotent goodness even to do good out of evil things rather than not to allow evil things to be at all, so ordained the life of angels and people that in it he might first of all show what their free will was capable of

---

[128]PL 41:751-52; cf. NPNF 1 2:479.   [129]Rom 5:6.   [130]PL 35:1924-25; cf. NPNF 1 7:411-12.

and then what the kindness of his grace and the judgment of his righteousness was capable of. Finally, certain angels, of whom the chief is the one called the devil, became by free will outcasts from the Lord God. Yet although they fled from his goodness, wherein they had been blessed, they could not flee from his judgment, by which they were made most wretched. Others, however, stood fast in the truth by the same free will and merited the knowledge of that most certain truth that they should never fall. For if from the holy Scriptures we have been able to attain the knowledge that none of the holy angels shall fall evermore, how much more have they themselves attained this knowledge by the truth more sublimely revealed to them! ON REBUKE AND GRACE 10(27).[131]

MANY ILLNESSES COME FROM THE DEVIL. AUGUSTINE: Many of the ills of the flesh are sent by the agents of Satan, but they cannot act without permission [from God]. Holy Job himself was tested in this way. EXPOSITIONS OF THE PSALMS 130(131).7.[132]

DEMONS DISCERN OUR THOUGHTS FROM OUR ACTIONS. JOHN CASSIAN: There is no doubt that unclean spirits can discern the thoughts of our hearts, but they can do this only by assessing external factors, for example, our attitudes, or the words and actions to which they see us more readily inclined. But they have no access to those thoughts that have not yet come out of the hidden recesses of the soul. CONFERENCES 7.15.[133]

THE PUNISHMENT THEY DESERVE. FULGENTIUS OF RUSPE: Those angels who turned away from God of their own free will . . . found that that turning away became the first part of their punishment, . . . which was nothing other than deprivation of the love of that blessed and good being. God ordered them to remain in eternal punishment, for

which he prepared eternal fire. . . . The evil of those wicked angels remains in them, and so the just retribution of eternal condemnation remains in them as well. TO PETER, ON THE FAITH 3.31.[134]

Satan

THE DEVIL CANNOT RULE GOD'S SERVANTS. HERMAS: The devil cannot claim dominion over the servants of God, who place their trust in him. The devil can wrestle against them, but he cannot overthrow them. If you resist him, he will be conquered and flee in disgrace from you.[135] SHEPHERD, MANDATE 2.12.5.[136]

THE DEVIL TESTS ALL GOD'S SERVANTS. HERMAS: The devil tests all God's servants. Those who are mature in the faith resist him strongly, so he withdraws from them . . . and goes to those who are weaker. He finds a way to get into them and then does what he wants with them. SHEPHERD, MANDATE 2.12.5.[137]

THE FORM OF A SERPENT. IRENAEUS: The apostate angel, having used a serpent to bring the human race into disobedience,[138] thought that he had escaped God's notice, but instead God assigned to him the name and form of the serpent. AGAINST HERESIES 4, PREFACE 4.[139]

JEALOUS OF GOD'S CREATION. IRENAEUS: The devil was jealous of God's creation and tried to pervert it so that it would become God's enemy. So God banished from his presence the one who stealthily sowed the tares. AGAINST HERESIES 4.40.3.[140]

THE DEVIL IS A CREATURE. IRENAEUS: The devil never created anything, but is himself a

---

[131]PL 44:932; cf. NPNF 1 5:482-83. [132]PL 37:1708. [133]PL 49:687-88. [134]PL 65:687; FC 95:80. [135]Jas 4:7. [136]PG 2:949; cf. ANF 2:29. [137]PG 2:949-50; cf. ANF 2:29-30. [138]Gen 3:1-7. [139]PG 7:975; cf. ANF 1:462. [140]PG 7:1113-14; cf. ANF 1:524.

creature, like the other angels. AGAINST HERESIES 4.41.1.[141]

THE MEANING OF THE WORD SATAN.
IRENAEUS: The Hebrew word *Satan* means an apostate. AGAINST HERESIES 5.21.2.[142]

WHY SATAN DECEIVED ADAM. TERTULLIAN:
I detect the origin of impatience in the devil himself, and it dates from the time when he could not bear the fact that God had subjected all his works to his own image, that is, to humanity. If he had been able to put up with that, he would not have been upset, and if he had not been upset, he would not have envied humanity. Thus Satan deceived Adam because he envied him, he envied him because he was upset, and he was upset because he could not endure God's action. ON PATIENCE 5.[143]

THE DEVIL SINNED OF HIS OWN FREE
WILL. TERTULLIAN: Where did the devil's malice of lying and deceit originate? Certainly not from God! God made the angel good, and before he became the devil, he stood out as the wisest of all the creatures. . . . If you turn to the prophecy of Ezekiel,[144] you will quickly realize that this angel was good by creation and that it was by his own choice that he became corrupt. AGAINST MARCION 2.10.[145]

THE CHURCH'S TEACHING ABOUT THE
DEVIL. ORIGEN: Concerning the devil, his angels and the opposing forces, the church's teaching is that these beings do indeed exist. However, the church has never explained with sufficient clarity what they are or how they exist. Most Christians, however, think that the devil was an angel who became an apostate and induced as many other angels as possible to fall away with him. ON FIRST PRINCIPLES PREFACE 6.[146]

SATAN ORIGINALLY DWELLED IN HEAVEN.
ORIGEN: Ezekiel compares Satan with lightning and says that he fell from heaven.[147] By this he shows that Satan had at one time been in heaven and had enjoyed a place among the saints. ON FIRST PRINCIPLES 1.5.5.[148]

EVEN IF THERE WERE NO DEVIL. ORIGEN:
Holy Scripture teaches us that there are invisible enemies that fight against us, and it tells us to arm ourselves against them.[149] Simple-minded believers think that every sin we commit is caused by the ceaseless efforts of these powers that prey on the minds of sinners. . . . In other words, they think that if the devil did not exist, no human being would ever sin. We do not agree with this, because we reckon with sins that clearly originate as a necessary consequence of our bodily constitution. The devil does not cause us to hunger or thirst, neither is he the cause of that desire that arises at the time of puberty, namely, the desire for sexual intercourse. ON FIRST PRINCIPLES 3.2.1-2.[150]

THE DEVIL DOES EVERYTHING HE CAN TO
DECEIVE US. CYPRIAN: The apostle Peter, in his epistle, forewarns and teaches us, saying, "Be sober and watch. For your adversary the devil goes about as a roaring lion, seeking anyone to devour."[151] He goes about each one of us. He is like an enemy besieging those who are shut up inside a city. He examines the walls to see if there is any part that is less firm and trustworthy, where perhaps he might make a breach and penetrate inside. He presents seductive pleasures to the eye, in order to destroy chastity. He tempts the ear with harmonious music, so as to weaken Christian resolve. . . . He promises earthly honors in order to deprive us of heavenly ones. . . . When he cannot deceive us secretly, he threatens us openly by

---

[141]PG 7:1115; cf. ANF 1:524. [142]PG 7:1181; cf. ANF 1:549. In fact, the word *Satan* means "accuser" or "slanderer." [143]PL 1:1256-57; cf. ANF 3:709. [144]Ezek 28:11-19. [145]PL 2:296; cf. ANF 3:305. [146]PG 11:119; cf. ANF 4:240. [147]Ezek 28:11-19; cf. Lk 10:18. [148]PG 11:104; cf. ANF 4:259. [149]Eph 6:11-13. [150]PG 11:305; cf. ANF 4:329-30. [151]1 Pet 5:8.

brandishing the fear of persecution. . . . He is always restless and hostile, crafty in peace and fierce in persecution. JEALOUSY AND ENVY 1-2.[152]

NO POWER OTHER THAN WHAT GOD HAS ALLOWED. CYPRIAN: The devil has no power except what God has allowed. Jesus said, "You could have no power against me unless it were given to you from above."[153] Also in 1 Kings: "God stirred up Satan against Solomon."[154] And in Job, first of all God permitted and then allowed the devil [to tempt Job].[155] To QUIRINIUS: TESTIMONIES AGAINST THE JEWS 3.80.[156]

THE PRIDE OF SATAN. ATHANASIUS: Humility is a great aid toward the salvation of the soul. Satan was not thrown out of heaven because of his fornication or adultery or thievery; it was his pride that cast him down into the depths. For he said, "I will go up and place my throne next to God's, and I will be like the Most High."[157] Because of this he was thrown down, and eternal fire was his inheritance. ON VIRGINITY 5.[158]

PRIDE THE CAUSE OF ENVY. AUGUSTINE: Some say that the devil fell from the heavenly places because he was jealous that humanity was created in the image of God. But envy follows pride, not the reverse. It is not envy that is the cause of pride, but pride that is the cause of envy. ON THE LITERAL INTERPRETATION OF GENESIS 11.14.18.[159]

RIGHTEOUSNESS CAN OVERCOME THE DEVIL. AUGUSTINE: The devil is to be overcome not by God's power but by his righteousness. What can be more powerful than the Almighty? What creature is there whose power can be compared with that of the Creator? But since the devil, by the fault of his own perversity, was made a lover of power and a forsaker and assailant of righteousness, . . . it

pleased God to conquer the devil not by power but by righteousness, and so human beings too should try to overcome him in the same way. It is not that power is to be shunned as if it were something evil, but righteousness must be accorded the priority it deserves. How great can the power of mortals be? Therefore, cling to righteousness and defeat the devil that way. ON THE TRINITY 13.13.17.[160]

THE SOURCE OF ALL EVIL. FULGENTIUS OF RUSPE: The devil is the source of all evil, because out of envy he led the first human beings to get involved in sin, infecting not only them but also their entire progeny with the sentence of death. . . . But God, who is merciful and just, . . . did not permit the entire human race to perish forever. His free goodness predestined those whom he willed to be brought back to the light. To PETER, ON THE FAITH 3.33.[161]

Hell

A PLACE OF PUNISHMENT. JUSTIN MARTYR: Our Master Jesus Christ said, . . . "Fear not them that kill you and after that can do no more, but fear him who after death is able to cast both body and soul into hell."[162] Hell is a place where those who have lived wickedly and who do not believe that what Christ taught will happen will be punished. FIRST APOLOGY 19.[163]

PUNISHMENT IN HELL DOES NOT HAVE TO WAIT. TERTULLIAN: All souls are confined to hell [after death], . . . where punishments and consolations are already being experienced, as the story of the rich man and Lazarus makes clear. . . . Why can you not accept this? . . . You answer that it is impossible because in justice there should be no inkling of the punishment

---

[152]PL 4:639-40; cf. ANF 5:491. [153]Jn 19:11. [154]1 Kings 11:23. [155]Job 1:6-12. [156]PL 4:772; cf. ANF 5:553. [157]Is 14:14. [158]PG 28:257. [159]PL 34:436. [160]PL 42:1026-7; NPNF 1 3:176. [161]PL 65:687; FC 95:80-81. [162]Mt 10:28. [163]PG 6:357; cf. ANF 1:169.

or reward before the final sentence is pronounced, and this should not happen until the flesh is restored to the soul, since it was a partner in the soul's actions and therefore ought to share in the judgment passed on it. What then takes place in that interval? Will we sleep? But souls do not sleep even when people are alive—it is the business of bodies to sleep and to die, since sleep is but the counterfeit of death. Are you going to say that nothing happens in the place where the whole human race is drawn to and where everyone's future expectation is postponed for safe keeping? Do you think this state is a foretaste of judgment or the start of judgment itself? Is it a premature encroachment on it or the first installment of it? Would it not be the greatest possible injustice, even in hell, if the guilty were still doing well there but the righteous had not yet received their reward? Would you make our hope even more confused after death? Would you have it mock us still more with uncertain expectation? Or will it now become a review of past life, and an arranging of judgment, with the inevitable feeling of trembling fear? Must the soul always wait for the body in order to experience sorrow or joy? Is it incapable of suffering either or both of these sensations on its own? . . .

Even in hell the soul knows how to joy or sorrow even without the body. In the flesh, it feels pain when it chooses to do so, even when the body is unhurt, and it can feel joy even when the body is in pain. If such sensations occur at will during life, why can they not happen after death by God's own judicial appointment? The soul does not need the flesh in order to act, and the judgment of God pursues its inmost thoughts and desires. "Whoever looks on a woman to lust after her has committed adultery with her already in his heart."[164] So you see that it is quite right for the soul to be punished for what it has done independently of the flesh, without having to wait for the flesh to catch up with it. In the same way, it will receive the reward for its pious thoughts, which it had without the aid of the flesh, without the flesh's participation in it. Even in matters done through the flesh, it is the soul that is the first to conceive them, the first to arrange them, the first to authorize them, the first to precipitate them into acts. Even if it is sometimes unwilling to act, it is still the first to treat the object that it means to effect by help of the body. There is no case in which an event can take place before it has been conceived in the mind. It is therefore quite in keeping with the order of things that that part of our nature should be the first to have the recompense and reward that it deserves on account of its priority. Since we understand the prison mentioned in the Gospel to be hell[165] and interpret "the uttermost farthing"[166] to mean the very smallest offense that has to be paid for there before the resurrection, no one will hesitate to believe that the soul undergoes some remedial discipline in hell without prejudice to the full process of the resurrection, when the reward will be administered through the flesh as well. ON THE SOUL 58.[167]

THE GEOGRAPHY OF HELL. HIPPOLYTUS: The souls of both the righteous and the unrighteous are detained in hell [for the time being]. Hell is a place in the created order, rough, a locality below the earth in which the light of the world does not shine. As the sun does not penetrate there, it must necessarily be a place of perpetual darkness. This place has been appointed as a guardhouse for souls, with the angels watching over it and distributing to each one the punishments that he has deserved. There is also a place set aside in hell where there is a lake of unquenchable fire, into which no one (I suppose) has yet been cast. It is waiting for the day determined by God, when one sentence of righteous judg-

---

[164]Mt 5:28. [165]Mt 5:25. [166]Mt 5:26. [167]PL 2:750-52; cf. ANF 3:234-35.

ment will be applied equally to everyone. The unrighteous . . . will then be sentenced to this endless punishment. The righteous though will obtain the incorruptible and unfading kingdom. For the moment they are being detained in hell, but not in the same place as the unrighteous. There is but one descent to this place, which is guarded by an archangel with his hosts. When those who are taken there by the angels appointed to the different souls have passed through this gate, they do not all go the same way. The righteous are conducted in the light to the right. . . . There they dwell in light and contemplate the blessings that they can see, waiting in expectation for even more wonderful delights still to come. . . . This is what we would call Abraham's bosom.[168] But the unrighteous are dragged off toward the left by angels who are ministers of punishment. They do not go there of their own accord but are dragged as prisoners. The angels reproach them and threaten them as they push them even further down into the lower parts. Those who get close hear the agitation and feel the hot smoke. When they glimpse the horror of the fire, they shudder at the expectation of future judgment, as if they were already feeling their punishment. Even the sight of the place of the fathers and the righteous merely adds to that feeling of being punished. For a deep and vast abyss is set there in between them, so that none of the righteous can cross over it in sympathy, and none of the unrighteous would even dare to try. AGAINST PLATO 1.[169]

THE TERRORS OF HELL. PSEUDO-CYPRIAN: There is a horrible place called Gehenna, where there is an awful murmuring and groaning of souls in mourning, with flames belching through the horrible darkness of thick night. It is always breathing out the raging fires of a smoking furnace, while the confined mass of flames is restrained or relaxed for the various purposes of punishment. Its violence has many

different degrees, as it gathers into itself whatever tortures the consuming fire of the heat it gives off can supply. Those who have rejected the Lord's voice and despised his rule are punished there with different penalties, in proportion to the degree to which the punishment is deserved. . . . Some are weighed down by an intolerable burden, some are hurried over the abrupt descent of a steep path by a merciless force, and the heavy weight of clanking chains bends over them in their bondage. Some are tormented on a slowly turning wheel, and others are squeezed together to the point of being smothered. ON THE GLORY OF MARTYRDOM 20.[170]

HELLFIRE CANNOT BE MATERIAL. AUGUSTINE: If the fire of hell is not immaterial, analogous to the pain of the soul, but material, burning by contact, so that bodies may be tormented in it, how can evil spirits be punished in it? It is undoubtedly the same fire that will serve for the punishment of people and of devils, according to the words of Christ: "Depart from me, you cursed, into everlasting fire, prepared for the devil and his angels."[171] Unless perhaps, as some learned people have thought, the devils have a kind of body made of that dense and humid air that we feel strikes us when the wind is blowing. CITY OF GOD 21.10.[172]

HELLFIRE IS NOT EVIL. AUGUSTINE: Eternal fire, which is meant to torture the ungodly, is not evil, because its measure, form and order are corrupted by no iniquity. It is felt as an evil torture by the damned, but it is the due punishment for their sins. Light tortures the bleary-eyed, but that does not make it evil. ON THE NATURE OF THE GOOD 38.[173]

---

[168]See Lk 16:22. [169]PG 10:796-800; cf. ANF 5:221-22. [170]PL 4:798-99; cf. ANF 5:584. [171]Mt 25:41. [172]PL 41:724; cf. NPNF 1 2:461-62. [173]PL 42:563; cf. NPNF 1 4:359.

PUNISHMENT IN HELL IS ETERNAL. FULGENTIUS OF RUSPE: The soul will always die together with the body, so that both may suffer together forever in hell. The death of the soul and body does not itself die, because their torture never comes to an end. The eternal death of the wicked is precisely this, that they do not die in the eternal fire and can never be at any time without punishment. Nor can anything be taken away from the burning body. The unhappy soul is constantly burning in its body, and the entire body continues to burn alongside the soul. The body in which the soul lived, either justly or wickedly, is the same one that will experience either eternal punishment or happiness without end. ON THE FORGIVENESS OF SINS 2.13.4.[174]

THE TORMENT OF LOVE. ISAAC OF NINEVEH: Those who are punished in hell are punished by the scourge of love. What could be more bitter or painful than that? Those who know that they have sinned against love feel this more deeply than they fear punishment. Sinners in hell are not deprived of God's love, which is given to all. Rather, the power of that love torments them by stimulating in them the most bitter regret [for what might have been]. HOMILY 28.[175]

---

[174]PL 65:564; FC 95:169. [175]Adapted from *AHSIS* 141.

OUTLINE OF CONTENTS

LIST OF ANCIENT AUTHORS
AND TEXTS CITED

Alexander of Alexandria
Epistle on the Arian Heresy

Ambrose
Cain and Abel
Duties of the Clergy
Exposition of the Twelve Psalms
On Abraham
On the Christian Faith
On the Holy Spirit
Six Days of Creation

Ambrosiaster
On 1 Timothy

Aphrahat
Demonstrations

Aristides
Apology

Arnobius of Sicca
Against the Nations

Athanasian Creed

Athanasius
Against the Heathen
Defense of the Nicene Definition
Discourses Against the Arians
Festal Letters
Four Letters to Serapion
On Synods
On the Incarnation
On the Incarnation and Against the Arians
On Virginity

Athenagoras
A Plea Regarding Christians

Augustine
Against Adimantus
Against Faustus, a Manichaean
Against Felix the Manichaean
Against Fortunatus the Manichaean
Against Julian
Against the Adversary of the Law and
    Prophets
Against the Argument of the Arians
Against the Letter of a Manichaean
Christian Instruction
City of God
Confessions
Enchiridion
Expositions of the Psalms
Letters
On Baptism, Against the Donatists
On Eighty-Three Varied Questions
On Faith and the Creed
On Free Will
On Genesis Against the Manichaeans
On Rebuke and Grace
On the Gift of Perseverance
On the Literal Interpretation of Genesis
On the Nature of the Good
On the Soul
On the Trinity
Predestination of the Saints
Sermons
To Orosius
Tractates on the Gospel of John

Bardesanes
Book of the Laws of Countries

Basil the Great
Against Eunomius
Ascetic Sermons
Hexaemeron

Homilies on the Psalms
Letters
On the Holy Spirit

Cassian, John
Conferences

Clement of Alexandria
Christ the Educator
Exhortation to the Greeks
Fragments
Stromateis

Clement of Rome
1 Clement

Commodian
The Instructions of Commodianus

Constitutions of the Holy Apostles

Cyprian
Jealousy and Envy
Letters
The Lord's Prayer
To Quirinius: Testimonies Against the Jews
The Vanity of Idols

Cyril of Alexandria
Against the Emperor Julian
Commentary on Isaiah
Commentary on John
Dialogue on the Trinity
Explanation of the Psalms
Thesaurus on the Trinity

Cyril of Jerusalem
Catechetical Lectures

Didymus the Blind
On the Holy Spirit
On the Trinity

Dionysius of Alexandria
Fragments

Fragments from the Books of Nature

Dionysius of Rome
Against the Sabellians

Ephrem the Syrian
Commentary on Genesis
Hymn on the Dead and the Trinity
Nisibene Hymns
Scattered Hymns
Self-Examination
Sermons Against Heretics
Sermons Against Rash Inquirers

Epiphanius of Salamis
Ancoratus
Panarion

Eusebius of Caesaria
Ecclesiastical History
On the Theology of the Church
The Oration of Constantine
Preparation for the Gospel
Proof of the Gospel

Fulgentius of Ruspe
Book to Victor Against Fastidiosus the Arian
Letter to Scarila
Letters
On the Forgiveness of Sins
To Monimus
To Peter, on the Faith
To Trasamundus

Gennadius of Constantinople
Book of Ecclesiastical Dogmas

Gregory of Elvira
Origen's Tractates on the Books of Holy
  Scripture

Gregory of Nazianzus
On Holy Baptism, Oration 40
On the Holy Lights, Oration 39
On the Holy Spirit, Theological Oration

5(31)
On the Son, Theological Oration 4(30)
On the Theophany, Oration 38
On Theology, Theological Oration 2(28)

Gregory of Nyssa
Address on Religious Instruction
Against Eunomius
Life of Moses
On Children Who Are Taken Away
   Prematurely
On Common Notions
On Not Three Gods

Gregory the Great
Forty Gospel Homilies
Homilies on Ezekiel
Morals on the Book of Job

Hegemonius
Disputation of Archelaus and Manes

Hermas
Shepherd

Hilary of Poitiers
Homilies on the Psalms
On the Councils
On the Trinity

Hippolytus
Against Beron and Helix [sp.]
Against Noetus
Against Plato
Refutation of All Heresies

Ignatius of Antioch
Epistles

Irenaeus
Against Heresies

Isaac of Nineveh
Ascetical Homilies

Jerome
Against Rufinus
Commentary on Ephesians
Commentary on the Gospel of Matthew
Dialogue Against the Luciferians
Homilies on the Psalms
Letters
Preface to the Books of Solomon

John Chrysostom
Commentary on Jeremiah
Homilies on Certain New Testament
   Texts
Homilies on 1 Corinthians
Homilies on Ephesians
Homilies on Genesis
Homilies on the Gospel of Matthew
Homilies on 2 Thessalonians
On the Divinity of Christ, Against the
   Anomoeans
On the Incomprehensible Nature of God
Sermons on Hannah

John of Damascus
Dialogue Against the Manichaeans
Homily on the Withered Fig Tree
On Divine Images
On Heresies
Orthodox Faith

Justin Martyr
Dialogue with Trypho
First Apology
Hortatory Address to the Greeks
Second Apology

Lactantius
Divine Institues
On the Workmanship of God
On the Wrath of God

Leo the Great
Letters
Sermons

Letter to Diognetus

Marius Victorinus
Against Arius
On the Generation of the Divine Word

Melito of Sardis
Discourse to Antoninus Caesar (Fragment)
Fragment of a Discourse on the Soul and the
 Body
Fragments

Methodius
Banquet of the Ten Virgins
On the Resurrection
On Free Will

Minucius Felix
Octavius

Muratorian Fragment

Novatian
On the Trinity

Origen
Against Celsus
Commentary on the Gospel of John
Commentary on the Gospel of Matthew
On First Principles

Phoebadius of Agen
Book Against the Arians

Prosper of Aquitaine
Replies to Objections

Pseudo-Clement of Rome
2 Clement

Pseudo-Cyprian
On the Glory of Martyrdom

Pseudo-Dionysius
Divine Names

Pseudo-Ignatius
Epistle of Ignatius to the Philippians

Rufinus of Aquileia
Commentary on the Apostles' Creed

Tatian
To the Greeks

Tertullian
Against Hermogenes
Against Marcion
Against Praxeas
Apology
The Apparel of Women
The Chaplet
On Fasting
On Idolatry
On Patience
On Prayer
On the Flesh of Christ
On the Resurrection of the Flesh
On the Soul
On the Veiling of Virgins
Prescriptions Against Heretics
To Scapula

Theodoret of Cyr
Commentary on Daniel
Commentary on Romans
Commentary on the Song of Songs
Cure for Greek Leanings
Letters

Theophilus of Antioch
To Autolycus

Treatise on Rebaptism

Victorinus of Petovium
Commentary on the Apocalypse

Vincent of Lérins
Commonitories

Author/Writings Index

Scripture Index

Genesis
1, *111*
1:1, *98, 115, 118, 133, 135*
1:10, *115*
1:26, *75, 82, 85, 121, 123*
1:27, *122, 123*
2:17, *127*
2:22, *122*
2:23, *122*
3:1-7, *144*
3:22, *75*
6:1, *128*
6:1-4, *131, 139, 141*
18:1-4, *131*
19:15, *131*
32:24-26, *131*
48:16, *138*

Deuteronomy
4:35, *73*
6:4, *12, 52, 53, 64*
6:13, *53*
32:8, *138*

2 Samuel
7:8, *88*
24:1, *58*

1 Kings
11:23, *146*

1 Chronicles
21:1, *58*

Job
1:6-12, *146*

Psalms
1:3, *16*
6:1, *58*
8:3, *9, 90*
14:1, *10*
18:11, *47*
19:1, *10*
25:10, *106*
33:6, *94*
34:7, *137, 142*
37:30-31, *8*
62:11, *54*
72:5, *64*
72:17, *64*
75:3, *114*
104:5, *114*
139:21, *15*
149:6, *15*

Proverbs
1:2-6, *16*
3:11, *17*
8:22, *69*

Ecclesiastes
10:13, *126*

Isaiah
1:2, *60, 65*
1:3-4, *64*
6:2, *41*
6:3, *51, 52*
6:10, *107*
7:9, *7*
9:6, *68*
14:14, *146*
40:12, *90*
44:6, *36*

45:5, *68*
51:6, *15*
53:1, *107*
61:1, *74*
64:4, *9*
66:1, *55, 64*

Jeremiah
7:11, *64*
10:24, *58*
26:3, *101*

Ezekiel
28:2, *137*
28:11-19, *145*
28:12-19, *128*
33:11, *65*

Daniel
3:1-30, *12*
7:10, *131*
7:13, *56*
10:13, *138*
10:13-20, *138*
10:20, *137*
12:10, *7*

Hosea
6:6, *65*

Malachi
2:10, *64*

2 Maccabees
7:1-41, *12*

Wisdom of Solomon
4:6, *138*

11:20, *111*

Matthew
4, *65*
5:18, *17*
5:25, *147*
5:26, *147*
5:28, *147*
6:8, *107*
6:9, *65*
8:23-27, *71*
10:28, *146*
11:21, *107*
13:36-43, *132*
13:41-42, *132*
16:18, *27*
18:7, *100*
18:10, *133, 137*
21:13, *64*
22:3, *104*
22:29, *24*
22:30, *134*
22:37, *65*
23:9, *65*
24:35, *15*
25:41, *139, 148*
27:46, *75*
28:19, *6, 51, 78, 80*

Mark
11:17, *64*
12:25, *134*
14:36, *60*

Luke
1:1, *14, 23*
3:38, *39*